On the Origins of Judaism

BibleWorld
Series Editors: Philip R. Davies and James G. Crossley, University of Sheffield
BibleWorld shares the fruits of modern (and postmodern) biblical scholarship not only among practitioners and students, but also with anyone interested in what academic study of the Bible means in the twenty-first century. It explores our ever-increasing knowledge and understanding of the social world that produced the biblical texts, but also analyses aspects of the Bible's role in the history of our civilization and the many perspectives – not just religious and theological, but also cultural, political and aesthetic – which drive modern biblical scholarship.

Recently Published:

On the Origins of Judaism

Philip R. Davies

LONDON   OAKVILLE

Published by Equinox Publishing Ltd.
UK: 1 Chelsea Manor Studios, Flood Street, London SW3 5SR
USA: DBBC, 28 Main Street, Oakville, CT 06779

www.equinoxpub.com

First published 2011

British Library Cataloguing-in-Publication Data

A catalogue record for this book is available from the British Library.

ISBN-13   978 1 84553 325 0 (hardback)
          978 1 84553 326 7 (paperback)

Library of Congress Cataloging-in-Publication Data

Davies, Philip R.
  On the origins of Judaism / Philip R. Davies.
     p. cm.—(BibleWorld)
  Includes bibliographical references and index.
  ISBN 978-1-84553-325-0 (hb)—ISBN 978-1-84553-326-7 (pb) 1.
Judaism—History. I. Title.
  BM155.3.D38 2008
  296.09'01—dc22
                                        2008023974

Typeset by S.J.I. Services, New Delhi
Printed and bound in Great Britain by Lightning Source UK Ltd, Milton Keynes

CONTENTS

Sources

1. The material in Chapters 2–9 is rewritten from earlier published essays. Below are the details of the earlier versions.

2. "Scenes from the Early History of Judaism," in D. V. Edelman (ed.), *The Triumph of Elohim: From Yahwisms to Judaisms* (Contributions to Biblical Exegesis and Theology; Kampen: Kok Pharos, 1995), pp. 145–82; reprinted by Eerdmans (1996).

3. "Biblical Foundations of Judaism," in J. Neusner, A. Avery-Peck and W. S. Green (eds.), *The Encyclopaedia of Judaism* (Leiden: Brill, 2000), I, pp. 113–20.

4. "'Law' in Early Judaism," in J. Neusner and A. J. Avery-Peck (eds.), *Judaism in Late Antiquity 3:1* (Leiden: Brill, 1998), pp. 3–33.

5. "The Place of Deuteronomy in the Development of Judean Society and Religion," in *Recenti Tendenze nella Riconstruzione della Storia Antica d'Israele* (Rome: Accademia Nazionale dei Lincei, 2005), pp. 139–55; "Josiah and the Law Book," in L. L. Grabbe (ed.), *Good Kings and Bad Kings* (Library of Hebrew Bible/Old Testament Studies, 393; London: T&T Clark, 2005), pp. 65–77.

6. "God of Cyrus, God of Israel: Some Religio-Historical Reflections on Isaiah 40-55," in G. Harvey, W. Watson and J. Davies (eds.), *Words Remembered, Texts Renewed. Essays in Honour of John F. A. Sawyer* (JSOTS, 195; Sheffield: Sheffield Academic Press, 1995), pp. 207–25.

7. "The Social World of the Apocalyptic Writings," in R. E. Clements (ed.), *The World of Ancient Israel* (Cambridge: Cambridge University Press, 1989), pp. 251–71; "Divination, 'Apocalyptic' and Sectarianism in Early Judaism," in I. Kottsieper, R. Schmitt and J. Wöhrle (eds.), *Berührungspunkte: Studien zur Sozial- und Religionsgeschichte Israels und seiner Umwelt* (FS Rainer Albertz; Münster: Ugarit-Verlag, 2008), pp. 409–23.

8. "Sons of Cain," in *A Word in Season: Essays in Honour of William McKane* (JSOT Supplements, 42; Sheffield: JSOT Press, 1986), pp. 35–56; "Women, Men, Gods, Sex and Power: The Birth of a Biblical Myth," in A. Brenner (ed.), *A Feminist Companion to Genesis* (Sheffield: JSOT Press, 1993), pp. 194–201; "And Enoch Was Not, for Genesis Took Him," in C. Hempel and J. M. Lieu (eds.), *Biblical Traditions in Transmission. Essays in Honour of Michael A. Knibb* (Leiden: Brill, 2006), pp. 97–107.

9. "Food, Drink and Sects: The Question of Ingestion in the Qumran Texts," *Semeia* 84 (2000), pp. 139–51.

Preface

The contents of this book are rewritten from essays previously published: in some cases drawn from more than one essay. This book is therefore neither "new" nor a set of reprints. The genre is unusual, perhaps, in current scholarly publication, but follows quite closely the way that ancient writers used to work.

I have tried, in rewriting, to produce a consistent level and style from sources that range from the highly technical to the more "popular," and aimed at a readable introduction to some of the many issues that the study of ancient Judaism offers. I have eliminated footnotes but taken as much account of more recent important work as possible, though to do justice to it would have required a completely new set of essays. In revising my earlier work, I discovered that I have not changed my earlier conclusions a great deal, though this is not something I am necessarily proud of, since it suggests I have not learned much recently. But I have been able to clarify some ideas and correct many details. Unfortunately, I have not found it easy to eliminate a certain amount of repetition and the reader is welcome to skip these passages, or read them while yawning.

I hope that over the years between first writing these thoughts and finishing this book I have managed to put questions better and to refine the answers a bit. But there remains a great deal to do, most of which will of course be done by others. Whether ideas are responsible for the people who have them (a comment attributed to Mark Twain) I am not sure. But ideas come more easily to those who ask questions.

Philip R. Davies
Sheffield, March 2008

This book is dedicated to two women, friends, publishers.

Jean Allen *was* Sheffield Academic Press from the moment she arrived and taught me about re-invention of the self, energy, walking, eternal youthfulness and management. I have not been the best pupil.
Janet Joyce is also part of the history of Sheffield Academic Press as well as the publisher of this book. From her I have had many years of professional support, loyalty, hospitality, trust and (over this book) patience.
Both have taught me a lot about the mixture of life and work and how to get the most out of both.

Chapter 1

INTRODUCTION

The problem that has occupied me for all of my scholarly life—and only now can I see it clearly—is the origin of Judaism. Ancient Judaism is the religious matrix of the three world religions of monotheism (or, if you prefer, monarchic theism) and one of the two parents, along with the classical Greco-Roman culture, that shaped Western civilization. Yet how it came into being is a mystery. Of course, it has its own canonized explanation, and a simple one: God created the world, chose Abraham and then Israel, rescued his people from slavery, revealed the law to Moses, gave them a land, guided them through the words he uttered to prophets, punished and forgave (in equal measure). But this account is, of course, itself part of the process of formation of Judaism and not an independent testimony to its real history. It explains only when interrogated. It may or may not give us much history (and we have few resources to verify or falsify it), but the tensions within its stories of the past—not least its varying definitions of "Israel"—betray competing and compromising interests (I have recently explored these in some detail in Davies, 2007a).

The scriptural canon of early Judaism was supplemented by the New Testament, the Talmud, and the Qur'an. Each of these writings defined one of the three "Abrahamic" religions: classical or rabbinic Judaism, Christianity and Islam. The first two grew alongside each other, the third arrived centuries later. Whilst Judaism retained the name of the mother, it is not for that reason typologically closer to its parent (Samaritanism, another often forgotten "Abrahamic religion," is probably the closest): the loss of the Jerusalem temple caused Judaism to mutate into a geographically decentred religion without priesthood or sanctuary or sacrificial cult. Christianity, thanks partly to its merger with the imperial Roman cult, retained a priesthood, altars, "churches" (temples) and a quite elaborate cult. Islam, by contrast, has neither priest, nor cult, nor temple. Any rational outsider would conclude that these three religions worship the same deity, the one named Yhwh in the various collections of books that constitute the Jewish Bible and the various Christian Bibles, some of the contents of which are re-presented in the Qur'an—but more commonly just called "God."

"Ancient Judaism" is the matrix of all these religions. It designates the rich complex of beliefs and practices that later crystallized into the three major forms (but also into others). Our understanding of this religious ferment has been revolutionized during my lifetime; most probably the discovery of the Dead Sea Scrolls was the catalyst. These documents have been claimed for Christianity (in a proleptic sense, as being "apocalyptic" or "messianic" and opposed to the temple cult, all less than accurate descriptions) as well as for rabbinic Judaism (from their concern with obedience to the Mosaic Torah and their obsession with continual purity). Both claims have some substance, but the tussle between these claims (which has been generally quite amicable) has shown how easy it is to trace the roots of both religions back to the complex of ideas and practices that constitute "early Judaism."

The Scrolls enabled scholars to work backwards towards the time of the Israelite and Judean kingdoms, via the province of Yehud, the successor to the kingdom of Judah and, with much less attention, via the Samaritan religion, the successor of the kingdom of Israel. Between the relatively illuminated history of these kingdoms and the much more illuminated world of the Greco-Roman era lies, if not a black hole, then a dark grey one. Of the crucial era in the development of early Judaism, from the fifth to the second centuries BCE, we knew very, very little. What happened in Yehud and Samaria as the Persian empire gave way to Alexander's Macedonians and Greeks, as Judah and Samaria fell under the Ptolemies, and perhaps were then reunited into a single domain, how "Judaism" and "Samaritanism" grew apart as separate cults—all this we can only approach by inference from canonized and uncanonized Jewish writings and scraps of information from other ancient writers. There are no narrative accounts from Judah or Samaria that cover the period between the end of the fifth century and the beginning of the second BCE, and few extant external sources that take any interest in it—until we come to Josephus, upon whom we have to rely more than we would like.

As for the Jewish literature emanating from the entire Second Temple period, the term "postbiblical" ("intertestmental" is now out of use) conveys the impression that the uncanonized writings are chronologically later than the scriptural, and this perception has survived relatively intact, though it is incorrect (parts of Daniel are later than parts of 1 Enoch), but, more importantly, that they are *typologically* "later," that they depend upon, or take for granted, a fixed scriptural canon. This perception is also mistaken, and, moreover, implies a single strand of evolution. But early Judaism almost certainly did not develop in a unilinear fashion (a state of affairs that makes relative chronology somewhat less important).

But the writings known as 1 Enoch, which have been known in the West since the nineteenth century and more recently the Qumran Scrolls, have revealed unexpected possibilities of "early Jewish" belief and practice, including, in the case of the Scrolls, not just the phenomenon of sectarianism but also features such as physiognomy, astrology, dualism, and mysticism—apparently accompanied by a rigorous adherence to scriptural law. These writings have also transmitted a kind of Judaism, or even "kinds of Judaism" that we would not have deduced from the canonized literature at all. There is still a tendency to embrace many of the features in these works within the orbit of "sectarianism," a relatively late and marginal feature. But such a view implies that there was a "mainstream" Judaism and that we know what that was. That, for instance, it is represented by the scriptural canon (and perhaps even delineated in the books of Ezra and Nehemiah). But the later stages of canonizing, including internal cross-referencing and, finally, closing its contents, are not a precondition of early Judaism but part of its development. How did some writings retain their status as canonical works (in the sense of being included in the closed canon) while others were not—though Greek-reading Jews apparently continued to regard other writings as scriptural, too? Who, in any case, had any authority to close the canon, and why was a need felt to do this, closed canons being the exception rather than the rule? There are several aspects of the formation and function of the scriptural canon that have not yet been understood; again, our evidence is mostly indirect and insufficient. Having worked on both canonized (especially Davies, 1998) and uncanonized "early Jewish" writings, I have found myself persuaded of generally later dates for the creation, and not just the completion, of the former, and earlier dates for some of the latter, to the point where I have found myself focusing on the areas of overlap, and these issues are especially prominent in the essays that follow.

One important respect in which the scriptural canon reflects the development of early Judaism is in the creation of "Israel." The Scriptures tell the story of a nation of "Israel," though on careful reading it can be seen that the texts represent different definitions. For example, we can see on the one hand a rejection of the people of Samaria (in 2 Kings 17 and in Ezra and Nehemiah), while in the books of Chronicles the "northern tribes" are included within an Israel governed from Jerusalem. We also find a kind of "Jewish penumbra" reflected in the land promised to Abraham, the territory assigned to David's empire and the area covered by Ezra's law—namely, between the Euphrates and the Mediterranean, "Across the River." In the second century we find much of Palestine annexed into the Hasmonean Judean kingdom. Whence this notion of a "greater Israel," as we might call it? Whatever the answer, it signals a rift between "Judean" and "Jew," one that may perhaps have already been developing. "Jew," at any rate, becomes an ethnic term. But how was "Jewish" definition understood?

The problem of defining "early Judaism" means asking "who was a Jew?" It seems fairly clear that both Judaism and Christianity helped to define the other as religious systems, with increasing clarity from the fourth century as Christianity became the official religion of the empire and rabbinic Judaism completed its redefinition of Israel in its own terms of "dual torah." I have been influenced by Neusner's model of a rabbinic Judaism inspired by catastrophe, creating something new and coherent but less connected to the past than transcending it. I have come to believe that the scriptural literature also represents the creation of an idealized nation, and one also born out of a trauma involving a loss of identity. But it uses the past much more than rabbinic Judaism. It creates a *nation* to which the Jews belong, and not just a cult. This nationalism may have been dormant or even non-existent until the second century BCE, but it exercised a decisive influence on the history of Judah and on Jews thereafter, until first the Jerusalem temple, then the land, was lost.

If Early Judaism—the best name we can give it, to distinguish it from classical, rabbinic Judaism, can be said to begin at any point, that point should probably be set in the sixth or perhaps fifth century. Its endpoint comes with the success of the rabbinate in securing its definition of Israel and of Judaism, in the fourth century CE or perhaps later. That period embraces much (most?) of the composition, and certainly the completion and canonizing of the Scriptures, the emergence and political conquest of Christianity. What still needs to be explored more rigorously, however, are the continuities with the Israelite and Judean monarchies, whose portrait in the Scriptures represents Early Judaism's own cultural memory, a memory that stretched back the origins of "Israel" to the time before any kings ruled or any temple stood in Jerusalem, or even (and this was always being disputed) before the Torah was revealed to them.

We have discovered new data in the last fifty years; but we have also broken much of the conceptual framework that connected Scripture and its "Israel," "early Judaism" and "Christianity," a framework maintained in both Christian and Jewish scholarship that held "early Judaism" to be a continuation or an intensification of legalistic Mosaism culminating in the "second torah" of the rabbis on one side and the abolition of torah on the other side. It is obvious now that this picture is wrong. The right picture, however, is something we are still working on. The gaps in our knowledge are still huge and consequently any critical reconstruction will be highly defective. It may be better for the present to offer partial narratives of aspects that we can perhaps discern and hope that the spaces between them will become clearer, if still remaining largely empty. That is a partial defence for what follows, still essentially a collection of separately conceived and undertaken essays. Two topics predominate: Chapters 3–5 deal mostly with "law," or "torah," and Chapters 7–8 with "apocalyptic." The remaining chapters, however, explore further issues and despite the limitations of what follows, I hope that putting questions together is the best way of finding the answers, or perhaps, of finding better questions.

Chapter 2

Early Judaism(s)

A large amount of important work has been published on topics covered in this essay since this essay appeared in its original form. The following publications are among those worth mentioning.

On the material culture of the early Persian period in Judah (note 27) see now Carter (1999), Edelman (2005), Lipschits (2005), Lipschits and Oeming (2006) and Lipschits, Knoppers and Albertz (2007).

1 Enoch has been particularly widely discussed. The first volume of George Nickelsburg's commentary has appeared and Gabriele Boccaccini has developed his thesis of Enochic Judaism further (1998), and also edited volumes from the ongoing "Enoch Seminar."

On Ezra-Nehemiah, see also Grabbe (1998), and on the development of Nehemiah tradition in 2 Maccabees, Bergren (1997). Bedford (2001) has examined the Ezra-Nehemiah temple building stories and identified in them some of the anachronisms to which I have also drawn attention, including confrontation with Samaria. He also casts doubts on the "exilic" roots of Judean institutions in the Persian period. Hultgren (2007) has identified the "new covenant" of the Damascus Document *with the covenant of Ezra and Nehemiah. The official edition of the Damascus Document (see notes 24 and 25) was published by Joseph Baumgarten (1996); see also the useful introduction by Hempel (2000).*

On the Samaritans and rivalry between Gerizim and Jerusalem, see also Hjelm (2000 and 2004).

On the construction of the biblical definitions of Israel as "cultural memory," updating and amending the conclusions of In Search of Ancient Israel, see Davies (2007). On Jewish ethnicity, see also Mendels (1992), and on Jewish cultural memory in the Hellenistic era, see Mendels (2004). On the development of Judaism in the Hellenistic and Greco-Roman period generally, the important books by Gruen (1998), Schwartz (2001) and Goodman (2007) should be mentioned.

Finally, a number of the topics covered below are treated in Etienne Nodet's (1997) book, which takes as its starting point the discrepancy between Josephus and rabbinic accounts of the foundation of Judaism on the one hand, and biblical accounts on the other. Nodet's explanations are on the whole slightly more radical, though they follow similar lines. In particular, he gives a substantial treatment to the Samaritan question and the significance of the "Maccabean crisis." Very highly recommended also is Cohen's (2000) account of the beginnings of Judaism There are several histories of the period: a systematic treatment of sources and synthesis is given in Grabbe (1991) and (1992); Cohen (1987) also approaches the topics very clearly and with the right kinds of questions.

Judaism and Judaisms

The Jews (Judaeans) of antiquity constituted an ethnos, an ethnic group. They were a named group, attached to a specific territory whose members shared a sense of common origins, claimed a common and distinctive history and destiny, possessed one or more characteristics (Cohen, 2000: 3).

This is an excellent definition, or rather description, as much for what it does not say as what it does. For the perception of Judaism in the Second Temple period has undergone a marked change in the last few decades. It is now frequently represented as a pluriform phenomenon; indeed, so much so that it has become commonplace to speak of the existence not only of various forms or types of Judaism but even of several "Judaisms" before rabbinic Judaism emerged as the authorized (though still not the only) form (Gnosticism, Hekhalot literature, Kabbalah and Hasidism attest to other streams within Judaism).

This new profile has emerged from research in different areas. The idea of a single or "normative" Judaism, which held the field earlier this century, persists in some quarters, but has been steadily undermined. The rediscovery and subsequent re-evaluation of Jewish and early Christian apocalyptic literature that flourished early in this century led to a dichotomy between "rabbinic" and "apocalyptic" Judaism which for a long time absorbed the attention of scholarship, especially a New Testament scholarship which was seeking to define the precise relationship between Jesus, the early Church, and their Jewish background (Collins' *The Apocalyptic Imagination* [1984] is subtitled *An Introduction to the Jewish Matrix of Christianity*). Among Old Testament/Hebrew Bible scholars, the thesis of Plöger, reformulated by Hanson, that two streams of Judaism developed from the early "post-exilic" period, has been quite influential. These scholars represented the dichotomy as one between "theocratic" and "prophetic" groups or "streams," in which rabbinic Judaism's supposed emphasis on legalism placed it on the "theocratic" and "non-eschatological" side. It was necessary to this kind of analysis that the eschatological/prophetic/apocalyptic stream was peripheral, and that the other element was therefore dominant, sociologically "central," normative. There is also a detectable bias in both authors in favour of the ("Christian" and especially Protestant) non-hierocratic, eschatological "stream."

More recent developments have disposed of this dichotomy. First of all, the relationship between the rabbinic literature and the Judaism(s) of the first century CE has been redefined: rabbinic Judaism is now treated by the majority of scholars as a post-Second Temple phenomenon that cannot be understood merely as a continuation of Second Temple period Judaism and which, moreover, as a system of thought and practice, has its own distinction and coherent programme. I refer in particular to the work of Jacob Neusner and his "Judaism of the Two Torahs." Neusner also opted to speak of Second Temple "Judaisms" (see, e.g., Green, 1987). The abuse of both Pharisaism and rabbinic sources in the study of first-century Judaism was also critiqued by Sanders (1977, esp. 33–75). Sanders also described a "common Judaism" (1992), though his assumption that shared Jewish practices in Palestine implied shared religious ideas is not necessarily justified, any more than observing the first day of the week, Christmas and Easter amounts to a "common Christianity"; but the question of common practice will be addressed at the end of this essay. There is currently no consensus as to the nature, role or importance of the Pharisees—or, indeed, their relationship to rabbis.

Second, the Dead Sea Scrolls, whether they are to be integrated into a single sectarian ideology or contain substantial amounts of literature from various sources within Judaism, have widened the range of ideas and practices recognizable as "Jewish." In contrast to the situation twenty years ago in Qumran scholarship, there exists no consensus on this point at present. Whether the Scrolls express one or more Judaisms is not important, though it is universally conceded that the range of ideas present in the Scrolls can hardly be the exclusive property of one sect, whatever sect it might have been (and there is now no agreement on this, either).The combination of cultic, legal, eschatological and apocalyptic elements in this archive has demonstrated clearly that the Judaism of the period cannot be easily sociologically (or ideologically) divided by means of these categories.

Third, if further evidence of great diversity were needed, the vast amount of so-called "pseudepigrapha" dating from this period provides a ready store of examples. Although a surge of interest in these writings can be witnessed in the first two decades of the twentieth century, it is only more recently that these writings have been used in the light of a new understanding of the plurality of early Jewish belief and practice rather than being assigned to one or other of the various distinct "parties" into which, following Josephus, it had been usual to divide Palestinian Judaism.

The outcome of these three developments is the now widely shared (though admittedly not unanimous) perception that what is called "Judaism" in the period before the fall of the Second Temple (and in effect a good deal later) was in reality a set of cultural and religious options. Sometimes these overlapped, sometimes they competed, and they ranged from what sociologists might nowadays call "civic religion" to quite exclusive sects.

Whether or not "common Judaism" is a useful term, the idea of a "common denominator" of Judaism, philosophically as well as historically, needs to be addressed. The replacement of the concept of "Judaism" by the concept of "Judaisms" solves one problem only to create another, perhaps an even more fundamental one—namely what it was that made any Judaism a "Judaism." On this question a good deal is taken for granted in modern (as in older) scholarship and some disagreement is also evident. The nature of the problem can be illustrated by two recent books on Judaism in the Second Temple period. One is Boccaccini's account (1991) of what he calls "Middle Judaism," which affirms that "Judaism is to be seen not as an ideologically homogeneous unit but...as a set of different ideological systems in competition with one another" (13–14) and which characterizes "Judaism" as a "genus" (18–20). The other is Schiffman's (1991) history of Second Temple Judaism, which states in conformity with the new paradigm that "Judaism is not a monolithic phenomenon," and speaks in the next sentence of "all these "Judaisms" (1), but nevertheless prefers to speak thereafter of "approaches" to (one) Judaism which stand "in a dynamic and interactive relationship to each other" (4).

What, in the case of Boccaccini, is common to these "different ideological systems" that makes them "Judaisms" or, in the case of Schiffman, what is the "Judaism" that all of these interacting manifestations "approach"?

Even if "Judaism" is, as Boccaccini says, something of a generic term, the genus itself requires a definition. In Boccaccini's treatment the essential nature of "Judaism" emerges differently, and indeed, only implicitly. At first glance, since his term "Middle Judaism" requires an "Early Judaism" of some kind, and since the character of Middle Judaism, according to Boccaccini, is divergence, "Early Judaism" ought to describe some common starting point for that divergence. By way of definition, he refers to ben Sira as "reaffirming the centrality of the covenant and the retributive principle" (80) and although he remarks that Job and Qoheleth challenged this centrally affirmed notion, the word "centrally" looks very much as if it is functioning here rather like "normative." Again dealing with ben Sira, Boccaccini speaks of "the postulates of a theology of the covenant being reaffirmed," defining these postulates as "the freedom of human will and the retributionary principle" (116). Here again there is a hint of "normativity." But it is nonetheless uncertain whether despite these remarks Boccaccini does intend to commit himself to a definition of "Early Judaism"; it seems to me both from some of his writings but chiefly from private conversations with him, that he is not prepared to identify any single "Early Judaism"; if so, then we are left without an account of what "Early Judaism" was, and thus without a definition of the genus "Judaism," historically speaking, though Boccaccini seems to suggest something rather like Deuteronomism as a "central" feature of it.

Schiffman, on the other hand, gives a direct definition of "Judaism": "the collective religious, cultural and legal tradition and civilization of the Jewish people" (1). This might be interpreted as a tautology, if the word "collective" means no more than "sum total," that is "whatever Jews do"; but in any event Schiffman means some kind of unity, or at least cohesion. His notion of "tradition and civilization" comes into view when he is discussing the penetration into Yehud of "Hellenistic cultural values." He speaks of the "rural peasantry" of Yehud having "no intention of abandoning their ancestral way of life for the new cultural symbiosis" (71). (Curiously, Schiffman describes this way of life as "Hebraic" rather than "Jewish"—perhaps trying to avoid further tautology.) Shortly before this, too, he writes of the "religious tradition" that the "Hellenizers" were challenging (68). Finally (98), where he is discussing "sectarianism," he observes that these divergent expressions of Judaism should not be taken as "independent Judaisms" because that term "ignores the vast body of commonality which united them around adherence to the law of the Torah" (98). Here the language is a bit evasive: Schiffman does not want to reject the plural "Judaisms" entirely, so he adds "independent." He also appears to regard the "ancestral way of life" as centering on the Torah.

For Schiffman, then, the various "approaches" to Judaism are versions of a common heritage, whose core is the Torah, and which can be defined over against the "Hellenizing" influences that tried to distort it. This perspective forms part of the central argument of Schiffman's book (against Neusner, though this is not explicit) that rabbinic Judaism is continuous with earlier "approaches" to Judaism and deeply rooted in the preceding "Jewish tradition." Whether a dichotomy can be made so neatly between "traditional" and "Hellenistic" is, however, questionable. Hengel's detailed treatment of this question, is not universally accepted, deserves some respect and at the very least a nuancing of the simple opposition. Are the Judaisms of Philo or of 2 or 4 Maccabees, traditional or Hellenistic? If such mixtures are possible in Egypt, then why not in Palestine?

If I am interpreting both Schiffman and Boccaccini correctly, they appear to diverge quite significantly in their assessment of "Judaism." Schiffman has replaced "normative Judaism" by "collective Judaism," but the change is hardly more than linguistic. There is in his account a "Jewish tradition" from which various "approaches" developed. Boccaccini's presentation of "Middle Judaism" as manifold and divergent does not, on the other hand, explain what the various Middle Judaisms diverged *from*, and in fact leaves one wondering what these often quite different Judaisms could have had in common, especially the "Zadokite" (Mosaic) and Enochic. But there is another difference between the two scholars. For Schiffman, Jewish civilization is a matter essentially of popular custom, while Boccaccini's agenda is "Jewish thought, defined by a set of theological writers. Both, however, are only aspects of a "Judaism." Neither aspect, in fact, can demonstrate a corresponding antecedent. We do not know much about "popular custom" in Judah either in the monarchic or post-monarchic eras. As for "Jewish thought," intellectual systems expressed by individual authors, we have no clear model. The scriptures do not provide a model of Judaism, but a very rich mixture of many kinds (as the comparison of Deuteronomy, Leviticus and Numbers in Chapter 3 illustrates). The Judaism of the prophetic books and of the wisdom books are not easily merged into a single "Judaism." The biblical literature, in short, does not provide a religious system nor does it display evidence of there ever having been a "core" Judaism. The "Judaism" of Boccaccini and the "approaches to Judaism" of Schiffman do not share a single common prototype. What can any antecedent "Judaism" be, then, other than "whatever was thought and done in Judah"? Quite apart from this, the divergence over the very *nature* of "Judaism" represented by these two works is not one that can be left aside. Can we mix together traditional social practices with the (inevitably elite, because written and copied and preserved) literature that provides most of what we know about early Judaism? And how is the relationship between the two rather different phenomena to be understood and expressed?

There is, then, much of a fundamental nature that needs to be said on the problem of Judaism—not merely what its content was, but what *sort* of a thing it was in the first place. Neither of these questions can be disposed of in advance of exploring the origins and evolution of "Judaism" in all its possible senses, because only by a very careful analysis of all the sources (which are in any case hugely inadequate) can we even define "Judaism."

Juda-ism and Judaisms

Schiffman's description of "Judaism" as "the culture of the Jewish people" seems, as remarked earlier, tautologous. But perhaps it isn't entirely. It is customary these days for "Judaism" to be classified as a religion. Yet nowadays the term "secular Jew" has some meaning. Schiffman's definition equates culture with religion, at least in the ancient world. But is "Judaism" the religion of the "Jewish people" or are the "Jewish people" those who adhere to the religion? Many Jews in the ancient world became so by voluntary or compulsory conversion to a religion that previously existed, so that in their case it was adherence to "Judaism" that made them "Jews." The "conversion" of so much of Palestine to "Judaism" under the Hasmoneans is curious, since it seems to have entailed both religious and political affiliation. The "Jewish people," by these actions, was, according to Seth Schwartz—who also understands this problem in the same way (2001: 4–14)—estimates a "two- to fivefold increase in the Jewish population of Palestine" in the wake of the Hasmonean expansion (2001: 41).

Another way of looking at the problem is to ask about the relationship between "Jews" and the Israelites of the "pre-exilic" period. The use of the term "Israel" as a self-description of the Jewish "people" implies continuity (or identity, if shared with Samaria). But the continuity in terms of population or even religious customs is only partial. The question of defining ancient Judaism is not so much philosophical or linguistic as *historical*. Let us begin the process of clarifying by making the distinction between "Jewish" and "Judean." Although neither in Hebrew nor in Greek is there any *linguistic* distinction between the two meanings, the terms are not synonymous in English, nor in most other modern languages in which Jewish scholarship is conducted. And this modern distinction does in fact correctly represent differences in meaning that the single Hebrew or Greek terms can convey. In our own time the debate as to whether the Fourth Gospel's "Jews" are members of the *ethnos* or "Judeans" has been pursued in the context of that gospel's supposed "anti-Semitism." Paul does not refer to himself directly as a "Jew," but only as an "Israelite"—because he was Benjaminite?

The word *ioudaismos* itself implies a self-conscious cultural and religious identity and first appears (several times) in 2 Maccabees where, as Daniel Schwartz notes (1992: 11), it "parallels and contrast with 'Hellenism' (*hellenismos)* and even 'foreignism' (*allophylismos)."* As Schwartz also rightly notes (13), it is only when such a concept as "Judaism" comes into consciousness, that is, becomes conceptualized, that there is a need to argue about what that concept denotes. Up to that moment, it may be a matter either of loyalty to a particular Temple and cult, or residence in Yehud/Judea, or perhaps of membership in a society ethnically defined in some way, or any combination of these. But the conscious "-ism" is a prerequisite, or at the least a symptom of the emergence of "Judaism" into historical consciousness. "Juda-ism" becomes a concept rather than an unreflected way of being. Schwartz notes (13) that "as long as 'being Jewish [in my terminology, 'being Judean']' was basically a matter of place or race, there was no reason to assume that all should agree about belief or practice, any more than all French or all women do." This means that we should not look to any *kind* of "Judaism" logically or historically until the emergence of "Juda-ism" as a concept, as the *idea* of a "Judean way of life." And at the "moment," logically and historically, there need be no common consent at all if the "Judean way of life" was experienced in various ways. We might therefore distinguish three stages in the emergence of the definition of "Judaism": first, Judean culture that is not homogenous and has not yet been conceptualized (and therefore is not a "Juda-ism"); "Juda-ism," the culture of Judea conceptualized, an object of various kinds of definition; and finally "Judaism," the definition of "Juda-ism" as a religion or a cult or a philosophy—a *system* of belief and practice rather than custom. In short: "Early Judaism" begins life as a plurality, and what makes any of these "Judaisms" a "Judaism" is whether or not they claim to be such. That claim might be geographical, cultural or ideological. One of the major elements in most Judaisms is an identity with "Israel," and this cannot be separated from the element of adherence to a common set of scriptural writings (though not necessarily a closed set). Whatever else these scriptures, they define Jews as "Israel"; more importantly, they also define "Israel."

A study of the origins and prehistory, of "Judaism" is possible and legitimate only if the above distinctions are recognized and we do not retroject later definitions into historical antecedent phases. Judaism *has* a beginning, but as a set of conscious ideas, reactions to some kind of crisis of identity. Its characterization of itself as a "revealed" religion" (so, e.g., Schiffman, 1991: 11) claims for it a theologically timeless quality but also a historical originated one: the "revelation" has its *moment.* Whatever the value of the claim religiously, it is not historical. The practical wisdom of a ben Sira, the mantic wisdom of the followers of the Enoch cult, the beliefs and rites of the Samaritans and the regimented lifestyle of the Qumranic *yahad* are Judaisms that have some shared common features but no single common origin. "Judaism" is not a "given" but something constructed by human imagination, participates fully in the ever-changing flux of human thought and behaviour. But the case of rabbinic Judaism (which is quite different in this respect from Christianity) shows how a constructed system can become a real one. The ideal "Israel" of the Mishnah is the one that united and preserved Judaism for centuries, and it is has been challenged only in relatively recent times by ethnic (culminating in an attempt at genocidal extermination), nationalistic (political Zionism) or cultural ("secular Judaism") alternatives. If nothing else, these alternatives remind us that from the outset "Judaism" was never a stable concept.

False Origins

It is a useful exercise to clear away a number of assumptions and theories about the origins of Judaism, because these are all built on ancient concepts of what Judaism was. A majority of scholars apparently still accept the view that the production of scriptures and the activities of Ezra and Nehemiah were original and definitive stages in the formation of Judaism. Can this view really been maintained?

Scriptures
The notion that the Jewish scriptures provide an account of a prototypical Judaism is unworkable on a number of grounds. First, the scriptures do

not have their own intrinsic religious system. Their contents cannot be transcribed into a coherent set of beliefs and practices without the aid of an *external* framework of systematic theology that controls a hermeneutical process, such as is the case with both rabbinic Judaism and Christianity. The possible religious systems that could be derived from the scriptures are numerous. It is true that both "torah" and "Israel" are major categories within the scriptures, but neither category is fundamental to the wisdom literature, although there are clear signs of occasional attempts to accommodate "wisdom" to "torah."

Second, the scriptures cannot have described, or arisen directly from, an actual historical religious system. Ancient Israel and Judah were not "communities of faith" as distinct from any of their neighbours, all of whom had their own deities also. We cannot know in much detail what the religions of these ancient societies were, but the books of Judges–Kings and the archaeological evidence agree that much religious practice in these two kingdoms largely conformed to local patterns ("worshipping the Baals"). The culture of the Israelite or Judean farmer seems to have been polytheistic, concerned with fertility and based on local and domestic shrines. Its folklore would probably have comprised such things as local legal practices, local stories about ancestors and places, and a collection of proverbial sayings and myths and legends associated with local shrines, not with a written torah, purity laws or belief in a corporate "covenant" with an exclusive national deity.

Third, not all Judaisms seem to have taken scriptures as their doctrinal basis. The literature of 1 Enoch, Tobit, the Hekhalot literature and the "Teaching of the Two Spirits" from the Qumran Community Rule do not do so. Ben Sira and the Mishnah do so partially. Many of the works translated in Charlesworth's two-volume *Old Testament Pseudepigrapha* are not doctrinally based on the scriptures, though they often use scriptural characters as pseudonymous authors. Most of these writings betray forms of religious belief or cultural behaviour that are minimally represented in the scriptures, such as messianic expectation or the belief that future events can be divined from texts. The scriptures function as an important *part* of most ancient Judaisms, but they do not *prescribe* them. That does not mean that as part of the created culture of Judah they did not play an important role in the cultivation of Juda-ism. They did: but as part of the complex process of *defining* what "Judaism" might be, or should be. Most—not all—of the scriptures, interestingly, define Judaism in terms of national identity: some as a cult, and some as a philosophy. In other words, they also reflect differences of opinion over what kind of thing "Judaism" might be.

Fourth, scriptures, as a corpus, and as religiously authoritative, do not predate Second Temple Judaism. Many of these writings are widely accepted as products of the Second Temple period. But the modern scholarly view that torah and prophecy are already firmly established in written (not necessarily final) form by the end of the Babylonian exile (and this "exile" is more of an ideological construct than a precise historical description) is precarious. It is fairly widely conceded that all of the scriptural books in their present form emanate from the sixth or even fifth centuries BCE onwards. Even allowing for earlier sources or earlier documents, the formation of this literature, which became canonical and finally constituted a closed canon and became "biblical" is contemporary with the formation of Judean culture(s) in the Persian period, and participated in that process. Scripture was not "inherited" but produced, within "early Judaism."

The accumulation of the above arguments means that the scriptures cannot be understood as a blueprint for the religion of Judaism, not a description of a culture or expression of a tradition. They are part of a cultural, obviously scribal and thus to some degree intellectual, process by which "Juda-ism" was negotiated; as they progressed towards their adoption as a formal religious canon, they played a more influential role in the self-definition of most Judaisms. It does not seem right, either, to conclude that the various Judaisms "adopted" the literature as scripture; rather we have an interaction between written (and rewritten) texts and cultural processes. No chicken and no egg.

Ezra and Nehemiah

One historical foundation of Judaism widely accepted in modern scholarship is the work of Nehemiah and Ezra. These two, and especially Ezra, are commonly held to mark the beginning of Judaism, the new "Israel" in Judah. The reading of the law, the (re)making of a covenant and the establishment of social and religious exclusivity represent either the beginning or the rebirth of a religion constituted by an exclusive, ethnically-defined, law-bound relationship between a people and its deity. The essential historicity of the events described in the two books has rarely been questioned; the famous exception of C. C. Torrey (1910) has attracted few supporters. Even Morton Smith (1971) abandoned most of his characteristic scepticism at this point and treated these books as largely historical reportage, though he recognized some divergence from what he construed as the real state of affairs. Significantly, he suggested that the events related to a community within Judean society, the self-styled "children of the Exile." Elsewhere (1961) he had suggested that sectarian tendencies were evident within Judean society from early on, and that the stories of Ezra and Nehemiah already portray this. Other scholars have also regarded this early "Judaism" as portraying a select group—Weinberg (1992, see further discussion in Davies, 1991) called it a *Bürger-Tempel-Gemeinde*—whose culture was gradually adopted by the society of Yehud as a whole, and, we may add, presumably by those in Samaria too, a factor that is given too little attention. Such a process, by which a certain culture and organization spread from an elite group outwards to encompass a society, might be essentially correct if we consider the Hasmonean political "Judaizing" of Palestine as its culmination (though Herod's furthering of the politicizing of Judaism beyond Judah by promoting himself as the patron of all Jews might represent a furthering of this process).

Nevertheless, the contents of the books of Ezra and Nehemiah present difficulties for historical reconstruction that have always been recognized. To begin with, there is no general critical consensus about the relative chronology of the two figures. This is a result of the confusion caused by the books themselves, which keep the two characters largely apart from one another but apparently date Ezra to the same time as Nehemiah. Though in the Masoretic canon the two books are treated as one, and while they do clearly show signs of having been integrated editorially, there must have been originally independent stories of the two characters and the connection of the two figures in a single story boils down to a single episode in Nehemiah 8–9. At what point were the two men brought together? Both ben Sira and the author of 2 Maccabees know of Nehemiah, but neither mentions Ezra, and 2 Maccabees associates Nehemiah with the high priest. This silence about Ezra implies at least that he was not associated with Nehemiah until the end of the second century BCE at the earliest, and perhaps that the Ezra story was not well known. Hence, Ezra's historicity falls under suspicion, being unattested elsewhere until the first century CE. But even in the case of Nehemiah, the enmity towards the Samarians probably reflects later conditions, and even suggests that the book has a purpose in denying any legitimacy to Samarians, and indicates a high degree of antagonism between Jerusalem and Samaria (rather than Jerusalem and Gerizim; the book is less interested in Jerusalem's religious authority than its political status). Political rivalry may have predated religious rivalry, and perhaps suggests political unification of the two under the Ptolemies (on the religious schism, see Purvis 1986).

Some recent trends in Ezra and Nehemiah studies have moved from questions such as the priority of one or other, the identity of Ezra's lawbook, the nature of the reforms of Nehemiah, or the authenticity of the Aramaic documents. Greater attention is being been paid to their literary and ideological aspects (see, e.g., Eskenazi, 1988; Clines, 1990; VanderKam, 1992, Kraemer, 1993). The increasingly common view that these books do not belong to the Chronicler's work has also reopened the question of their purpose. Consequently, attention is being diverted away from the historicity of the details described and towards the more promising quest for the historical circumstances that prompted these writings. Indeed, this approach also seems the best way to account for the literary form of the books of Ezra and Nehemiah. Such an approach might begin with the observation that the two books, or the tales attached to the two characters, claim to describe *the origin of Judaism*; two stories, which inherently contradict one another by assigning functions to each that undermine the functions of the other, have been flimsily entwined by an editor, and no earlier than the second century BCE. Hence, it appears plausible that *competing* claims about the origin or the true founder of "Judaism" (and in each case the "Judaism" is differently conceived) have been reconciled editorially, with the happy result not only that these ancient rivals were accommodated into a single and perhaps mutually acceptable legend, but also, unhappily, that some modern historians are chasing historical scenarios that never existed. An investigation into these books might be better shifted to, say, the second century BCE, to a time when a hitherto unknown (to our extant sources) Ezra confronted Nehemiah for the post of "founder of Judaism" and the two stories were blended, achieving compromise in a series of acts that were largely shared. Thereafter Ezra seems to have been the more popular figure, nevertheless, perhaps because the "Ezraite" definition of Judaism prevailed, as indeed, it seems to have in the form of rabbinic Judaism, whereas the builder of the walls of Jerusalem under imperial patronage perhaps looked suspiciously like a predecessor of Herod the Great. Or, more simply, those for whom Ezra has originally stood as "founder" survived the end of Jerusalem as a Jewish city.

This perspective can be carried further by involving another account of the origins of "Judaism," outside the scriptural canon but chronologically perhaps not far removed from the others. According to the *Damascus Document* (CD), the exilic punishment on Israel led to the restoration of a remnant, to whom the true divine will about Sabbaths, feasts and laws was given. While the rest of Israel went astray, this chosen remnant remained to await the divine judgment on Israel and on the Gentiles, anticipating salvation and vindication for themselves (for details, see Davies, 1982: 56–104). The revelation of the law and the foundation of this "true Israel" is credited to a figure known as the "Interpreter of the Law" (*doresh ha-torah*). The account is different in scope, in literary form and in some details, from both Ezra and Nehemiah. But these differences are mostly attributable to the literary genre in which the story is embedded, and to the fact that CD's "Judaism" is yet again different from that implicitly advanced in either Ezra or Nehemiah. The similarities between the three accounts are even more striking and significant; they presuppose the same story of Israel's "pre-exilic" past (though the historical narrations of that period in Nehemiah 9 and CD 2:14–312. have quite different emphases) and the exile as punishment for that past. All three accounts, significantly, speak of a covenant with the members of the elect group that is based on a lawgiving, and all three allude to a process of interpretation of that law and deal with issues of holiness and separation from "outsiders" (and indeed from other Judeans, the "people of the land" or "builders of the wall"). In these respects the accounts all reflect a certain common perspective on "Judaism."

The *Damascus Document* seems to share with Jubilees, Enoch and Daniel the notion that there was no historical "restoration" in the sixth century BCE and ignore or belittle the building of a Temple at about that time. They betray a wider conflict over the matter of the origins of "Judaism" ("Judaism" being represented by the name "Israel," though the new "Israel" and not the "pre-exilic" one). Rather than understanding the history of Judaism to begin with a firm historical tradition, what we see in the literature is a set of competing traditions, appearing around the same period, with only Nehemiah attested before 200 BCE, as a builder of Jerusalem (ben Sira 49:13).

The case of Ezra and Nehemiah is a microcosm of the issue outlined earlier about the relationship between scriptures and Judaism: a literary text that does not relate history directly but indirectly, that does not produce "Judaism" but reflects the development and even the negotiation of "Judaisms." Ezra and Nehemiah presuppose the existence of what they are supposed to be founding and can provide information only about a period much later than the Persian era, contributing to a quite different story about the origins of "Judaism."

Juda-ism Outside Judah

Some recognition, however brief, should be registered of those who regarded themselves as "Judean" but lived outside Judah. During the Second Temple period these Judeans grew to be more numerous than those within Judah—though not, as modern Jewish myth still has it, largely as a result of forced exile, but by conversion, economic migration, military service and other motives. Since we cannot identify with certainty any literature from the Judeans who *were* deported, to Babylonia (despite many scholarly hypotheses), the earliest perspective we have is provided by the letters from the colony of Elephantine around 400 BCE. The writers, who address their letters to both Jerusalem and Samaria, call themselves "Judeans" and preserve religious customs that appear to be continued from monarchic Judah (when the colony was created), together, perhaps, with some degree of local assimilation. Since it had been probably been founded under the Assyrians, few if any of this military colony were native Judahites or Judeans but they retained this identity largely, it seems, by adhering to the cult of the Judean god Yhw, to whom they had built a temple. The preservation of such an ethnic identity is known to have been the case with other military colonies in the Hellenistic period and was presumably sustained by its difference from the surrounding population of the kind that a military colony might require.

Those who preserved a Judean ethnic identity in Mesopotamia pose some interesting questions to the historian. Presumably they adhered initially to the customs of their homeland. But when we encounter them later they seem to have been influenced by the developments taking place in Judah itself. We should presumably consider that under the Persians and their successors communication between Judah and Babylonia was good, as it was also between Judah and Judeans in Egypt. We do not know how or why Judeans came to be in Egypt (apart from the Elephantine colony) but the book of Jeremiah records a story that they fled there after the murder of Gedaliah. Most likely, this is largely a legend embraced by these Judeans to explain their presence and link their history to the history of Judah itself. There are various pieces of evidence to suggest that Egyptian Judaisms had their own temple(s), one being at Leontopolis (*Tell el-Yahudiya*: see Isa. 19:18; Hayward, 1982; Bohak, 1996).

Aspects of Juda-ism in the Hellenistic Period

Hecataeus of Abdera

From about the beginning of the Hellenistic period (c. 300 BCE), several references to Judeans by non-Judean authors are known. Of these the most interesting, and the most discussed, is that of Hecataeus of Abdera (for discussion, see Grabbe, 1991: 1.173, 216–18; Stern, 1976: 20–35; Hengel, 1974: 1.255–56 [2.169]; Schürer, 1986: 3,1.671–77). A summary of his accounts of Judean history and constitution is preserved in the work of the first century BCE compiler Diodorus Siculus (40.3); a further excerpt from a book attributed to him and "written entirely about the Jews" is preserved in Josephus (*Contra Apionem* 1: 183–204; Stern [1976: 1.35–44], followed in Schürer, takes the work as authentic). Because of its uncertain attribution, it will not be considered here. According to Hecataeus, a pestilence in Egypt at some time (Hecataeus gives no chronological clues) prompted the inhabitants to expel certain strangers who practised alien rites; of these deportees, some landed in Greece, but the larger number in Judea, which was then uninhabited. They settled under the leadership of Moses, who founded several cities, including Jerusalem, where he established a temple. He also set up "forms of worship and ritual," laws, and political institutions. He divided the people into twelve tribes, forbade images to be made of their sole deity, and appointed priests, who were to be not only in charge of the cult but also political leaders and judges. Thus, he says, "the Jews have never had a king" but are ruled by a high priest, who enjoys great power and prestige. Moses also instituted a military education and led the people to many conquests against neighbouring tribes, after which he apportioned the land equally, but reserving larger portions for the priests. The sale of land was forbidden, specifically so as to avoid oppression of the poor by the rich through accumulation of land. The people were also enjoined to reproduce. In marriage and burial their customs differed from those of others, though their traditional practices were disturbed under the Persians and Macedonians. The Judeans' laws claim to have been words heard by Moses from God.

This account demonstrates some Hellenistic features. For instance, Moses appears as a typical colony founder. There is also a patently Egyptian legend underlying the account of the origin of the Judeans in Egypt. In a passage almost certainly reproduced from Hecataeus, Diodorus elsewhere (1.28:1–3) reproduces an Egyptian legend or myth that most of the civilized world came about through colonization from

Egypt: thus Belus led colonists to Babylon, Danaus to Greece, and others to Colchis and Judea (for the text see Stern, 1976: 1.169). A few elements in Hecataeus' account are also present in Manetho's stories preserved in Josephus, notably the name Moses and the immediate connection between the departure from Egypt and the foundation of Jerusalem (for a comparison, see Davies, 2001).

How accurately might this account reflect (a) the profile of Judean culture at the end of the fourth century and (b) any accounts of their history that Judean themselves had? It has been widely surmised that Hecataeus must have had some information from Judeans, whether living in Egypt or in Judah itself. A study of this account by Mendels (1983: 96–110) has proposed that Hecataeus' account is fairly accurately preserved and reflects ideas emanating from Judean priestly circles from his own time. Mendels' contention is based on correspondences between the account and the situation described in Ezra and Nehemiah, which he takes to be a reliable portrait of Judah in the Persian period. Although I have earlier argued against this view, many of Doron's observations and arguments nevertheless suggest that Hecataeus was fairly closely reflecting the state of affairs in Judah during his own time. Mendels notes that the Judeans are said to have occupied a land that was "utterly uninhabited" after leaving Egypt. This, as he notes, conflicts with the Pentateuchal tradition, but is in accordance with the ideology represented in Nehemiah and Ezra that maintains that the returnees from exile had come to a desolate, if not quite empty, land. He cites Nehemiah 2–4 and Judith 5:19, but, as noted by Carroll (1991), the ideology of the "empty land" appears even more emphatically in Jeremiah 32 and Leviticus 25–27 and can be seen as a wider perception within Juda-ism. Indeed, Ezra and Nehemiah do not stress the concept of the "empty land"; in them we meet the "people of the land" on several occasions, though in an entirely negative sense. But at any rate, Hecataeus' view is reflected in some biblical texts, giving support to Mendels' contention that he reports a genuine Judean perspective.

As for Moses having founded Jerusalem, and other cities, Mendels suggests that because of the authority of Moses during the Persian period, and particularly the authority of his "law," Hecataeus may have understood Moses also to have been a city-founder. To support his explanation, he claims that the role of David is underplayed in Ezra–Nehemiah. But rather than focusing on unconvincing parallels in Ezra–Nehemiah, we could consider divergences from what became the canonical version of Judean history. Moses is credited with conquest, with the creation of twelve tribes and with the division of land among the tribes. These activities correspond in some measure to the story in the book of Joshua, where, however, another hero has come to be credited with conquest and land allotment (account of a Mosaic conquest and land distribution east of the Jordan remain in Joshua 12–14). The statement that the Judeans had always been ruled by priests and never by a king is blatantly contradicted by the canonical writings. Hecataeus' source did not seem to know of the books of Samuel, Kings or Chronicles, but did know of some stories that appear in Joshua. He also knows of something like an "Exodus." The reliability of Hecataeus' information may be simply erratic, but that should not automatically be assumed. He may just as well be preserving what some Judeans believed to have been the case, giving us a precious insight into the early stages of the formation of the Pentateuchal tradition, a national history of the people of Judah in the process of being written and—most curious of all—the prominence of a hero with an undoubtedly Egyptian name. Perhaps a Judean source from Egypt after all?

Indeed, some degree of credence ought to be given to Hecataeus' account simply because he appears to be quite accurate in many details regarding the Judeans' account of their history. He knows that the laws governing cult and ritual are ascribed to Moses and even that Moses is claimed to have heard them from God. In calling this cult monotheistic and aniconic he is presumably also observing correctly. He even knows that Moses appointed judges (see Numbers 11). He is also correct, as far as is known, about the high priest being the ruler of the Judeans, and his observations about land tenure fit with the scriptural sources. Of course, the sorts of changes in land tenure often posited for this earlier period are just as plausibly set in the Persian and Hellenistic periods, so that some, or even all of the "prophetic" material in the Bible protesting at the accumulation of land must at least be considered as possibly emanating from this later period (on this see Kessler, 1992; Kreissig, 1973; Kippenberg, 1978). But that is not the point.

Finally, there is the matter of military education. The widespread use of Jews as mercenaries is well-known from the Assyrian period (when the Elephantine colony was set up) to the Hellenistic period. The likelihood that Judeans were trained in the military arts is quite high, in view of this and of their initial success during the Maccabean wars, when a quite effective militia seems to have been organized. In any case a military aspect to Judean culture is probably betrayed in its literature, in the elaboration not only of the military victories in Joshua and the "holy war" ideology of Deuteronomy and Deuteronomistic writings, but also in the depiction of the Israelites in the wilderness as a nation-army (see the discussion of the "Israel" of Numbers in the next chapter). That material strongly suggests a self-image of Judeans as a nation of warriors. Indeed, one title given to their deity, *Yhwh Sebaoth*, probably means "Yahweh of armies."

The account of the Judeans by Hecataeus thus furnishes an extremely important source of information about the culture, and especially views of their past at the dawn of Judeans in the Hellenistic era. If Hecataeus is reliable in most matters, his work reflects "Juda-ism" at a relatively early stage of formation; the Temple cult, priesthood and a distinctive land tenure system have been established, but only a rudimentary history has yet been formed to explain who these "Judeans" are, where they came from, and how they got their deity. Between the beginning of the third century and its end, when ben Sira wrote, the extent to which practices, beliefs and historiography have developed can perhaps be traced, if with some hesitation. The more or less contemporary descriptions by Theophrastus, Clearchus and Megasthenes should also be consulted. (Theophrastus [c. 370–285] describes Judeans as philosophers, performing burnt offerings, looking at the stars while praying, and fasting; Clearchus [early third century] also classes the Judeans as "philosophers" and traces their origin to India; Megasthenes [c. 300] associates the Judean philosophers with India.) Rather than an ancient Judean "tradition," we encounter a dynamic process of ideological formation, the end product of which is a conscious "Juda-ism," a developed identity of which any Jerusalem *literatus* could be proud. No doubt the impact that the Ptolemaic administration made, notably in respect of economic exploitation, urban development and bureaucratic intrusion even into the rural areas, facilitated that development by presenting Judeans with a culture in the face of which their own identity needed to be more strongly defined and articulated.

Ben Sira

Ben Sira is a key figure in the evolution of Judaism, both because of the time and place he occupies (c. 200 BCE) and also because of the influence his writings had in different kinds of Judaism. A wisdom teacher whose work belongs to a well-known Near Eastern genre, he was also devoted to the cult and the priesthood of Jerusalem. He was aware of a Mosaic lawbook, the "book of the covenant of the Most High God" and also spoke of "the law" (*torah*), which will be considered presently. He was familiar with the cultural world of Hellenism, which he did not oppose, though his writings demonstrate above all a desire to fuse the traditional scribal ethos of wisdom with other Judean elements: cult, priesthood, scriptures, and a little of the Hellenistic culture. Perhaps he is one individual of whom we know that personifies the process by which Jud-aism was being constructed at this time.

Behind the whole process of creating a Judean literary canon lay several impulses, no doubt: but two of them can be connected with the spread of Hellenistic culture. One was to generate a cultural and social identity in the form of a national history and constitution: several nations and groups were fashioning such accounts at this time, though usually in Greek (Manetho, Berossus, Philo of Byblos). The other, which the retention of the scribal literary language of Judah betrays, is the desire to counter Greek education with a Judean one. Such motives do not necessarily explain the creation of the individual writings, but they explain how a literary canon, in Hebrew, developed and how it developed, as a canon, alongside the notion of "Juda-ism."

Ben Sira does not know the five books that now constitute the Pentateuch in their present canonical form. He seems to have a different evaluation of Adam and Enoch than the scriptural text finally offered. He had also apparently not heard of Joseph's exploits in Egypt, either, but only a story about Joseph's bones being carried back. But his canon of texts contains what was later finalized, and probably a bit more. However, he does not cite or exegete any passages from the literature: he only alludes to their content, in a way, as Middendorp (1973: 90–91) observes, that "would have been familiar to a reader with a Greek education." In his bringing together the concepts of "wisdom" and "law" he does not equate wisdom with a canonized text, but something broader, perhaps closer even to "custom." He is "Judaizing" a universal value, or perhaps, more modestly, teaching that for a Jew, "wisdom" means Jewish customs, including its cult, or "fear of the Lord"—"fear" meaning "devotion," signifying, as it does in Jonah, worship of a divinity and the nearest that ancient Judaism comes to a word for "religion." The "law which Moses commanded" (likewise 42:2: "the law and covenant of the Most High"), is probably a reference to Deuteronomy (in some form), since this book is the only one that claims to be "commanded" by Moses, and the terms "words" and "commandments" (1:26; 2:15) echo especially the vocabulary of Deuteronomy. Ben Sira's view is thus close to those other Hellenistic writers (both Jewish and non-Jewish, and including Hecataeus) who regard Moses as the writer of the Judean "constitution."

Of course ben Sira regards the words of Moses as divine commandments of God: Hecataeus, too, wrote that the Judeans regarded the words of Moses as heard from God. But does he regard Moses' writings as divinely originated in an essentially different way from his own words, which, according to the same discourse (24:30–32) are "prophecy" and elsewhere are "wisdom" and will be a "bequest to future generations" (24:33)—just as Moses' words are (24:23)? (Is this what is meant by 2 Tim. 3:16; "all scripture/literature is divinely inspired"?) "Torah," as ben Sira uses the term, represents divine wisdom much as ben Sira's own words do. When in 41:8 he condemns those who have "forsaken the *torah* of the Most High God" we should perhaps not think in terms of halakhic deviation, or even of disobedience, but closer to the Stoic meaning of *nomos*. Both *hokhmah* and *torah* are in fact divinely given insights into how to live in accordance with the created order. The identification of the two is not forced at all; they are different words for the same thing: Judean ethics. It is significant that his description of the scribe who "seeks out the wisdom of all the ancients, and is concerned with prophecies; preserves the sayings of the famous and penetrates the subtleties of parables; he seeks out the hidden meanings of proverbs and is at home with the obscurities of parables" *does not include Torah*. The accumulation of wisdom from literary tradition has little in common with the Qumranic or Pharisaic Torah. His wisdom is not halakhah.

Nevertheless, ben Sira's equation illuminates how scripture and "Judaism" are converging. Ben Sira's Judaism is not a revealed religion in Schiffman's sense: "... based on the belief that God revealed himself to the Jewish people through the agency of Moses." If that were so, his book would not be, as it so obviously is, a genuine book of wisdom, such as the *Wisdom of Solomon* is not (a comparison of the two writings is highly instructive). Ben Sira's Juda-ism draws on the Mosaic covenant book but also on other writings for a cultural resource; it includes the cult and priesthood but most of all cherishes wisdom. Ultimately, it is not a Judaism of Torah, nor is it predominantly Mosaic.

Juda-ism in Conflict

The importance of the Maccabean wars for the definitive transition from the kind of Juda-ism found in ben Sira to Judaism is that the *casus belli* was *religious*. While its root causes were as much economic and political, Antiochus IV and his supporters were seen by the Judeans who resisted him to have attacked the foundation of *their* Juda-ism, the major symbols of national identity, including national customs, the high-priesthood and the cult. The conflict underlined the extent to which the Juda-ism of the resisters was essentially religious. We cannot say the same of the so-called "Hellenizers" since we do not really know, in their own words, exactly how they understood Juda-ism. 1 Maccabees represents the protagonists as "Israel" on the one hand and "the nations" on the other, and narrates the conflict as a replay of the time of the Judges, with the family of Mattathias as divinely appointed saviours. Mattathias himself wears the mantle of the xenophobic and anti-idolater Phinehas.

Alongside the conflict between Israel and the nations is one between "apostates" and "pious" within Judah, and naturally, righteousness lies with the victors: a dispassionate assessment is no more to be expected than historical accuracy in a Judean historian of this period. Certain elements of "Juda-ism" are depicted as definitive—temple, circumcision, diet, sabbath, holy books. These practices (presumably fundamental to Schiffman's "traditional Judaism") become dominant characteristics of Judaism in due course. But how representative were they before the conflict? Rather than defending the essence of traditional Judaism, the Maccabees brought to a head the disagreements about what it was. Even after their success, the conflict continued, but we can see it more clearly represented by distinct parties: Pharisees, Essenes, Sadducees, and no doubt others. As for "Hellenism," the Hasmoneans set a good example of how to be at the same time Judean, nationalistic and Hellenistic, and Herod followed them. "Traditional Judaism" can no more be defined *after* the Maccabean success than it could before. But an independent Judean state required some degree of orthodoxy, or rather orthopraxy.

Circumcision is a good example to consider, as the most prominent identifier of a Jew. According to 1 Maccabees, some Jews tried to conceal it, others abandoned it, and the Maccabees enforced it. The custom was practised among many people in the Levant during all preceding periods, and while a distinguishing feature of being Judean, it was not entirely distinctive; certainly it cannot always have been an outward sign of the covenant of god and people that it later came to be. (Most of the people "Judaized" by the Hasmoneans already practised the rite.) What caused it to become a central feature of Juda-ism, and the major religious symbol of all Judaisms—and when? The scriptural evidence allows us to see it being transformed from a cultural practice into a sign of the "covenant" (and not all Judaisms had a covenant). Joshua 5:2 contains an account of a circumcision of all Israelites after crossing the Jordan (not after birth). Although Josh. 4:2 accords this some importance, circumcision is not connected with any covenant ceremony nor given any religious rationale. Exodus 4:26 gives an aetiology of some sort, which continues to defy explanation, though it has suggested to some commentators that circumcision was thought to be connected with marriage and that failure to circumcise might cause divine retribution. The text that was to become definitive is Gen. 17:10–14 where circumcision is named as a mark of the covenant. Unfortunately, none of these passages can be dated; nor can the expression "circumcision of the heart," that seems characteristic of Deuteronomistic Judaism.

But what about social reality? Circumcision can be a mark of *public* difference only when visible. Public nudity does not seems to have been a custom of any of the peoples of the Levant; rather it was a feature of the Greek, and Hellenistic, city (as 1 Maccabees implies), in the gymnasium, the baths and the stadium, Nudity was normal and natural among Greeks, and circumcision seen by them as a deformity. Judeans who encountered this cultural contradiction (hardly a majority, one supposes) could become for the first time self-conscious about circumcision, regarding it a cultural aberration and not a norm. They could give it up or cover it up on the one hand, or reassert it with pride as a mark of their own culture. While circumcision was, then, a cultural norm, its significance specifically as a crucial mark of membership of "Israel" is most likely to have emerged after contact with Hellenistic city life. Like circumcision—when Juda-ism became "Judaism." Perhaps it was even Antiochus who decided that it was a major barrier to the progress of Greek civilization in his realm, and so made it a badge of Judean pride and resistance.

The Sabbath is a not dissimilar case: here too is a custom of considerable antiquity which assumed at some point a strong religious character. How and why did this Sabbath become a matter of observance for every Judean, leading to a proliferation of observances and non-observances? Unlike the case of circumcision, we have a fairly large spread of biblical texts forbidding work on the Sabbath or implying no work: laws in Exodus, Deuteronomy and Leviticus, texts in Jeremiah, Ezekiel, Amos and so on. What is not so well established is the fixing of the Sabbath as a day of *religious activity*, that is as a day on which certain things *were* done, liturgical acts *outside* the Temple (on this question, see McKay, 1994). In literature such as *Jubilees* and CD, we see violent accusations of Sabbath violation and regulations or norms about what is or is not to be done on that day. Unfortunately we are almost wholly in the dark as to what Judeans in Palestine *did* on Sabbaths (we are just a little better informed about the Diaspora).

Did Jews not fight on Sabbaths? Hecataeus presented the Jews as training their young in warfare, and there is ample evidence of the service of Jewish mercenaries in foreign service from the Assyrian period onwards. It is hard to believe that these soldiers refused to fight every seventh day, or would have been allowed to refuse. Jewish traders, too, probably did not refuse to sail or go to market on the Sabbath. Hecataeus does not comment on what would have been a remarkable custom; abstinence from normal human activity every seventh day, nor does any other observer from the early Hellenistic period.

With abstinence from certain foods we also encounter a custom whose antiquity need not be questioned, but whose adoption as the mark of religious loyalty again poses historical questions. Diet, circumcision and Sabbath illustrate the transformation of culture into religion, of Juda-ism into Judaism(s).

"Official" Judaism

Another dimension to the issues of "Judaism" and "scripture" is provided by Neusner's distinction between what he calls "testament" and "torah" (Neusner, 1988). "Testament" refers to a religious system, or a text or texts, that do not have a potential for engendering a total religious system, whereas "torah" does. Neusner traces the evolution from testament to torah in the case of the scriptures over the period 500–700 CE. A similar kind of distinction might be made on a more limited scale between a testament that belongs with a certain group, and operates only within a restricted social and temporal boundary, and a body of texts that is given the status of a national symbol, and thus acquires the possibility of becoming the nucleus of a religious system that embraces "Israel" in a fuller sense than any testament.

In an interesting study of the Qumran *Temple Scroll*, McCready (1993) has argued that this document represents an attempt at creating the "Jewish worldview" which many looked to its authors to describe. Hence, while the Hasmoneans created the matrix for a "Jewish worldview" through their establishment of a politically united and independent "Israel," they did not in fact fulfil this potential, and it was left to "sectarian" groups to articulate that vision, and inscribe the "torah."

In large measure I think that Neusner's distinction and McCready's application clarify the issue of scripture as it developed in the Hasmonean period. Neusner is correct in insisting that the development of a fully-fledged "torah" (in the form of a dual, literary Torah) does not occur until much later than our period, but McCready is probably correct to see in what we call "sectarian" circles the earliest attempts to define a torah, albeit for a group that consciously set itself against the political and religious authorities of their time. The *Temple Scroll* itself, and the attempt in the *Damascus Document* to organize a community around the laws of "scripture" show, nevertheless, that a certain body of literature was being taken by many Judeans as a benchmark against which all systems had to be judged (and this, I have suggested, was partly the purpose of this canon). It is, I suggest, in the aftermath of the Maccabean revolt that dissenting groups can attack each other on the basis of their understanding and application of an agreed set of texts. The establishment of such a benchmark partly reflects a set of negotiations between competing definitions of "Judaism" and an ongoing attempt to harmonize them (that is to say, embracing as much variety as possible), but closing this canon (and, I would say, excluding a certain number of writings in the process) was a political and act of enforced "consensus." The canonizing of documents of "Juda-ism" thus became a religious canon constitutive of several Judaisms, and we have the evidence for such conscription in the Qumran texts and the Mishnah, as well as in Christianity.

The conversion of an open literary and cultural canon into religious "scripture" is perhaps the most accessible index of the mutation of Juda-ism into Judaism(s). Josephus is able to say in the first century CE that "we have twenty-two books" (including histories written by prophets and therefore true, unlike non-Jewish ones). But we know, however, that the Jews had many more, including some used by Josephus himself. Is he inventing a convenient alphabetic figure, or had some authority been able to decide on this number, and on what books? If so, which authority, and why would such a decision need to be made? 2 Maccabees 2:13 narrates that Judas collected the "scattered books" just as Nehemiah had once done "to found his library"; according to 1 Macc. 1:56–57 they had been targeted for destruction by Antiochus. We might deduce from this that the Hasmoneans set up a library of books which were regarded as authoritative or definitive; such a policy would have matched the library-building of other cities (e.g. Alexandria, Rhodes) in the Hellenistic world (and so again we find Judaism developing in imitation of Hellenism!)

but also have establishing a literary archive capable of functioning as a monument of "Juda-ism," every bit as good as any Greek canon. But this canon would not have been sufficient: parties devoted to different Judaisms had to be appeased, controlled, or marginalized; we are told that several changes of allegiance took place under the Hasmoneans as those called "Sadducees" and "Pharisees" came in and out of favour with the rulers, while other groups, represented in the Dead Sea Scrolls, removed themselves from the established cult and priesthood and either preserved or invented other versions of "Judaism." While "Judaism" had been defined in the mid-second century by external conflict, now it was being defined in numerous ways, by internal conflict, yet somehow governed by more or less the same canon. Thus specific Temple rites, festivals, calendar, taxes, laws—everything "Jewish"—were now a matter of political, even *royal* decision, and could not be changed. The Hasmoneans were forced to make their own rather political "Judaism" more explicit—and export it to their neighbours. From this moment on, there are not only several "Judaisms" but authorized and unauthorized Judaisms, central and peripheral Judaisms, priestly and non-priestly Judaisms—even *normative and non-normative,* because of the identification of certain religious practice with the state. The banner under which the Maccabees and their allies had fought was now enshrined at the centre of their political ideology—Juda-ism, but still expressed in various forms of "Judaism."

"Common" Judaism and the Temple

Can we speak of Hasmonean (and post-Hasmonean) Judaism as "common Judaism"? Sanders (1992) has argued for, and described, such a phenomenon for the period of Roman administration. His description draws largely on the Mishnah and Josephus and thus inevitably representing certain beliefs and practices at the expense of others. But his attempt to find what was common in Judaism, what made Judaism "Judaism," is an important contribution to the problem discussed above and intended, it seems, as a further challenge to those scholars who overemphasize the variety of Judaisms in the first century CE.

Unlike his earlier volume on Palestinian Judaism (1977), Sanders' book attempts to grasp the reality rather than the theory of Judaism, and he plausibly suggests the Temple as a practical and symbolic expression of "Judaism" for many people during the period of Roman administration, including the reign of Herod. The Temple cult is in any case one of the oldest and most important ingredients of "Judaism" and capable in most cases of retaining loyalty in practice regardless of philosophical differences. When claims were made on its behalf for an exclusive status, and when this exclusivity came brought conflict with the Samarian temple at Gerizim we cannot know. But these claims testify to its increasing importance, an importance that the scriptures underline with their elaborate (and probably fictional) accounts of Solomon and his building. It can also be found at the centre of most Judaisms that we know about, including Enoch and the Qumran Scrolls, both of which, however, seem to regard it as an imperfect counterpart of the heavenly dwelling.

I have some reservation, however, about his chapter on "common theology," which attempts to explore what the "common Jew" thought when performing the "common acts." The more we address the texts, however, the further we seem to move from the "common Jew." The strength of the great religions, dare I suggest, is where they unite through ritual but permit theology to roam as freely as possible. The point about ritual is perhaps not what it means in itself but what it means to perform it (a very un-Protestant observation). The chief significance of the Temple as a major pillar of Juda-ism and of all Judaisms is surely that it was a political symbol as well as a religious one. One could reconstruct many Jewish theologies of the Temple, as the divine palace, the navel of the universe, the core of holiness, the place of paradise or of Isaac's near-sacrifice, the national assembly.

The examples of popular loyalty to the Temple and its cult are many (as Sanders points out). Herod's rebuilding encountered very little opposition that we know about during a period that was politically turbulent and even violent (Rhoads, 1976; Horsley, 1987; Goodman, 1987). Herod aimed to consolidate the cultural unity of his Judean subjects and reconcile them to the Empire, just as by his displays of munificence outside his territories, he sought to consolidate an empire-wide "Judaism" as a secure and respected philosophy within the Hellenistic culture of its environment and to bind the Judean *ethnos* outside his geographical kingdom to its "homeland." Virtually all of the elements of Sanders' "common Judaism" gain their rationale from the Temple. This increased fervour for the Temple carried through a process that can be observed from the beginning of the current quest. The Temple cult had long been a central feature of Judean life and even a symbol of political sovereignty. The Chronicler manages this quite well in making it the *real* "house of David." He also comes close to portraying "Israel" as a cult community: the Temple and its cult define Israel's *raison d'être*. Here (in the late fourth century perhaps) we can see Judaism defined in religious terms, but not, as in Ezra or Nehemiah, in terms of law or covenant. In the 160s BCE the "pollution" (as some saw it) of the Temple became a focus of resistance and by the first century CE, it was the central and unifying symbol for all forms of Judaism, including those in the Diaspora. The symbols of the Temple—holiness, agricultural festivals, tithing, priesthood, divine presence, atonement—became so pervasive that its removal in 70 CE necessitated the creation of a Judaism based on those symbols. Paradoxically, because it symbolized so much, its loss offered numerous paths of survival. For the majority of Jews in the late Second Temple period it was in any case a distant place to visit now and then, and otherwise present through its absence. I would agree with Sanders, then, that if any one single institution defines "Juda-ism" it is the Temple, a symbol itself capable of sustaining a great variety of Judaisms.

Conclusion

My suggestions in this paper (which will be amplified in the following chapters) have been that the emergence of Judaism, though problematic and under-evidenced, can be plotted by a series of probes that point to several related developments. Customs become symbolic of something perceived consciously as "Juda-ism," as a distinct way of life, mainly, perhaps, in opposition to "Hellenism"; the central elements of this Juda-ism was probably the temple in Jerusalem and finally as a set of competing and ever more religious definitions of that culture (Judaisms). The engagement of the Hasmoneans in religious (not exclusively cultic) matters through their adoption of a religious ideology in support of their bid for power, their assumption of the high priesthood, and the lobbying of groups with whom they had been obliged to associate in their bid for power, enhanced the religious definition of Judah's culture and introduced further political implications and social differentiation. "Juda-ism," in other words, became a national ideology to which not all Jews subscribed equally, though the Temple itself remained as a unifying symbol, even when its priesthood was being opposed.

The pictures I have sketched (there can be no single picture) do not constitute a history of Early Judaism, but suggest some issues that ought to be paramount in writing and that cast doubt on a good deal of current reconstruction. I have also largely ignored non-Palestinian Judaism, where Judaisms assumed varied forms, such as those that Hellenistic associations and societies took, or as a philosophical system that absorbed Stoic, Platonic, Pythagorean and Epicurean metaphysics and ethics (not that these developments were exclusively non-Palestinian). I have mentioned other Jewish/Judean temples: at Gerizim (strictly, non-Judean), Elephantine and Leontopolis: others, for example in Cyrenaica, may have existed and if so outlasted the one in Jerusalem. Of the elements in Judaism that have been overemphasized by Christian scholarship, scripture is the most prominent. Only among certain kinds of Judaism (including Christianity, some of the Qumran Scrolls, the Alexandrian allegorists), did the scriptures serve important dogmatic and philosophical purposes. Rabbinic Judaism embraced it from the second century CE as a definitive expression of Torah.

The elements that formed and defined Juda-ism and its Judaisms—cult, culture, nationalism (see Mendels, 1992), Hellenism, reaction to Hellenism, political independence, loss of Temple, the imposition of the *fiscus iudaicus*, which required Judaism to be defined in a way that was not previously necessary, and Christianity, first as a sect, later as imperial power—all these factors can to a greater or lesser extent be mapped as influences on the history of Judaism. Judaisms remained, of course, plural and still are—from a religious denomination in the USA, something else in the Yeshiva, different again in various forms of Zionism (social, religious and imperialist): as a nation-state, as recognizable and influential sub-cultures in Hollywood or New York or London. Jews are definable as a race, as a religion or just as heirs of a cultural identity; often "Jewishness" is only part of an individual's descent, because of mixed marriages. "Judaism" remains to this day as elusive as ever. To some extent, that is simply a feature of ethnicity. But for all kinds of reasons, the fact of variety takes second place to the belief in a single essence, both past and present.

Chapter 3

Scripture and Early Judaism(s)

Judaism, Scripture and "Biblical Israel"

Any discussion involving the relationship between "Judaism" and "Bible" (or "scriptures") must centre on the question: did "Judaism" arise from its scriptures or vice-versa? Which is the foundation for the other? Or, in what ways did one promote the other? "Foundation" is perhaps not the most appropriate image for this kind of enquiry (as in the original title of this essay), since it is most likely that the two evolved interactively. But we can talk about scriptural elements that are foundational in the sense not of being chronologically or even logically "prior," but of furnishing a definition, or definitions to which the various ancient Judaisms accommodated themselves.

The notion of a Judaism without scriptures may seem strange, as it would be also for Christianity or Islam: all are "religions of the book." (Christianity came into existence without any New Testament, but could not have done so without the Jewish scriptures.) But behind all three religions lies "early Judaism," and the relationship between the systems that make up this productive ferment and a scriptural canon are more complicated. We cannot assume a given scriptural canon at the beginning; the Torah, the prophetic collections, the great historiographical narratives, all presuppose that the monarchic era is over and thus have to be dated (let alone regarded as canonical) from the sixth century BCE onwards. Even then, from writing to canon includes a few intermediate steps.

The scriptures do, of course, provide an account of the foundations of Judaism, in the form of a history of the "people of Israel" and a description of their laws and customs. Until fairly recently (a matter of decades) it has been usual to incorporate a version of this history of "Israel" into modern accounts of Judaism itself. There is obviously continuity in the history of Judah during its monarchy and afterwards, but the differences between the religions of ancient Israel and Judah (the plural is deliberate and drawn from Zevit, 2001), and the religion(s) of Judah in the Second Temple period have become increasingly obvious. The same might be said of the population mix, too. It is as plausible to suggest a quite radical break at the beginning of the Persian period, not just in political circumstances but in religious belief and practice. If the scriptural presentation of "Israel" is wholly or largely a product not of the monarchies of Israel and Judah but of their successors in Judah (and we should not overlook the Samarians in the former kingdom of Israel who share the Torah with Judaism) the biblical "Israel" is in part a retrojection, a "prehistory." As such it is predominantly a history of failure, since both kingdoms disappeared and the populations deported; but it is also a history to be revived by a new "Israel" in the land of Judah. Hence we can view the scriptures not as a *given* "foundation" of Judaism, but a constructed one. They are, in short, essentially to be interpreted as Jewish writings, and not as Judean or Israelite ones, regardless of whatever earlier sources they may draw upon. The scriptural profile of "Israel" is very rich, and encompasses ethnic, political and cultural characteristics. But it is not uniform or free of contradiction. Obviously Judah and Samaria at some point diverged in their definition of "Israel"; but there were also divisions within Judah, as we know from the books of Enoch and the Qumran scrolls. Such variation, however, illustrates perfectly the inclusive function of a canon.

Let us then consider the profile(s) of Israel in the Jewish (and as far as the Pentateuch is concerned, the Samaritan) scriptures.

The Scriptural Definition of Israel

Having set out the adventures of humans from a single creature (Adam) in a restricted environment (a garden) to a set of nations distributed throughout the world, the Pentateuchal narrative describes the creation of Israel first in terms of genealogy. Israel is one of the families of Abraham, who is shown on his way from the core (Mesopotamia) to the periphery (Canaan) of the inhabited world, in accordance with the divine programme of human settlement (see Gen. 1:28: "fill the earth") and subsequent to the scattering of humans from the city of Babel. The initial definition of Israel is as part of a family. But it is important to note that "Israel," the family of Jacob, coexists with other Abrahamic families— Ammon and Moab (via his nephew, Lot), Aram, via Abraham's father's family, Edom and Ishmael, and in friendly relations with those outside the family, Philistines, and the indigenous Amorites/Canaanites.

It is in Exodus that this family becomes separated both from the land and from these neighbours and at the same time grows into a nation. It receives what is constitutive of every fully-fledged nation: a leader and a law. It is also led from Egypt towards a land it is going to occupy. The land is not as large as that which was promised to Abraham (which included the territory between Egypt and the Euphrates) but the "land of Canaan," which is, curiously, left undefined until Numbers 34. Relations with not only the existing inhabitants but also those (Abrahamic) nations on their borders now becomes one of hostility, and this attitude persists throughout the remainder of the Pentateuch. The contrast between Genesis and the remaining Pentateuchal books in this respect is quite striking: on the one hand the geopolitical area "Across the River" (west of the Euphrates) is "Abrahamic" and embraces many nations in peaceful coexistence; on the other hand the "land of Israel" is a distinct territory within this larger unit in which a single nation lives in some tension with its neighbours. The contradiction in these profiles can be replicated in the Second Temple era in the conflict between an exclusive and an inclusive view of the extent of "Judaism." On the one hand the books of Ezra and Nehemiah suggest an exclusive definition that certainly rejects Samaria, while the Hasmonean realm (which may have reconstituted a single Ptolemaic region) suggests much more a "Judaized" but multi-ethnic "Abrahamic" domain. The divisions that led to the Maccabean wars and, in turn, the Hasmonean dynasty, can also be seen partly in these terms, and indeed this is how 1 Maccabees presents them (1:11):

> In those days certain renegades came out from Israel and misled many, saying, "Let us go and make a covenant with the Gentiles around us, for since we separated from them many disasters have come upon us."

It is also worth observing that the "nation" that Israel is now becoming acquires its own distinctive culture as part of the process of separation from all other nations. Yet while nations usually acquire their own customs over time, Israel does not (circumcision is practised by *all* descendants of Abraham). It is *given* a culture from its deity and, as Deuteronomy stresses, that culture so exclusively defines Israel that separation from its immediate neighbours is required so as not to dilute them.

With the possession of its own land, the nation soon becomes a nation-state, or two states. Although this history lies outside the

Pentateuch, it is worth remarking that this duality is also reflected in the history of early Judaism. It is obvious that Judah and Samaria at one point constituted a religious unity of some kind: the Samaritans and Jews share the Pentateuch. The books of Chronicles, though insisting on Jerusalem as the centre of all Israel, seem to include Samaria within the nation even after the division. The books of Kings, on the other hand, lay little stress on "Israelite" unity and regard Samaria after the fall of the kingdom as no longer populated by the "descendants of Jacob" (2 Kings 17, esp. v. 34).

The narrative structure of the Torah, then, is an account of the foundations of a *nation*, Israel, in stages: family, people, nation, state. It has recently become clear that this story is not to be regarded as history: the ancestral legends, the Exodus and the conquest are contradicted—perhaps not totally, but substantially—by the evidence that the core of what was to become "Israel" came into existence in the Palestinian highlands in the thirteenth century. But that conclusion only forces us to reread the stories more carefully for what they are really saying, which is how "Israel" is to be defined and what kind of memory of the past defines each and every Israelite. Notably, it is one that leaves choices regarding the interaction of "Israel" with other nations and peoples.

But the Torah contains more than narrative. It also includes sets of laws that prescribe how the nation will behave. These laws, however, also convey a definition of how Israel as a society is constituted, and, as with the narrative, they leave open certain choices. More than one "Israel" is proposed. There are three places in the narrative at which the nation is formed, and at these points three different approaches to the constitution of Israel are found: Sinai, the wilderness trek, and the plains of Moab. These places and these moments correspond approximately to the books of Leviticus, Numbers and Deuteronomy. The Sinai narrative of Exodus itself, centring on the so-called "Book of the Covenant" (or *Mishpatim*) does not, by contrast, afford a systematic description: no "constitution of Israel" can really be derived from it. But each of the last three books of the Mosaic canon projects a definition of the nature of Israel, its society and its world

The three "constitutions" are treated below not in *narrative* order, but in order of, as I see it, their importance as "foundations" of Judaism. We do not know which of the three came into written form first, but they should in any case be interpreted synchronically.

The Israel of Deuteronomy

Thanks to the influence of Deuteronomy on the books of Joshua–Kings, the dominant biblical narrative of the founding of Israel as a polity (for this definition, see McBride, 1987) comprises the following elements: a law book; a law-reading; a covenant ceremony, including blessings and curses. The relationship between the people and the deity is construed as a formally legal one, in which rescue from slavery is a "down payment" and land is promised in return for obedience to the terms of the covenant document (i.e. the laws). The equation, for the last two millennia, of "Judaism" with obedience to divine laws is so obvious that it may escape attention that such an equation is a Deuteronomic invention. The framers of this Deuteronomic theory built, in all probability, upon an existing narrative in which Moses received laws at Sinai, and may have expanded upon (as well as glossing: the term "covenant" appears here and there in Exodus) an already existing collection of laws; but the laws have been put into a new context: a *legal religion* according to which obligations on either side cease if the conditions are broken. The entire concept is then framed literarily in the form of a testamentary address by Moses immediately before the Israelites cross to possess the land in fulfilment of the deity's part of the contract.

The patron-client relationship that underlies nearly all ancient Near Eastern (one might even say, Mediterranean) social exchange is here applied to a nation and its god, and the (usually) implied conditions of such relationships are constituted by the divinely-originating lawcode (a stereotype of ancient Near Eastern monarchies). The conditions of the Deuteronomic covenant boil down to a rigid maintenance of both cultic and racial identity, implying a community surrounded by peoples who are cultically and racially very similar.

Deuteronomy's model is replicated elsewhere. The covenant-making scene recurs elsewhere. It is repeated in Joshua 24, Nehemiah 8–10, and, outside the scriptures, at Qumran in the *Damascus Document* and 1QS, where Israel is being reconstituted as a sect. By means of this ceremony, Israel is constituted by allegiance to a particular deity. The concept of a "covenant" has also found its way into other parts of the Torah, where covenants abound: with Abraham, with Noah, with Phinehas. These covenants, however, are with individuals rather than nations, and they have more the character of a one-sided (divine) *appointment*, without any freedom on the part of the human to accept or reject, but without any obligations on the part of humans either—in other words, the notion has become embedded so firmly that it is even used of relationships that are not properly covenantal at all!

The Deuteronomic definition of Israelite religion as the obligation of a legal contract between a whole people and a god is a *theory*, but one that directly links piety to historical fate and defines Israel/Judaism as a monarchy, but with a divine king. The amendment of this notion to include a royal dynasty (later to become one of a number of messianic candidates) is possibly a concession to memory, but also can be seen as an area of contention in that both pro- and anti-monarchic sentiments are present in the Joshua–Kings corpus, while the ending of 2 Kings can be interpreted as either the death of native monarchy or as a hint of its rebirth. The most blatant ambiguity resides in the laws about the king, who seems to be a purely constitutional monarch, expected to rule by the book of the Deuteronomic law (Deut. 17:14–20). The ambiguity may be deliberate, and certainly can be understood in the context of adaptation to initially benign or neutral imperial political systems under which Judaism emerged with its own priestly leadership, the priests effectively replacing the royal courtiers.

The Israel of Numbers

Numbers reads less as a coherent composition than Deuteronomy, but it has a fairly consistent presentation of Israel. The book opens directly with a census of those "able to go to war" (1:3), and from that point onwards the portrait of the nation offered is a military one. Such a portrait suits well the narrative context chosen for it, in which the nation is, like a campaigning army, on the march towards a destination to be conquered, living off the terrain and constantly on the alert for attack. Thus, chapter 2 describes the disposition of the camp and the order of marching. The following chapters deal with priestly and cultic matters, but the section ends (in chapter 10) with instructions for the priests to blow the trumpets in time of war as well as on cultic occasions—linking the two kinds of activity. There follows a description of the Israelite army marching from Sinai, following their divine leader's cloud. The closing words of this opening section also link the central cultic object, the ark, *and its deity*, to warfare: whenever it was moved, Moses was to say "Arise, Yahweh, let your enemies be scattered and your foes flee before you," and on its stopping, "return, Yahweh of the massed armies of Israel (*ribebot 'alpey yisrael*)."

The organization of Israel, then, according to Numbers, is military. The nation is divided into families and tribes, but these are all reconfigured as military units: they provide specified numbers of young men to fight. The spatial arrangement of Israel is also important, for it assumes the form of a military camp; on each of the four sides is a group of three tribes. The camp as a whole apparently represents the land, since as far as geography allows, the tribes occupy positions corresponding to their regions of settlement, with Reuben, Gad and Simeon on the south, Dan, Asher and Naphtali on the north, Benjamin, Ephraim and Manasseh on the west and Judah, Issachar and Zebulon (somewhat unsatisfactorily grouped) on the east. At the centre of the camp/land is the temple/tent of meeting, with the three Levitical families camped on the north, south and west, and the priests guarding the entrance on the east. Towards the close of Numbers, (chapter 34) attention moves to the imminent occupation of the land and its divisions and the disposition for the tribal allotments is given, followed by allotments for the Levites, as the geography of the camp is converted in anticipation into the geography of the land.

A military disposition is also reflected in the attitude of Numbers towards discipline. The "rebellion" (*mrd, mrh*) of the people, wishing to go no further, is a constant theme (see chapters 14, 17 and 20), and the issue of Moses's leadership stands very obviously as a motif of the entire book, climaxing in a challenge by Miriam (chapter 12) and by Korah, Dathan and Abiram (chapter 16). Such disobedience to the appointed leader is, naturally, harshly punished. The military discipline recalls the book of Joshua, in which Achan's breach of the ban (Joshua 7) is punished with even more severity. Both Numbers and Joshua in fact describe the events of a successful military campaign ending with the distribution of land, reminding one of the Greek institution of cleruchies, whereby troops were awarded allotments of land to sustain them, or, possibly, the more generally followed custom of allotting agricultural and residential land to military colonies. Both Numbers and Joshua clearly wish above all to demonstrate the necessity of firm leadership and the rewards of obedience, and both go out of their way to demonstrate the perils of insubordination. The theme of both books is not so much obedience to the covenant as to the military leader.

What kind of "foundation" does Numbers provide for Judaism? We may recall the observation by Hecataeus of Abdera (c. 300 BCE, and introduced in the previous chapter) that Moses had instituted a military education and led the people to many conquests against neighbouring tribes, after which he apportioned the land equally, but reserving larger portions for the priests. These data look like a *precis* of Numbers. But whence comes the idea of this military constitution? Was it devised merely for the narrative of the wilderness itinerary, or does it have a historical basis? The military aspects of the scriptural Israel and the historical Judah of the Second Temple period have not been as greatly emphasized in scholarly research as has the theological notion of Yahweh as the "divine warrior," which is, nevertheless, one part of the phenomenon. For the name *Yhwh Seba'ot* probably means "Yahweh of armies" and the title should be given due weight, for whether the armies in question are heavenly or human, it seems probably that this deity had, or contained elements of, a warrior god, or has a very strong military component to his cult.

Indeed, there is a good deal of evidence, if not conclusive, of the military reputation of Israelites and Judeans (for details, see Hengel, 1974: I.15ff.; II.11–12). The military colony at Elephantine, probably set up by the Assyrians, was composed of Judeans, who continued to serve under the Persians. If we are to believe the claims of Josephus (*Apion* I:192ff.), Alexander, Ptolemy I and Ptolemy Philadelphus likewise recruited Jewish mercenaries. There were Jewish garrisons in Egypt, Libya and Cyrenaica. The city of Leontopolis, founded by Onias IV, included a military colony, while in Asia Minor, Antiochus III settled two thousands Judean soldiers from Babylonia. As is well known, Caesar's concessions to the Judeans also stemmed from military assistance rendered to him by forces led by Antipater. Thus, if not a major occupation of Judeans, military service as mercenaries seems to have been something of a tradition, and accordingly, it can be concluded that the success of the Judeans in the Maccabean wars and the subsequent expansion of the Judean kingdom was built on considerable native military experience. Hengel's suggestion that such military colonies may have been a major factor in the spreading of the Jewish Diaspora should be seriously considered, though such an explanation throws into doubt the strength of sabbath observance among certain Jews. Perhaps, as Hengel also suggests, Hecataeus's comment about Jewish military education stems not from any data derived from Numbers or Joshua, but from the many Judean military colonies in Egypt (and elsewhere?).

At all events, there is certainly adequate evidence to suggest that among the Judeans of the Persian period (perhaps earlier as well), a strong military ethos was present, and such an ethos is a plausible context for the insertion into the Mosaic "constitution" of an Israel organized like a mobile military colony.

Whoever was the creator of the Israel of Numbers, his definition of Israel was, at all events, revived in the Qumran *War Scroll*, where the powerful and direct influence of Numbers 1–10 is evident (especially in cols. 2–19) and in these columns a surprising degree of knowledge of military hardware, manoeuvres and regulations seems to be evident behind the ridiculously choreographed performance of the army itself. The military ideal elaborated in the book of Numbers, then, constitutes an enduring influence on the character of Judaism towards the end of the Second Temple period and may go some way to explaining the motivation, and the considerable success with which the Jewish war was conducted against the Seleucids and, initially, with Rome.

The Constitution of Israel in Leviticus

Like Numbers, Leviticus describes the dwelling place of its ideal Israel as a "camp"; but not a military camp. The camp is an ideological cosmos on which the contours of purity and pollution are drawn. The emphasis here is primarily on the social relations pertaining between the members of Israel and their god, but not, as in the case of Deuteronomy, in terms of the administration of justice. The vision is not that of the legal but the priestly scribe. As Mary Douglas has argued (Douglas, 1966), the underlying organizing principle is "order," which is achieved through a series of taxonomies. Animals are divided into "clean" and "unclean" and also into their proper spheres: land, sea, air. From Douglas's view, taboo ("unclean") animals are those seen not to fit the classification. However, the explanation does not fit very well, although the underlying perception is sound. An alternate account suggests that carnivorous animals are unclean (and this coheres well with Genesis 1, in which vegetation is suggested as food for humans and beasts). Whether any anthropological explanation can entirely fit the data of Leviticus, the notion of an *ordered* world in which things clean, holy and proper are kept separate from those that are not, both conceptually and, where appropriate, practically as well seems the best analysis of the system—and it is supported to some extent by the account of creation in Genesis 1, where order is made out of chaos by the creation of categories (light–darkness, dry–wet), the placing of the appropriate creatures in its proper domain and the marking of divisions of time. Such classification in Leviticus extends beyond animals to the types of sacrifices, bodily emissions and human sexual relations. It extends, indeed, beyond Israel (beyond "the camp") to the unclean word beyond, and constitutes Israel, like the sanctuary itself, as a centre of holiness relative to the unclean environment in which it lives. The function of the land in this scheme is different from either Deuteronomy or Numbers. The land is not to be enjoyed, Canaanite-free, as a covenant gift; nor to be overcome by a disciplined army, but it is to be maintained as an ordered cosmos which is kept holy by the separation of clean and unclean; separation of kinds of things; separation of Sabbath from non-Sabbath and of tithed produce from non-tithed. The "camp" of Leviticus embraces the ark, the tent, the area of the priests, of Israelites, then of the world beyond: concentric spheres of holiness to be mapped onto the land in Leviticus. This is not the "camp" of Numbers, nor is it Israel.

Central to the well-being of Leviticus's Israel is the sacrificial system and the priesthood, because Israel's holiness is directed to, and sustained by, the holiness of its god; and the sacrificial system regulates Israel's contact with its deity, while the priesthood ensures that this contact is maintained in an orderly way, for the contours of holiness must not be ruptured. Hence, the first five chapters of Leviticus deal with the various kinds of sacrifice, and the next two with the ordination of the priests (with chapter 10 as a warning against illegitimate priestly behaviour). Then various other issues are covered: animals, childbirth, skin diseases and bodily discharges, culminating in the ceremony by which all Israel can be atoned for (chapter 16). The so-called "Holiness Code" (chapters 17–26), in which it is possible to detect slight differences in ideology, rehearses the uncleanness of blood, sexual relations, sacrificial laws and, finally, the holiness of times and seasons.

The system represented by Leviticus is concerned above all with regulating the transition of humans between various states. The sanctuary, and its trappings, and the priesthood must be holy; but the remainder of Israel may, and will, contract uncleanness from time to time: sexual emissions, blood, and corpses, for example, will impart uncleanness (for all of these, significantly, have to do with life: its creation, preservation, and withdrawal). But such uncleanness must be removed with reasonable promptness, because it has the capacity to affect the holiness of the sanctuary, and thus threaten the continuation of the divine presence within it. The second part of Leviticus appears to extend the realm of holiness over the entirety of Israel, however, thus reducing the distinction between priesthood and laity and raising the responsibility of each Israelite to maintain a holiness which, moreover, is not limited to the cultic.

But the literary history of Leviticus is not our concern here (for discussion, see Milgrom, 1991: 42–51, nor the dating of its composition or completion. The origin of its classifications system, and its relations to an actual cult, are all matters much discussed, with both pre-exilic and post-exilic dates being defended. Whatever its origin, however, its definition of Israel as a society dedicated to holiness came to be extremely influential in a community where the presence of the Temple and a large priestly population probably dominated the life of the city of Jerusalem, from which no part of the province of Judah in the Persian period was more than a day's walk. Indeed, the issue of priestly holiness played an important role in the development of the Jewish "schools" or religious parties such as the Pharisees and the communities of the Dead Sea Scrolls. Both groups seem to have been concerned, perhaps following the trend observable in Leviticus 17–26, to extend the regulations regarding priestly holiness more widely. The associations known as *haburot* devoted themselves in particular to strict observance of tithing and dietary rules, and extended the remit of Levitical purity beyond the priestly sphere. As for the Qumran scrolls, differences of interpretation of the rules of purity between the writers of the text 4QMMT and their addressees (those then in power in the Temple) may have led to the former separation from "the way of the people," perhaps founding the kinds of "camp" communities encountered in the *Damascus Document*, in which text accusations are made that the temple is being defiled by breaches in the laws of sexual relations (uncle-niece marriage, intercourse during the period of "uncleanness"; see CD 4–5). This clearly reflects the Leviticus principle that impurity defiles the Temple whether or not such defilement takes place in or near it. But the "city of the sanctuary," according to CD, does require a special degree of purity from its inhabitants, and sexual intercourse is entirely forbidden within its walls.

It is also clear from the analyses by Neusner and his students of the development of the Mishnah that the issue of purity (including tithing) formed the earliest stage of that document's growth. The Mishnah as a whole legislates for a holy people in a pure land, and while by the middle of the second century CE the land itself was not accessible to most members of Israel, and the priesthood had disappeared, the ideal of such an Israel remains at the heart of rabbinic Judaism.

The Heritage of the Mosaic Constitution(s)

The essence of early Judaism may be said to reside in the three definitions contained in the Mosaic canon. By virtue of their fusion into a single canonical narrative they were capable of being fused into a single vision, and yet the differing perspectives could not be entirely harmonized. From the Deuteronomic constitution, the word *torah* was perhaps the most important bequest, for it is Deuteronomy that describes itself as a book of *torah*. The word then spread to cover the Mosaic canon, and other sacred writings as well. But the notion of covenant remained fundamental to the characterization of the religion of Israel, though it extended beyond the episode at Sinai to embrace a wider (and perhaps largely Diaspora) Judaism which traced the origins of its identity to Abraham and *his* covenant (and even to the Noachic covenant with non-Jews). The *legal* basis of the bond between humanity and the god of Israel and its god remained, and thus rabbinic Judaism is a religion of law, because that is the mode of human response to the divine will. Yet because of the vision of Leviticus, the law is transformed into a mechanism of holiness: this gives torah its *purpose*, and extends the goal beyond obedience towards the ideal of human perfection, and beyond doing the will of God to becoming *like* God.

The influence of the unique vision of Numbers on the whole *Gestalt* of Mosaic Judaism has been less evident than either Deuteronomy or Leviticus. But it remains the one ancient constitution for an Israel *without land*, and Israel surrounded by enemies and caught between a past that seems temptingly luxurious (as the "rebels" claim) and a future that is precarious, for the destined land is full of giants. The spectre of destruction in an alien environment that implicitly justifies the militarism of Numbers, is raised both by Esther and Daniel, where the Jews rely respectively on the benignity of the foreign king to allow them to kill their enemies, and the hope of a final heavenly vindication. If Deuteronomy and Leviticus deal with the nature of Israel, Numbers raises more acutely whether there is to be an Israel—and it also shows that the greatest threat to Israel can come from within. It might be said that Numbers proposes, among other things, how internal division should be dealt with. And internal division was an abiding characteristic of Second Temple Judaism, at least to judge by what we know of its history and literature.

Ideal Israel and Material Judaism
That a gap exists between the various communities called "Jewish" and an ideal "religious" community called "Israel" and delineated in the scriptures is clear enough: that gap allows for multiple Judaisms to exist. But when "Israel" is used in a material, or empirical sense to designate an actual society (and it is how "Judaism" was usually rendered

in Hebrew or Aramaic) the gap opens up around a Judaism that we can call "sectarian." By sectarian I mean a society that claims exclusively the identity of its parent. Thinking of oneself as a "Pharisaic Jew," for example, does not betray a sectarian attitude: thinking of one's group as the "true Israel" does. Now, the sectarian literature from Qumran cannot escape the use of "Israel" as a term for the people of which it is a part, yet these other "Israelites" outside the group are not really Israel, which is defined by proper religious observance (Davies, 2007). This absolutely vital distinction can also be expressed historically. In several writings from the late Second Temple period, the early history of Israel is written off—either ignored or dismissed as an era of wickedness. The scriptural "return from exile" is correspondingly denied; there has been no general restoration, only a partial one. The "Israel" now in Palestine does not constitute that Israel with whom God made, or renewed, his covenant after the punishment of exile. The "new" covenant (and the new "Israel") must distinguish itself from the old one, yet plausibly retain the right to its identity as "Israel." One way to do this is to reiterate the "law" given to the old Israel but in different textual forms, such as the book of Jubilees (whose author may not yet have become a sect but have the ideology in place), or the Qumran Temple Scroll. In the case of the Enochic literature, however, the "true" Israel is not defined in terms of torah but of another tradition: revealed wisdom. The "Instruction on the Two Spirits" in the Qumran Community Rule likewise replaces the scriptural categories by which Israel is defined by a doctrine of dualistic predestination.

One difference between Enochic or Qumranic and other Judaisms was, of course, the calendar. But while it was fundamental to the observance of the divine will, the difference was neither rooted nor reflected in scripture, whose Israel has more than one calendar. In Genesis 1, where the Sabbath is present as part of created time, dispute over the priority of sun and moon is nicely resolved by separating their domains and according neither of them a determinative calendrical role—though the new moon remained a festival. Yet the "solar" calendar is clearly present in the Flood story with its 30-day months, and the start of the year is set in both spring (Nisan) and autumn (Tishri). Nevertheless, the conflict between Judaisms regarding the origin of sin *is* represented in Genesis— though only in a discrete section (see chapter 8).

Israel and the scriptures in the late Second Temple period
Let us conclude this chapter with a reminder of the major ways in which
the scriptures functioned as "foundation" in the late Second Temple
period.

1. As a Source of Individual Piety

Ben Sira (early second century BCE) celebrates the scholar who has the
leisure to study not only the "law of the Most High" but also prophecies,
parables and proverbs (39:1–2). The introduction to the Psalms collection
(i.e. Psalm 1) advocates the achievement of the wisdom ideals by means
of studying torah: the pious man will, like a luxuriant tree "yield its fruit
in its season, and its leaf does not wither. In all that he does, he prospers."
Psalm 119 advocates rather more fully (and less aesthetically) adherence
to the divine *torah*, which for this writer consists of "commandments"
(*mizvot*), "ordinances" (*mishpatim*) and "precepts" (*piqqudim*), all of
which are presented as God's "word" (*dabar*). The ending of the book
of Hosea recommends the book's contents as an object of study to the
wise ("Whoever is wise, let him understand these things; whoever is
discerning, let him know them": Hos. 14:9). Even within the existing text
of the Jewish scriptures, then, we see evidence of the learned study of
sacred writings ("torah") for the purpose of achieving the traditional goals
of wisdom, discernment, prosperity, repute, happiness, peace, and so on.
While the books of Moses provide the core of this study (so ben Sira),
prophecies and proverbs were also read, apparently as commentary on,
or support for, the Mosaic canon. This use of holy writings, for personal
development, to inculcate a certain lifestyle, cannot be dated precisely,
but probably belongs somewhere in the Hellenistic period, a period that
witnessed in Judah both growing literacy and growing individualism.
We are not, after all, viewing here a corporate scribal education but
a self-education based on scribal values but expressed in the form of
self-cultivation as a Jew. (We find the same concern with cultivating a
personal lifestyle in Qoheleth, but he does not base his recommendations
on *torah*.)

If we turn to other Judaisms of the Hellenistic era, we also find the
Mosaic canon playing a fundamental role. Philo of Alexandria elaborates
it with a panoply of Greek philosophical ideas (especially Stoic and
Platonic), making it into a regulatory principle for the preservation
of the immortal soul. Here again, the culture is one of individual self-
enlightenment: for Philo the law of Moses does not impart a communal
ethic (or rather, this is a secondary purpose) but guidance toward the

perfection of the individual soul. In the Qumran scrolls, on the other hand, and notably in the *Damascus Document* and its related texts, we encounter the "law of Moses" as an explicit basis for a sectarian *society* that claimed to have received its own revelation of the divine will—by which was meant the proper manner of interpretation of the Mosaic law. By virtue of this strict adherence to the divine will, and because of the disobedience of the rest of Israel, the "Damascus" sect lived apart, either in specific quarters of cities or in their own villages (called "camps"). Likewise, it can be argued that other groups, such as the *haverim*, formed societies for the purpose of cultivating a Jewish piety based on Mosaic laws. These usages both feed into the Judaism of the rabbis, in which not merely obedience to torah, but study of it, are part of Jewish piety.

2. As a Historical and Political Record

The torah also contains the story of Israel's origin, including the origin of its religion. Indeed, the "lawgiving" on Sinai/Horeb is also the provision of a national constitution; it is the birth of a nation out of a family. (Such a role for Moses is celebrated by Philo and Josephus, and many other Hellenistic writers: in the Greco-Roman world city founders, founders of philosophical schools and lawgivers were all highly venerated.) The unity of law and narrative may have any number of literary-historical reasons, but the structure is a grand one. The laws are given in a specific time and place to a nation whose history is being formed also by other events. It is indeed part of the creation of that nation, endowing it with a formal constitution, with which the ideal Greek or Roman society was blessed.

The character of the Mosaic canon as a *narrative* definition of Israel occupies a secondary role within rabbinic Judaism's Torah, but was very important in the Second Temple period. It would be a fundamental mistake to form an impression that in the Second Temple period either "Israel" or "torah" were purely what we would nowadays call "religious." The antiquity of the Jewish people was important, as well as the superiority of its philosophy. Thus ben Sira (chapters 44–49) rehearses at length the great figures of his people's history and completes it with a description of the splendour of the contemporary high priest. That the scriptures were both records and instruments of nationalism must also be recognized and in the second century BCE the two were explosively combined. The "Maccabean revolt" was not simply a political uprising; it was also a civil war, and a struggle for a definition of "Judaism" as either a superior Hellenized religion or a cult that venerated its exclusivity and antiquity. Ironically, while the victors were ostensibly the "traditionalists," the Hasmonean dynasty that emerged from the victories against Syria were scarcely less Hellenized than many of their contemporary rulers. Was it religion or nationalism that underpinned these events, the large expansion of Judah and the two wars against Roman hegemony? Were the various "messianic" hopes (among those Jews who entertained them) political or religious aspirations? The ambitions that led to the loss of Temple and then land were a quilt made up of various patches of piety and nationalism. But when did this nationalism surface? Was it present among the Judeans of the late sixth and the fifth centuries, whose hopes for a revival of local kingship have been suspected by many modern historians? Or did it arise later as a response to the new cultural and political configurations that followed the arrival of Alexander and his successors, a phenomenon that has also been noted by historians?

The scriptures reflect wide differences of opinion over the relationship between religion and politics. The wisdom literature, despite its concern with personal social behaviour has been seen as promoting political virtues of prudence, foresight, modesty, honour, truthfulness and reticence. The books of Chronicles seem to present Israel as a cultic society in which the priesthood is dominant and the king is a lay arm of that cult. But the Deuteronomistic literature, including much of the prophetic corpus, regards politics as a dimension of Israel's own religion and closely links social and religious behaviour with political and economic welfare and indeed the survival of the nation as a political entity. The entire scriptures also deal indirectly with Israel's relationship to other nations and to the purposes of history and Israel's place in, fluctuating between the annihilation of other nations to their embrace within the Jerusalem cult. The intellectuals of the tiny province of Judah did not, on the evidence of these writings, reconcile themselves to quiet obscurity, but dreamed of the wealth of the nations flowing to the Jerusalem Temple (Haggai) or foreign kings worshipping its god (Isaiah 40–55), or a final great battle in which the spectre of foreign domination would be forever banished (Ezekiel). The political aspirations evident in the writings should not be divorced from the political and religious imperialism of the Hasmoneans. Religion and political nationalism turned out to be a lethal prescription, and in rabbinic Judaism it became necessary to conceive a *people* whose Judaism transcended individual piety, but which also shed national-political ambitions. Christianity might almost be seen to travel in the opposite direction (if we leave aside the vexed question of its founder's execution); spreading as politically less confrontational, it ended up as an imperial cult in which personal salvation itself became, in Deuteronomic fashion, a matter for the rulers to take care of.

3. As a System of Signs (Omens)

The idea of ancient writings as a system of signs is essentially *mantic*; it belongs to that (priestly-scribal) culture built on the notion that earthly events are controlled by supernatural powers that either deliberately or not leave traces in the material word that can be decoded so as to discern the future. Divination is the general term given to this technique; it took as specific forms the examinations of the entrails of sacrificial animals, or the interpretations of dreams, or of the movements of stars or other meteorological phenomena. Observations and deductions about them were recorded in omen-lists. Although divination was practised in all societies, despite being condemned in the Jewish scriptures it was also popular in Jewish societies in the Second Temple period. The Qumran texts include brontologia, physiognomies and horoscopes; in the gospel of Matthew magi learn of the location of the Messiah through a star and are warned in a dream to take a different route home. But important for our purposes is the use of holy books as a source of signs about the future. The book of Daniel is thoroughly mantic in that it presupposes the destiny of the world to be fixed and thus knowable in advance by divine revelation, which takes the form of dreams (chapter 2) or visions (chapters 7ff.) or writing on a wall (chapter 5). But in Daniel 9, it takes the form of an *already written* text: the scroll of Jeremiah is being read (for reasons of individual piety or in search of an oracle?) and found to contain not a *literal* prediction of seventy years but a coded one of 490, requiring angelic interpretation to be understood. In the Qumran Habakkuk *pesher*, this hermeneutic is made explicit; Habakkuk, it explains, did not know the time when the events of which he spoke would transpire, but the "Teacher of Righteousness" was given the knowledge to understand. Reading scriptures, then, requires a hermeneutical technique of decoding.

Among the Qumran scrolls and in the earliest Christianities the scriptures are indeed exploited as an encoded message about the eschatological scenario. The Melchidezek fragments from Cave 11 and the *pesharim* (and indeed the Admonition of CD) show scriptures functioning as predictive of events contemporary with the writer, but also requiring an interpretation that only a select few can possess. Some of these writings also show the extent to which a collection of holy books was beginning to be seen as providing the possibility of a *system*, with the principle already established that one sacred text could illuminate another. While the *pesharim* adhere to one scroll each, other midrashic works range across torah, prophets and writings (or whatever categories were then in force) in constructing a single plot, namely the great final Day of Atonement by Melchidezek (or, as in the case of the New Testament gospels, the Great Day of Atonement and Vindication by Jesus).

This use of the scriptures fed into rabbinic halakhic hermeneutics, through the ingredient of *charismatic interpretation* characteristic of the Qumran manuscripts (and, I would say, of Christianity, for which the true understanding of the scriptures was imparted by a divine gift) was eliminated. But it was established by the rabbis (a) that scripture was a *self-explaining* system, and (b) that its statement of the law was incomplete. Hence by means of a system of deductive and inferential rules, the *implicit* meaning of the scriptural system could be made *explicit*, and the entire will of God be made known. In an analogous way, the diviners of Babylon had for centuries compiled copious lists of signs and their meanings, based, apparently, on experience. If rabbinic exegesis, then, was in a sense mantic, it shared with the ancient omen-lists of Babylon a quasi-scientific character, though one based not on collections of recorded cases but a set of exegetical rules.

Conclusion

The foregoing discussion does not make a systematic case for exploring the development of the scriptures against the background of the emergence of early Judaism. But we do not know when the scriptures were compiled, and the evidence we have for their existence does not go much earlier than the third century BCE, a time in which the Enochic literature also seems to have begun. The evidence of the Qumran scrolls shows us very clearly, however, that the Torah was functioning canonically (which does not necessarily imply a *closed* canon), and that attempts were being made to integrate and systematize the contents of Exodus, Leviticus and Deuteronomy especially. In particular, the originally distinct Deuteronomic concept of covenant and the Levitical concept of holiness are being merged into a system that will provide the model for rabbinic Judaism, though in the absence of a geographical centre and a Temple cult, the arena and the agencies of "holiness" inevitably become transformed into the domestic.

However, these comments, while they may assist a pre-third century date for the Torah substantially as it has been canonized, do not require it, and the model of "biblical" and "postbiblical" literature is one that should be carefully reconsidered and perhaps replaced by one of overlap. If, as can be argued, we can trace the beginning of both scripture and "early Judaism" to the early Persian period, then indeed they do need to be studied as simultaneous developments, in constant interaction.

Chapter 4

"Law" and Early Judaism(s)

This chapter deals rather with the interrelated questions of (a) what "law" might mean in the context of formative Judaism(s) and (b) what we might know about it. "Law" is embraced by various terms in Hebrew: *torah, mishpat, huqqim* and *mitsvah*. The last three are used of individual commandments or stipulations and they represent to some extent variants between different literary sources: torah can function as an all-embracing term for the divine law and this is its usage in rabbinic Judaism; but its scriptural use can also be wider, including priestly instruction.

Scriptural law is by definition a literary phenomenon, but in any case I use it in the sense of "jurisprudence," legal theory. The *administration* of justice is a separate matter, which will no doubt be affected by (and affect) literary formulations, though in varying degrees. I am not concerned here with how justice was actually dispensed in the Second Temple period; it was controlled by custom as much as decree (as the evidence relating to divorce shows; there is no scriptural law about the process of divorce), and also varied from place to place and from instance to instance. But Judaism increasingly defined itself in relation to a body of divine, scriptural law. Understanding the origin and nature of this "law" must precede any conclusions about what Jews did or did not do according to their "laws" in the Second Temple period.

Legal Theory versus Legal Practice

No direct link necessarily exists between the behavior envisioned by a law and the behavior practiced by members of the community...It is not even valid to assume, without further evidence, that the law was actually made known to the members of the community (Flesher 1988: xii).

This is a judgment on the Mishnaic laws of slavery, and behind it stands a whole programme of research promoted by the work of Jacob Neusner, and it is difficult to deny that the great rabbinic enterprise represents a conspicuous case of legal theorizing. Though it does no doubt reflect *some* actual practices, its relationship to foregoing or contemporary *realia* is complex and often irretrievable. Its "generative problematic" (to use Neusner's well-known phrase) is a theoretical and systemic one, that is it derives from the explication of a system based on an ideology of land, people and purity. It is manifestly utopian, its Utopia being a land of Israel of a kind that its framers did not occupy and their successors even less so. Its Israel is not a concrete Jewish society, but an eternal and ideal "people of God." Despite these ideal features, the Mishnah's system, predicated on a people living in the land of Israel and maintaining a Temple cult, formed the basis for a way of life that is not utopian at all. The Mishnah (and its successors) expounds a system of law *subsequently* elaborated by exegesis and made more applicable to everyday life by exegesis and by the application of individual rulings. By the time we come to the literature of *responsa*, we are dealing with practical applications, and we can in most cases deduce practice from them, even though the dynamics of Mishnaic theory continue to exercise a control. But between the Mishnah and the regulations that later govern Jewish life lies some considerable distance.

The Mishnah uses only partial evidence of what was adopted as practice before it was written or even while it was written. Actual practices have to be carefully sought out in each case, with the aid of archaeological or comparative data. It draws on actual historical practice, but also elaborates previous literary legal materials (i.e. scripture) and introduces complete innovations (such as the procedure for capital cases and for execution). Yet it *does* determine legal practice in later times and places. Its theory does not follow practice, but practice does follow its theory. Can this conclusion be applied in some sense also to biblical law?

The Nature of Biblical Laws

There are broadly three views that one might take regarding the relationship between the biblical laws and the actual administration of justice in ancient Palestine. One is to regard the biblical material as descriptive in intent and in effect. This was once a dominant assumption of biblical scholarship, so that "Israelite law" and "biblical law" were interchangeable terms, and prescription and practice held to be mutually entailing. The laws, both social and cultic, describe for us how Israelite society functioned.

A second view recognizes that the biblical laws are in a form that has been shaped by a process of scribal editing and influenced by wider ideological interest, but that nevertheless individual laws by and large do reflect actual social practice. In other words, while the literary law compositions may not be entirely descriptive (or even prescriptive in the sense of being intended to apply directly) in *intent*, individual laws are in fact a reflection of social practices or norms, and thus to an extent the biblical laws may *in effect* be descriptive.

A third view considers that while the evidence of scribal composition, intellectual and theoretical motivation, and literary contextualizing is perfectly obvious in the biblical laws, the relationship between individual prescriptions and actual practice is both probably marginal and also often unprovable, and that these literary creations reflect essentially the contours of their scribal authors' thinking. It was, on this view, no part of their intent to describe social reality, only to theorize on what ought to happen, or ought to have happened, in an ideal world. On this view, scriptural law is a mode of social philosophy, or of theocratic theory.

The first view is not widely defended (though see Phillips, 1983 for the view that the *Book of the Covenant* [*Mishpatim*] was or contained "ancient Israel's criminal law") but the second view is prevalent, and it may be helpful to expand, however briefly, on the issues and evidence. Broadly speaking, the two main avenues of research into the "practicality" or "actuality" of biblical laws are (a) ancient law codes and legal documents, and (b) non-legal biblical material such as prophetic and narrative literature.

Since we have very little extra-biblical material *directly* attesting to legal praxis in ancient Israel or Judah, a good deal of weight has come to be attached to ancient Mesopotamian law codes and their parallels with biblical laws. Certainly such parallels exist, and different explanations are possible. On the one hand, scholars such as Paul and Westbrook (Paul, 1970: 99–105; Westbrook, 1988, 1991: 12) accept what Westbrook terms the "diffusionist" view of ancient Near Eastern law, whereby a common legislative culture or tradition, facilitated by a range of common economic features, permeated the Fertile Crescent during the second millennium. Such "diffusion" may have taken place through the medium of written sources, but also could have spread through migration and general social and political interaction in the form of basic concepts and practices. Although Westbrook acknowledges that the writing of laws always owes something to scribal discretion, selectivity and ideological bias, he accepts (as I understand) that biblical legislation represents broad social-legal tradition stretching from the Tigris to the borders of Egypt (but not including Egypt, where the picture is different).

However, such a pattern relates in the first instance to legal theory and not necessarily to practice. The great Mesopotamian law codes are not prescriptive, that is to say not intended to regulate legal praxis in a direct way. "Non-legislative" is Fishbane's neat description of them, and he refers to them as "prototypical collections of cases" (Fishbane, 1985: 95–96). This might still allow them to be regulative, however, and Jackson (1989: 186) goes further in characterizing such codes as "didactic, sapiential, monumental." Legal practice (as evidenced by the extant *mesharum* acts, temporary and specific acts, usually of debt-relief, and corpora of court decisions) was, he argues, to a great degree unaffected by these codes (see especially Krauss, 1960).

Jackson's view is endorsed by some who accept the "diffusionist" view (e.g. Paul, 1970: 23–25), who therefore think of a pattern of legal theory across the Fertile Crescent. Such a pattern is likely to have been established, in this case, not from common custom but from the diffusion of a *literary tradition* whereby the scribes of Jerusalem (or wherever) drew upon earlier literary sources in composing their own codes. Such an opinion has long been entertained, but it needs to be remarked that although the Code of Hammurabi is in origin an ancient source, it was still being copied well into the first millennium and can therefore be regarded as a contemporary source even for Second Temple literature (as is true, of course, for much Sumerian and Akkadian literature and for Canaanite mythological literature). We cannot derive from the parallels with the Mesopotamian codes any dating for the biblical ones.

For Carmichael, the evidence of the Roman legal system is also pertinent. His conclusion that the construction of laws is "an intellectual exercise" (Carmichael, 1992: 15–21) appeals, as well as to Mesopotamian law codes, also to the work of the Roman jurists in the late Republic period (Jolowitz and Nicholas, 1992: 91–96; Watson, 1974: 101–10). But although these jurists did not enact laws, nor participate in court hearings, they did advise on the *interpretations* of law and issued *responsa* on individual matters; their work was not entirely theoretical. Nevertheless, it is important to note the existence in Rome of a tradition of legal exegesis which operates in formal independence of a tradition of legal judgments. That is to say, on the one hand we have a body of *theory* being developed, and on the other a continuing *practice*, each overlapping, but (and here lies the importance) each practised by different persons and institutions. Theory is not necessarily or even typically the business of the practitioner, and vice-versa. That may well have been the case in the ancient Near East. Hence, the biblical laws represent a scribal tradition and not a judicial one related to actual practice.

The mention of exegesis brings us to the work of Fishbane (1985), who accepts that the biblical law codes are a product of scribal drafting and interpretation, and indeed emphasizes the exegetical nature of much of it. Nevertheless, he insists that the biblical codes are presented as divine revelations intended to regulate life, and notes that Lev. 10:10 (cf. Mal. 2:7) enjoins priests to teach laws, with judges enjoined to follow them (Deut. 16:18–20; 2 Chron. 19:6–10). He thus maintains that they have a closer relationship to the practice of justice than the ancient Near Eastern codes: the internal traditions of the Hebrew Bible present and regard the covenantal laws as legislative texts. However, it needs to be asked whether this particular device is really so different from the depiction at the head of the law code of Hammurabi receiving laws from Shamash. On this issue, Jackson has made an especially important and interesting set of observations. Focusing on the semiotics (communicative functions) of law codes, he asks: who are the recipients of the "message" of these law codes? His answer is: apparently not judges. The Mesopotamian law codes contain no instructions that they should be enforced or enacted, nor have there been found separate texts that contain, or allude to, such instructions. Jackson's point is that until a certain stage of social development, law is exercised by means of custom and tradition, not by written documents. In support of his position he cites (1989: 188) Deut. 16:18 (cf. 1:16) and 2 Chron. 19:15–17, where commands to judges are general and do not include reference to any written text as a basis for judgment. We may add that the role of the elders in administering justice is indicated elsewhere in Deuteronomy (e.g. 21:19, 22:15, 25:7) but the contents of Deuteronomy are addressed to the people as a whole.

A further parallel between Mesopotamian and biblical law codes is that both offer only a selection of legal cases. But these are not always "typical" cases, as one might expect if they are intended to be used for guidance, but often unusual and infrequent cases; and they do not cover the entire range of legal matters. The parallel makes it unlikely that such a feature of the biblical laws can be explained by a later process of editorial selection, but rather as the outcome of exegetical reasoning, of which the Mishnaic laws provide copious examples. In some cases, such as the laws of slave release (Exod. 21:2–6) or the rebellious child (Deut. 18:21) or the remarrying of a previously divorced wife (24:1–4), allegorical meanings can easily be suggested (with Israel as the slave, the son or the wife); theoretical or theologically-inspired cases are also evident in the case of exemptions from war (Deuteronomy 1–9).

But did texts ever exist relating to legal administration from the territories of Israel and Judah? Jackson comments (1989: 185) that "archaeology has not served well the study of legal institutions of biblical society. We lack 'court' records—using that term in both its legal and politico-administrative sense." He then goes on to make a further point: "what we possess is a rich literature, into which it is *possible*—to put the matter at its highest—that some original sources from the real and administrative milieux may have been incorporated. Certainly we cannot assume without careful argument that the biblical codes come from any such milieux." Should the absence of documentation about actual cases support the argument that the biblical literature is not about praxis but theory? Or should we, despite the absence of evidence, assume that such documents existed? The most that can be assumed is that some Israelite Judean kings may have had law codes written, but not that these, if they did exist, were in fact enforced in practice. As we shall see, Jackson is in any case not basing his argument entirely on silence.

Marshall has attempted (1993) to apply an anthropological analysis of the *Book of the Covenant*, beginning by sketching out the social structures that would have characterized Israelite society before and during the monarchic period, and, building on the theories of K. S. Newman (Newman, 1983) concerning the relationship between law and economics, to assess the likely social setting of the law codes from the implications they offer about the economic basis of society. His opening discussion of theory is informed and lucid: he accepts that laws develop over time, that they are multilevelled (i.e. they are mediated by families, elders, and chiefs) and that "law" does not simply equal "custom" but includes scope for rational and improvisatory functions. He then seeks to extrapolate social structures from the contents of the *Book of the Covenant*, looking at climate, geology, flora and fauna to determine the material context of pre-monarchic "Israel" and then extrapolates the likely legal issues in such society/societies. The next step is to inspect the legal issues dealt with in the *Book of the Covenant*, and his analysis shows him that Exod. 20:24–22:16 reflects a (dimorphic) pastoral/agrarian society, with free, non-slave, and debt-slave classes. In Exod. 22:17–23:19, however, private ownership and accumulation of wealth appear, implying landowners, landless people and indentured slaves, plus slightly more developed cultic operations. Marshall's conclusion is that the two law codes, or the two parts of the law code, that he separates in the *Book of the Covenant* "could have been operative in pre-monarchical Israel" (181).

The method seems promising, though Marshall's application is problematic. First, for his history he relies mostly on Finkelstein's (1988) reconstruction in dealing with the Iron I ("premonarchic") period but uses biblical material for Iron II (the "monarchic" period). Can the different kinds of evidence really be mixed in this way? Should Marshall not have followed Finkelstein for Iron II, and arrived at a rather different (and much more meagre) picture than the biblical one? Marshall also believes that by allowing for the existence of different "legal levels" one can dispense with the need to posit a complex literary history, and thus be able to posit a single "BC [*Book of the Covenant*] society." Furthermore, he limits his contexts to the pre-monarchic and monarchic periods, without making it clear that he cannot rule out the possibility that we might be dealing with different contemporary and co-existing social patterns or, indeed, with the Second Temple period, which he does not even consider as providing a possible social context for a written law code. Finally, and most importantly, his thesis does not explain why we have a *Book of the Covenant*, why a written law code for this society should have been created and how it would have functioned.

How far should we assume that an "ideal" society, such as a law code *might* address, corresponded to the author's own? A major flaw in Marshall's conclusion is the move from "might" to "was," and a failure to give a satisfactory account of the production of a pre-monarchic law code and its preservation, unadapted to later social structures, in later periods. In theory, however, it remains a valid proposition that the assumptions of even theoretical and idealizing lawmakers (to state the issue as strongly as possible) might be influenced by their own concrete social contexts. The problem is to discern where these contexts are distinctive enough. The role of elders, the lack of a monarch, the existence of slaves: all these conditions hold for centuries of history. On the other hand, one of the features of utopian legislation is that its vision, its society does *not* exactly mirror the present. Yet again, we can return to the Mishnah: for what sort of real society could it possibly have been formulated? From its contents, we would infer one living in the "land of Israel," with a functioning Temple cult. We happen to know, however, that this impression is entirely misleading.

The Function of Biblical Law

If we cannot demonstrate a close relationship between the literature and legal praxis, we must infer a historical context and function in less direct ways—as we would with the Mishnah. We must examine the nature of the biblical codes with respect to (a) their literary character and (b) the substance of their individual stipulations. Here the work of Carmichael and Jackson makes an important contribution. Carmichael's well-known (but not widely-adopted) thesis (1992) is that the biblical laws are the product of intellectual reflection on incidents recorded in narratives. I will not rehearse his evidence here, but I would suggest that if accepting them is difficult, then refuting them is no easier. Carmichael makes an impressive case for many of the laws being dependent, for both the issues they address and their language, on episodes preserved in the Pentateuchal narrative. Having myself been initially unwilling even to countenance such an unlikely argument, I have pondered for many years on how to disprove them; and finally I have arrived at an understanding of the biblical laws that makes it possible for Carmichael's suggestions to be at least part of an explanation. But for the moment I merely note that a similar aporia seems widespread: Carmichael's work has received an uneasy reaction from all quarters, as if its ideas and argumentation were irrefutable and unacceptable at the same time.

Jackson has highlighted the literary features of biblical law codes, proposing a number of cases where the *Book of the Covenant* exhibits "chiasmus, thematic reiteration through a sequence of interlocking double-series, and various allusions to the immediate narrative context" (Jackson, 1989: 198; actual examples are provided in Jackson, 1988). Similar observations have emerged from the study by Sprinkle (1994), who argues that the *Book of the Covenant* is an "artfully crafted unity, being well-integrated internally and in relation to the Pentateuch of which it is a part" (206). I am not necessarily endorsing Sprinkle's conclusion, but the arguments he deploys can be added to a number already advanced that raise questions about an original and retrievable "Book of the Covenant" prior to its present setting in the Pentateuchal narrative. The most striking of these is the opening section on slavery, including the law on a runaway slave. The connection of this theme to the Exodus narrative has been noticed often enough.

As to their legal *substance*, we can point to abundant evidence that the laws of Deuteronomy and of Leviticus 17–26 (or however else it is demarcated) are generated *as a whole* by a theory about the nature of Israel and its relationship to its deity (see the previous chapter). For example, as noted earlier, the metaphor of Yhwh and Israel as husband and wife has inspired the only biblical law about divorce in Deuteronomy 24, and the motif of Israel as a rebellious child similarly for the law in Deut. 21:18–21. And what about the law (Deut. 23:15) that if a slave runs away from his master he should not be given back? Are we not to think of the freeing of Israel from Egypt by Yhwh? Each of these laws might reasonably be considered as the product of reflection on wider issues, such as the disobedience of the nation to its father-god or husband-god, and its right to be punished. Or, conversely, of its right not to return to Egypt for enslavement. Even the Jubilee legislation may be a reflection on an exile calculated as lasting fifty years (one of two calculations that can be extracted from biblical texts).

For it cannot be denied that these stipulations are to various degrees impractical and need to be explained as the result of some kind of theorizing or deduction. If we add this kind of motivation to those suggested by Carmichael and Jackson we may be getting close to the mentality and the spirit of much of biblical law. Certainly, to regard them as reflecting by and large ancient Israelite praxis runs the risk of putting a utopian society onto the pages of history. Rather, we should look for the historical context and function of a utopian law code.

For instance, many laws express the logical outcome of certain basic premises. The Deuteronomic laws about holy war are derivable from a premise about authorized ownership of land: Yhwh owns it and gives it as a dowry or a bequest to Israel, dependent on the fulfilment of covenant obligations. Likewise, Leviticus exhibits a clear ideology of purity based on proximity to the presence of the deity, the world within and without the "camp," and a universe and lifestyle divided into degrees and states of cleanliness. There is no ancient society in Palestine devoid of "Canaanites," nor can "holiness" be detected so readily as to dictate everyday life. There *are*, of course, cases where such laws might reflect practice, or vice-versa; one interesting case is the fallowing of land every seventh year. This may be good agricultural sense, and even followed. But if so, it was not hardly followed because of a law such as that in Leviticus, nor would all farmers follow the same cycle: the notion of a sabbatical year is utopian—though we have some evidence that it was observed to some degree in the later Second Temple period in the case of Hillel's *prosbul* (*M. Shevi'it* 10:3). Perhaps the practice, if it were such, inspired the writer of Leviticus—for whom it becomes part of a sabbatical system, including the jubilee), and the writer of Deuteronomy (for whom it functions according to a different ideological scheme). But we could not argue on the basis of the written law itself that a fallow year, or jubilee year, was observed. We cannot argue that adulterers or rebellious sons or runaway slaves were handled as written down.

In sum, it seems that we should accept (1) that the institutions connected with the *administration* of law and those connected with the generation of the *legal literature* in the Bible are quite distinct, even if some actual practices are reflected in the latter and (2) that the social worlds implied by at least Deuteronomy and Leviticus are products of their author's ideologies and related only indirectly (if at all) to social norms at the time of their creation.

Written Law Generating Praxis

During the late Second Temple period literary laws began to provide the basis for study, and then praxis, within certain Judean societies, sects and individuals. We can see the process clearly taking place in the Qumran scrolls, though applied to a small and exclusive society, with the aid of halakhic exegesis. But I have noted earlier that even in the Mishnah we do not have a record of Jewish legal praxis. The process by which scriptural laws became the explicit basis of actual Jewish behaviour was a long one, extending beyond the Second Temple period and even well beyond the Mishnah. But the process begins to take place much earlier, if only partially or occasionally. In the Gospels (Mk 12:18 and parallels) we have a case where a legal opinion is sought: the levirate marriage of a woman to seven brothers in turn (and a similar dilemma is found in Tobit). Do we infer from these reports that such laws were enacted? The world of Tobit is make-believe, so we cannot be sure whether in a make-believe world make-believe laws apply. In the case of the gospels, are we dealing with a writer ignorant of Jewish law, and wrongly assuming that what is in the scriptures is actually done? Or is there an historical encounter between different schools of thought on a legal opinion, unrelated to realia? The same is perhaps true of the episode (Jn 8:1–11) of the adulterous woman, where Jesus is asked to give an opinion on the scriptural ruling that she should be stoned. These stories imply that scriptural laws were being argued about; they were taken seriously as the divine will. This suggests the adoption of their "utopian" vision as a programme, yet it does not imply that adulterous women were stoned, nor married their brothers-in-law when occasion required. In the case of tithing, or levitical purity, however, we do find such laws being adopted, and, in cases where they applied only to the priesthood, extended beyond the priesthood. We find, even in poems subsequently included in the scriptures, the ideal of the righteous man as one who studies "the law" and "walks in it" (Psalm 1). That corresponds to the view of ben Sira (38:34), who also includes wisdom sayings and prophecies as among the studies of the scribe. Ben Sira's comments, taken with Psalm 1, suggest that the scribe studied the laws for the purpose of obeying them (just as Hos. 14:9 implies that prophecy as well was recommended to the wise for their consideration). We can therefore show evidence that written texts were the basis for the (self-?) education of scholarly and religious elite. It is commonly assumed that we are here dealing with the interpretation of a "Jewish law" that already had some authoritative force, but whose implications were still being worked out. This rather oversimplifies the picture. But the Qumran scrolls (and other near-contemporary Judean literature) attest the notion of a "law of Moses" as something that at least some groups regarded as self-evidently authoritative for the way of life of "Israel."

But if, as I have suggested, the law codes in Exodus, Deuteronomy and Leviticus did not have that status (or that purpose) when they were drafted, how did such a status come about? That is, or so it seems to me, the one under-investigated gap in scholarly treatment of "biblical law." However, before closing that gap, or part of it, we need to define the gap chronologically, to review the date at which the biblical law codes came into existence. Here, too, some long-established conclusions should be challenged.

The Origins of Judean Written Law Codes

Classical source-historical analysis placed both the *Book of the Covenant* and Deuteronomy in the monarchic period and the Holiness Code in the post-exilic. Some of these views have of course been challenged: P is currently considered to be substantially monarchic by a few scholars, while the *Book of the Covenant* has been placed in the sixth century by van Seters. It also remains the prevailing view that Ezra returned from Babylon and read out a law book, so that the Second Temple period is held to have witnessed only exegetical development and practical application of a body of legislation that already existed in written form. The purpose and function of such a body of written law, either in the Judean monarchy or the community of deportees in Babylonia, really has no convincing explanation and no convincing content.

I shall suggest in the next chapter that Deuteronomy most plausibly originated in the post-monarchic era, and not as often held, in the seventh century, and there is no point in anticipating the arguments here. I merely suggest that it has no convincing context in the late seventh century and that a biblical legend to that effect is as insufficient a pretext as a story about tablets handed down from Sinai. But one feature that Deuteronomy shares with the story of Ezra is highly significant: the notion that laws are the terms of an agreement made directly between a deity and the people. In the narrative of Ezra we find a priestly-scribal figure who is placed at the origins of Second Temple Yehud society and who returned from Babylon with a law book. Indeed, even before he appears in Ezra 7, the law book is present in Yehud, It is surprising how many textbooks wrongly claim that he returned *with it*, since the first mention of the law book is at 6:18: "And they set the priests in their divisions, and the Levites in their courses, for the divine service, which is in Jerusalem; as it is written in the book of Moses"; then we read (Neh. 8:1): "And all the people gathered together as one in the street that ran in front of the water gate; and asked Ezra the scribe to bring the book of the law of Moses, which Yahweh had commanded to Israel." Nowhere is it said that Ezra brought the law book from Babylon. Certainly, he was fluent in the "law of Moses" (7:6) but the text gives no hint that this law book was not well known in *both* Palestine *and* Babylon: "Then Jeshua ben Jozadak stood up, and his fellow-priests, and Zerubbabel ben Shealtiel, and his colleagues, and they built the altar of the god of Israel, in order to offer burnt offerings upon it, as written in the law of Moses the holy man" (3:2). Ezra makes his appearance (7:6, 12) as "a scribe fluent in the law of Moses [later of the "law of heaven"], which Yhwh, the god of Israel, had given: and the king granted him all he requested, under the influence of Yahweh his god upon him."

In 10:3 Ezra is addressed by Shecaniah with an appeal to put away foreign wives and children ending "let it be done according to the law"; in Nehemiah 8 the people ask Ezra to bring out and read the law, and as (or after) he does so, the Levites "give the meaning." In Nehemiah 10 the people take an oath to obey this (written) law. Thus, the relationship between the divine law and the people is now direct, and we find the process of interpretation, which characterizes the scribal tradition of revising and editing and commenting on texts, an activity so clearly exposed by Fishbane (1985; though I think his somewhat diachronic conception is wrong) now being applied not to the rewriting of texts by way of learned commentary, but spoken directly to people. The congregation is addressed, not just by the law, but by the interpretation; they oblige themselves to keep it, not just as a society but as individuals—just as

Ezra himself had (7.6): "For Ezra had set his heart upon studying the law of Yahweh, and to observe it, and to teach the statutes and ordinances..." Whether or not such a ceremony, or anything like it, ever took place, the scene depicted conveys the belief that the law is to be obeyed by every Judean, who will learn of it directly, and understand it by means of learned exegesis, from the priestly caste.

Assuming that such an arrangement, bypassing the traditional role of the monarch as a mediator between the people and the deity, enacting laws and upholding justice, is extremely unlikely to have had any antecedent before the end of the monarchy, at what point in the Second Temple period might such a context for a law emerge? And from what circles does it emanate? I have suggested earlier in this book that Ezra and Nehemiah are quasi-sectarian figures in that they represent the founder-heroes of different Jewish groups, and not the people of Judah as a whole. I also pointed to the adoption of the Pentateuch by the Samaritans, which suggests the recognition of a canonized text in the neighbouring province. Between the reconstruction of Jerusalem as capital (mid-fifth century) and the Judean/Samaritan split (third century?), the notion of a law for the followers of Yhwh in Judah and Samaria emerged. This law did not depend upon a single sanctuary, and the Pentateuch does not indicate any such role for either Shechem or Jerusalem, though both may have come to exercise an authoritative position. In other words, we are looking at the largest black hole in the history of early Judaism—the fourth and third centuries, a time in which it was perhaps possible (for the first time ever?) for "Israel" historically to embrace both communities. For there is no good evidence that Judah and Israel were originally united, before their respective kingdoms were formed. During the Neo-Babylonian period, however, the role of Mizpah and Bethel in respectively the political and religious leadership of Judah may have brought together the ancient Israelite cult of the "god of Jacob/Israel" and that of Yhwh Sebaoth from Jerusalem. The two names are combined as a single title for the syncretized deity in the book of Jeremiah, while Judah is also addressed as "sons of Jacob"; such a unity is reflected in the Pentateuch itself and in the books of Chronicles (in Joshua–Kings the position is more complicated; see Davies, 2007). The creation of this "biblical Israel" is a presupposition of a body of law agreed between "Israel" and the deity Yhwh.

Law, Cult and Temple

There is another characteristic of biblical law that also helps to clarify the social context in which they were originated and developed. Deuteronomy and Leviticus include cultic and non-cultic laws, in varying ratios. It is also clear from subsequent interpreters and students of these laws (the authors of Ezra and Nehemiah, ben Sira, the Pharisees and "Damascus Covenanters") that no distinction is made between the areas of cult and those outside. What happens in the Temple, what the priests do, how the people observe their festivals, vitally affects the fabric of the whole society. This ideology is not without precedent in the ancient Near East, of course (see e.g. Blenkinsopp, 1991), but the biblical laws as a whole bring together political, social and cultic in an especially dramatic way, submerging the royal function under the priestly and the palace under the Temple. The Nehemiah narrative seems either to preserve the memory of non-priestly authority over Sabbath activities, perhaps reflecting a Judean political governor under the Persians (Neh. 13:15–19), or to argue for a division of powers between priests and non-priests that was not in effect. Indeed, both Deuteronomy and the Holiness Code develop an ideology which integrates the sanctuary and its holiness into the political and social character of the nation. This is a characteristic of priestly legal theorizing, in which all of human private and social activity is understood in relation to cultic activity, to an overriding divine presence, whether legal (Deuteronomy) or "holy" (Leviticus). Thus priests (on their own assessment) sustain the nation by their service. The dominance by the Jerusalem Temple of all "Israelite" life is equally emphatic in the books of Chronicles, though the Chronicler makes full use of royal ideology in undergirding the status of the Temple.

A society in which temple and economy were in actual fact inextricably bound together, such that priests actually exercised decisive local political power is not necessarily implied by these characteristics, though such a context will explain how priestly legal theorizing came to be preserved and canonized. The monarchic Temple in Jerusalem probably functioned mainly as a part of the royal establishment, its religious activities dependent upon the wishes, and the deity, of the incumbent monarch, and its revenue, such as it was, subject to royal consent and oversight. The Persians do not seem to have exercised close oversight of cultic matters: but, as imperial taxers, they regarded the Temple as the focus of economic activity and probably of tax collecting itself (Blenkinsopp, 1991: 23–24; Schaper, 1995). The loss of the secular, royal power is echoed with some regret in the literature of the Persian period in which a Davidic successor is briefly present (Haggai, Zechariah) but equally it is bemoaned as the cause of the nation's political evils; Second Isaiah prefers Cyrus as Yhwh's "messiah"; Ezekiel prefers a *nagid*.

How far, then, do the laws of Deuteronomy and Leviticus reflect Second Temple praxis? Could they not actually *derive* from the actual laws of a Temple society? Weinberg's view (Weinberg, 1992; cf. Blenkinsopp, 1991) is that an initially rather small society, which developed or preserved its own laws, was centred on the Temple and enjoyed imperial patronage, gradually extended and imposed itself throughout Yehud, and beyond. The power of the Jerusalem Temple no doubt did wax considerably, but if the biblical laws applied once to a *Bürger-Tempel-Gemeinde* and then were imposed on the surrounding territory as part of a process whereby the authority, and economic benefit, of the Jerusalem elite was enhanced, they must have either been extremely ambitious at the outset or substantially enlarged over time. For these laws embrace a whole ideal society (Israel), and do not even consistently favour the interests of a *Bürger-Tempel-Gemeinde*. The merging of cultic and non-cultic laws into a single conception is influenced by the configuration of the contemporary social structure. The integration of cultic and social in Deuteronomic and Leviticus requires us to date the composition of these law codes, as well as their incorporation into the larger Pentateuchal narrative, *and* the process by which they began to be adopted into various Judean lifestyle, as the work of two to three hundred years.

But this discussion cannot end without considering the *Book of the Covenant* (Exod. 20:18–23:33). It has no cultic legislation and no mention of priests; there is only a law about the altar (20:24–26), a single mention of "house of Yhwh your god" (23:19) and laws on celebrating the three great festivals. Van Seters' arguments in favour of its exilic setting and its dependence on Deuteronomy are not entirely convincing, and the thesis of dependence on Deuteronomy is unnecessary if Deuteronomy itself is redated. (It remains mysterious why Van Seters, having redated so much of the Pentateuch, leaves Deuteronomy alone!) There are, of course, obvious Deuteronomic or Deuteronomy-like passages in 23:23–24 and 28–33, probably additions. There are otherwise no particular clues to the date of this collection. I suggested earlier that its connection with the Exodus theme through the topic and treatment of slavery was intrinsic, and the departure from Egypt is connected with the Unleavened Bread feast (23:14–15). It is equally difficult to associate it with First and Second Temple Jerusalem, and with exilic communities; but the exclusion of these options does not necessarily make it pre-monarchic. That implies too simplistic a view of the history of Israelite and Judean religion. It is an interesting collection that invites us to consider the plurality of Israels, Judaism and their contexts and in particular the times and extents to which the religions of the area were predicated upon central sanctuaries.

Law and Ethnicity

Regardless of the precise historicity of Ezra or Nehemiah, it has been argued that Persian policy toward Yehud, as towards other provinces and peoples, was to authorize the production of a more or less autonomous legal system. We must remember that in a multicultural empire, unless there is an imperial law universally enforced in all areas (the "law of the Medes and Persians," somewhat mocked in both Esther and Daniel), a clear connection between law and ethnicity is logical, since both are functions of social identity. It has been argued that the Achaemenids promoted the creation, or reconstitution, of law codes governing various *ethne*, including Judah (and on the assumption, Samaria). The well-known case of the Egyptian Udjahorresnet has be invoked as an instance (Blenkinsopp, 1987): he seems to have been responsible, under the direction of the Achaemenid king, for the restoration of at least one cult centre in Egypt, and of the "houses of life," scribal institutions devoted to the composition and preservation of texts, including especially cultic and medical. These "houses of life" were generally, though not exclusively, associated with temples. Its activities also included teaching (Williams, 1990: 27).

Blenkinsopp suggests that the mission of Ezra follows closely that of Udjahorresnet: commissioned as a Persian sympathizer, he restores the Temple cult, restores the scribal schools and promulgates the local law. The parallel is attractive, but there are several difficulties (see Watts, 2001). First, the portrait of a law-bringing Ezra may, as argued earlier, reflect a much later perspective, retrojecting what was later seen as a law to be interpreted and adopted as the law of Judah to a written text imposed at the birth of Second Temple Judaism. The second and more substantial objection lies in the difficulty of matching any particular biblical material with such a law. Much has been written about this problem, if it is indeed a real problem (i.e. assuming there was an Ezra), and while a minority of scholars think of an early Pentateuch, the majority think rather of something more restricted, such as Deuteronomy or the

Priestly Code. But neither of these is a plausible law for a province or for an *ethnos*.

Another problem is the extent of this law's jursidiction. The decree from Artaxerxes according to Ezra states that Ezra was to appoint judges throughout the province of Abar-Nahara itself. This again looks like a reflection of a later situation, when what can be called a "Jewish" population was spread beyond Palestine into Transjordan and Syria. "Jewish" (i.e. "Judean") implies a sort of ethnic-religious identity by which persons in the Levant could be defined as adherents of the cult of Yhwh. This is in fact precisely what Jonah claims; although he is apparently an Israelite and not a Judean, he claims allegiance to a temple that is probably to be understood as Jerusalem; but he also calls himself a "Hebrew" (*'ivri*), meaning a resident of the satrapy of "Beyond the River." In Genesis this territory is converted into the lands of the Abrahamic nations. But within the narrative boundaries of Ezra and Nehemiah this larger territory is hostile and not to be engaged with.

Interpreting Scriptural Law

We find among the literature of the Second Temple period successive interpretations and reinterpretations of laws that over a period become canonized. But this canonization does not entail universal obedience. The laws define "Judaism"—all or most forms of it—though Jews within the Roman Empire (and presumably under the Parthians) could employ other legal systems: we have (limited) evidence of this. Among the sects represented in the Qumran scrolls, the Torah was clearly the divine will and its correct interpretation an index of being true Israel. The development that comes to its completion in the classic rabbinic documents is, as we can now see, anticipated in the Second Temple period, and betrays a general movement in the direction of turning theory into practice. This is not, however, to affirm some continuous unbroken line between scripture and rabbinic Judaism, nor to argue for a normative "Judaism" defined by the text of Torah. It might be fair to say that among the things that made a Judaism into a Judaism was the belief that it was defined by a "law." But the changing definition of *torah* from "teaching, religious instruction" to "precepts" accompanies the progression from theory to praxis that I have been tracing, though it does not match it precisely. Nor is that changing definition a simple one: rather it remains complex, not least when translated into Greek.

Concluding Observations: The Wider Historical Context

Between the composition of the law codes, a process that, like most canonical documents, involved copying and editing, and their reception (in theory and then in practice) as laws binding on each and every Judean's way of life lie several stages. The entire process, I would suggest, only begins with the society of the Persian province of Yehud because this is a society in which identity requires such a definition, as it does not in a monarchic state. The development of the Torah represents a literary exercise in creating "Judaism" or rather, in creating "Israel," of which a part becomes "Judaism" and eventually dominates. How far this process advanced before the advent of Alexander and his successors is impossible to say; but the Hellenization of the Persian empire—something already underway but not politically realized until the end of the fourth century—probably accelerated such a development. The breach with Samaria is likely to have begun under the Ptolemies, possibly as a result of Egyptian preference for Jerusalem over Samaria as the capital city of the unified region.

The events leading to the Maccabean wars, the religious aspect of that struggle and the foundation of a national state under the Hasmoneans added a new dimension to the process of constructing "Judaism," as did the expansion of the state to cover much of Palestine. I have not considered the role of Judean education in cultivating the study of Hebrew texts, nor the impact of Greek education in encouraging this process. But the structure of Torah as a *definition* of "Israel" seems to me to correspond very well with the social, religious and political imperatives of the third and second centuries BCE. The emergence of Jewish "parties" is probably to be understood as neither a direct result of political or cultural warfare, nor to imply a previous unity, but as a response to the need to define what "Israel" is and a lack of a clear definition. The Israels of the scriptures are not records of a historical nation but formulations of answers to questions of identity that rose only after the end of the Judean monarchy.

The home of "biblical law," Torah, even in late second Temple times remained for the most part, I suspect, the social space of the Jerusalem intellectual, the school or marketplace. Judaism as observance of *torah* is still in a certain sense a "Judaism" within Judaism, even within Palestine.

Chapter 5

DEUTERONOMY AND THE ORIGIN OF JUDAISM

In the opinion of virtually every scholar, Deuteronomy marks a crucial step in the evolution of the religion of Judah. This may be an understatement: "revolution" could be more appropriate. At any rate, its dating has long been a linchpin. For a long time (even before De Wette: see Paul [1985]) that question has been widely regarded as solved; the book (or its core) emerged in the late seventh century BCE in the reign of Josiah, as 2 Kings 22 narrates. The questions of why it emerged then and what its purpose was are less emphatically agreed, and several hypotheses have been produced. These, in my view, are not satisfactory. There have always been challenges to this long-established dating, going back to Hölscher (1922), who also stressed the utopian character of the book.

I want here to re-examine the date and purpose of Deuteronomy. In doing so I would like to illustrate several facts of how the past is created, both by biblical authors and by modern biblical scholars; for at issue here is not only how and why biblical narratives convey and exploit "the past" but also how "biblical history" is reconstructed by modern critical scholarship using these texts. I want, therefore, to explore first how Deuteronomy itself constructs or implies a history and how other scriptural texts construct a history for it, and then how modern scholarship has constructed a history for Deuteronomy. Finally, I will give my support to an alternative theory about its date that I think makes better sense, both of Deuteronomy itself and of the narrative of 2 Kings.

Biblical writings point away from their own time, away from the historical contexts that generate them. This is obvious in the case of the so-called "historical books," including the Pentateuch; but we also find it in the prophetic books, in novellas like Ruth, Jonah and Esther, and explicitly in the technique of pseudepigraphy—works ascribed to

Daniel, Solomon, and of course David. Modern historical scholarship, by contrast, orientates itself towards the time of the text itself, believing that the literature is properly understood only if we know when it was written, by whom, for whom, and why. To achieve this scholarly aim we have to construct a critical historical framework into which the biblical literature can be fitted.

The Projected History of Deuteronomy

Two levels of historical focus are projected by the book of Deuteronomy. Suppose that we begin with the main part of the book, the law code itself, chapters 12–26. a nation once engaged in forced labour in Egypt and being brought out (13:5, 10; 16:1–6); having assembled on the mountain of Horeb (18:16) and moving towards a land to destroy its inhabitants and their culture and settle there. There are references to details of a story apparently already known: a lack of hospitality from Ammonites and Moabites, cursing by Balaam (23:4), an engagement with Amalekites (25:17–19).

The introductions to this central section, in 1:1–4:43 and 4:44–11:32, provide a sharper focus, creating an immediate geographical and temporal setting for the speech that follows them: beyond the Jordan, in the wilderness, in the plain opposite Suph, between Paran and Tophel, Laban. Hazeroth, and Di-zahab… In the fortieth year, on the first day of the eleventh month (1:1, 3). Other incidents are added: rebellion, the reason for the prolonged journey to Canaan, and success against the kings of Heshbon and Bashan, a testing at Massah (6:16), the calf image made at Horeb (chapter 9) and the second set of tablets (chapter 10) as well as other rebellions. The epilogues to Deuteronomy (chapters 27–34) add brief allusions, too: "boils of Egypt" (28:27)…"Sihon of Heshbon and Og of Bashan" (29:7).

Deuteronomy thus invokes a narrative of Egyptian oppression already familiar to its readers: lawgiving, wilderness wandering and land occupation. The opening of the book also prescribes the precise past moment of the origin of the speech, on the plains of Moab just before entry into Canaan, just before Moses' death. The past is thus focused in two perspectives: the speech containing the laws implies a temporal context—escape from Egypt, lawgiving, wandering in the wilderness. But the text surrounding the speech also provides a precise moment for the speech itself. This focus is what provides Deuteronomy with its own historical setting. If, as most scholars maintain, the prologues and epilogues are later than the core of laws, then we can reconstruct these into two separate sequential processes; first, the composition of a speech that invokes a narrative; then a framework that freezes that speech into a Mosaic pseudepigraphon and gives it a precise moment of delivery. In the words of Clements (1989: 36):

> We can then see how the law book, which must originally have been set out in a more or less timeless fashion as the law of God for all generations of Israelites, has been given a strengthened authority, and has been modified in its character, by being given an author (Moses) and a unique and very specific historical setting.

Modern scholarship does not accept that historically Moses uttered this speech, but, more importantly, neither do we believe that the implied narrative reports historical events. But we also know that pseudepigraphy was common in the ancient world, and that this device was not understood as "deceit": such a view is modern and in the case of biblical texts usually stems from a misguided and literalist piety. The narrative implied in the book of Deuteronomy and the figure of Moses both convey an important part of the meaning of the text. But to understand the meaning more precisely we need to know when and why Deuteronomy was first composed. Yet the book, as noted already, obscures from us the actual historical circumstances of its composition.

The Projected History in the Book of Kings

On the way to finding the historical time and place of Deuteronomy's composition, we encounter another layer of concealment. The story in 2 Kings 22, usually attributed to a "Deuteronomist," a writer or group inspired by the book of Deuteronomy, relates a story of how a law book was discovered in the Jerusalem Temple in the days of Josiah. There is little doubt that this law book is intended to be understood as all or part of Deuteronomy; the language of the account and the description of the ensuing reform point clearly enough to Deuteronomy. But while there is no contradiction with a Mosaic attribution, this law book is not explicitly associated with him. 2 Kings 23:25 refers to "all the law of Moses," but does not necessarily mean the law book, which in the preceding verse is called simply "the book that the priest Hilkiah had found." The formula in v. 25 closely follows what is said about Hezekiah in 2 Kgs 18:6, and may in any case date from a later point in the production of 2 Kings. So for the writer of the narrative(s), the law book was probably *not* regarded as a Mosaic pseudepigraphon. Had it been so understood, then that would surely have been stated, in order to enhance its authority. So when and from where did the author (or authors) think this law book actually originated? We are not told; the information is apparently unimportant. What *is* important is that its contents were endorsed by a "good" Judean king and its stipulations implemented. The law book, then, needs Josiah, but not Moses.

Most scholars think that the writer of 2 Kings 22 gives us a reliable historical account and they thus assign the composition of most or all of Deuteronomy to the time of Josiah. While Deuteronomy's own story about the origin of its laws on the plains of Moab is rejected, another biblical story about its origin is accepted. But would the Josianic date have been *deduced* by scholars without the story of 2 Kings 22? Perhaps that is impossible to answer, but, the story having been accepted as historical, scholarship has set about rationalizing and embellishing the data. It has thus been speculated that Deuteronomy was composed shortly before its discovery, whether by writers in the kingdom of Israel who later moved to Judah (Welch, 1923; Alt, 1953; von Rad, 1953; Weinfeld, 1991: 44–50; cf. Nicholson, 1986) or by a priestly clique in Judah itself, seeking to minimize royal power, or by a scribal school of the period (Weinfeld, 1972: 158–78; 1991: 62–65). Josiah's reform—which 2 Kings 22 explains solely as a result of the law book—now becomes the centrepiece of Josiah's reign, either as part of a royal political initiative or as a bid for power, a major episode in modern critical histories of Judah and of the Jewish religion. Sweeney, for example, (2000: 137–69) suggests that the "people of the land" stood behind what was an economic as well as a religious reform, and that the priests were in fact deprived of income and thus power. But Deuteronomy places power over the law with the priests and it seems unlikely that any religious reform could have been realistically effected without their cooperation and support. Even Finkelstein's archaeologically based history (2001, 2006), bases a great deal on a scholarly elaboration that itself rests on little more than a biblical story.

But we know the inclination of ancient Judean writers to create stories about the past, including the Mosaic origin of Deuteronomy itself. Why might the story of Josiah's "discovery" not be compared with Chronicles' story of Hezekiah's Passover or even, more pertinently, 1 Kings' own story of Solomon's dedication of the Jerusalem temple— namely as a programmatic fiction? What reason do we have for reading 2 Kings 22 as being intended to narrate historical information rather than a legitimating legend? For this we need some form of additional argumentation concerning Josiah's reign and a plausible purpose for such a law book. Neither of these, despite the volume of scholarship devoted to them, can be established.

The Projected Scholarly History of a Josianic Renaissance

The backbone of the generally accepted date of Deuteronomy is, as already observed, a hypothesis about the reign of Josiah. He has been made to preside over a golden age both culturally and politically, a briefly but wonderfully reconstituted "pan-Israelite" domain. He has been credited with the policy of reviving the empire of David (now widely thought to be non-existent or hugely exaggerated). According to some scholars, he reclaimed the territory of Israel and promoted a new literary renaissance, a golden age of Hebrew prose (Weinfeld, 1972; see also Sweeney [2000] for a wider treatment of Josiah). But the biblical account actually says none of this. Josiah's "golden" reign is not a biblical, but a *scholarly* portrait, constructed to explain a biblical story in terms of modern historiography. Josiah's reign has indeed now replaced the "Solomonic Enlightenment" as a time of fervent literary activity.

But are the contents of Deuteronomy compatible with late monarchic Judah? We can compare what we now know of the reign of Josiah from biblical and other sources, with the political, social and religious ideology of Deuteronomy and with what we know of the ideology and structure of monarchic states in the ancient Near East.

The theory of a Josianic political restoration takes its starting point from 2 Kings 23, which says that Josiah pulled down the altar not only at Bethel, next door to Jerusalem, but also "all the shrines of the high places that were in the towns of Samaria which kings of Israel had made" (v. 19). From this it is deduced that Josiah reasserted control over the territory of the former kingdom of Israel. It has long been understood that this was possible because of a power vacuum in Palestine created by the decline of Assyrian power (e.g. Weinfeld, 1991: 65–68 for an over-confident account of the archaeological data). But such a power vacuum probably did not exist, as has been argued by Na'aman (1992). Na'aman has demonstrated that there was an orderly transfer of power in Palestine from Assyria to Egypt *before* Josiah came to the throne. In this case, a Judean political resurgence cannot have happened, nor realistically have been envisaged. Na'aman's suggestion that Josiah was executed by the pharaoh on suspicion of seditious activity and not in warfare would mean that Josiah had behaved in a way unacceptable to

Egypt, but hardly an occupation of a large tract of territory. The general scholarly consent is that Josiah did close down the sanctuary at Bethel, and that 1 Kings 13:1–10 has been included by the "Deuteronomistic" historian to anticipate Josiah's actions recorded in 2 Kings 23:17 (for contrasting assessments of Bethel's fate see Blenkinsopp, 2003: 93–95; Negev and Gibson, 2003:78). But that argument need not imply that Josiah actually *did* destroy Bethel, only that such a deed was in accord with a divine punishment on a sanctuary that in Deuteronomistic eyes was an illegitimate rival to Jerusalem. The information in 2 Kgs 23:19 that Josiah destroyed sanctuaries in cities of Samaria is separate from the note about Bethel and a programmatic statement similar to those found throughout 2 Kings when summarizing the reigns of Judean and Israelite monarchs.

The more detailed account of Josiah's religious reform within Judah (23:4–14) has to be assessed separately. The attribution of a religious reform is in itself unremarkable, since 2 Kings attributes changes in religious practice to virtually every king of Judah since Solomon (e.g. Ahaz, 16:1–4; Hezekiah, 18:1–4; Manasseh, 21:1–9). However, the scale of this description exceeds any other, and it is clear that the author of 2 Kings wishes to present Josiah as an exceptionally righteous king. But against this glorious account must be set the lack of any clear reference in other biblical literature. We would expect to find traces elsewhere in the biblical writings of such a reform as Josiah is said to have instituted. But there is no unambiguous hint of any such reform in other biblical literature that might perhaps be assigned to the period, for instance the books of Jeremiah or Zephaniah, despite the intensive efforts of Sweeney to demonstrate otherwise (2000: 179–313).

The glorious profile of Josiah does not make it more probable that Deuteronomy dates from his reign, for the reverse argument is equally valid: that such a reputation explains the attribution of the law book discovery to him, as the only truly righteous monarch since Solomon. Josiah's reform is "remembered" only by the author of 2 Kings 22 and/or 23, unless, as argued by Würthwein (1976), an original account of a religious reform of the kind known from elsewhere in 2 Kings was subsequently embellished in an attempt to link it to Deuteronomy (a strong possibility, perhaps supported by the evidence of 2 Chron. 34:3–7; but see also the analysis of 2 Kings 22 in Hoffmann, 1980: 169–270; Sweeney, 2000: 40–51).

Hence, the story of Josiah's religious activity is at the very least exaggerated (see Spieckermann, 1982: 18–24 for the argument that the reform was limited and essentially anti-Assyrian). Still, some kind of religious reform need not be ruled out, even if only on the grounds that the relaxing of Assyrian control suggested that some Assyrian features of the Judean royal cult might be eliminated. Whether such a reform was originally connected in 2 Kings with the discovery of the law book is, however, a disputed literary-critical issue (for a relatively recent discussion of this long debate, see Lohfink, 1985a).

The figure of Josiah clearly bears a lot of symbolic value for authors promoting a Deuteronomic ideology. His sponsorship of the law book endorses the transfer of power from king to priest: royal command gives way to a written code. His destruction of all shrines (throughout both Israel and Judah) except Jerusalem also authorizes the exclusive status of that sanctuary. Just as in Chronicles it is the Temple that fulfils, replaces and continues the "Davidic house," so in 2 Kings Solomon and Josiah are used to confirm the commitment of Judean kingship to what will later be referred to as "torah" alongside their allegiance to the Jerusalem Temple. Josiah endorses the contents of Deuteronomy as a blueprint for the religion of Judah and gives a written law that is already, or perhaps will later be, attributed to Moses, the Davidic *imprimatur*. A Judaism that we can call "Mosaic" (or a Torah-Judaism) is depicted as being enforced by the most righteous king of Judah—and one whose reign closely preceded the end of the monarchy. He is not therefore a figure of remote antiquity. Regardless of the question of whether, or how far, the story about Josiah is historically correct, it has a purpose beyond the narration of fact. We can interpret and explain the story of Josiah's reform without needing to rely upon an historical event to do so.

The History of Deuteronomy

On the argument so far, we have no reliable date for Deuteronomy. From the use of elements of Assyrian ideology and literary convention (see especially Weinfeld, 1972: 59–157) we have a *terminus a quo* but given that Assyria supplied the diplomatic repertoire of West Semitic scribal schools over a long period, we do not have a *terminus ad quem*. We need, therefore, to consider the ideology of Deuteronomy and deduce the most likely political, religious and social context for it. Deuteronomy proposes the idea of a covenant, or treaty, with its deity, but one imposed on society and the individual, not on any institution or figure. The mediator, if there is one, is Moses (or the anonymous speaker of the core of the book, if Mosaic attribution is secondary). The conditions are written in a book, not enshrined in traditional practice and the book does not have the form of royal code or decree. Deuteronomy divorces state religion from the royal patronage that even according to the books of Kings it had always enjoyed, and also reduces prophecy to endorsement of this written text. It furthermore registers a strong cultural hostility between Israel and its immediate neighbours "in the land" and upholds a strongly monotheistic ethos. It seeks to regulate the use of sanctuaries for sacrifice, either to a single sanctuary or to authorized Yahwistic sanctuaries.

Let us consider three of the issues among those just raised: king; law; and Israelites/Canaanites: these, I think, are sufficient to justify some conclusions about the date of the original contents of Deuteronomy.

King

Does Deuteronomy imagine a society ruled by a king? The answer is technically "yes":

> When you come to the land which Yahweh your God is giving you, and possess it, and inhabit it, and say, "I will set a king over me, like all the nations that are about me, you shall in any case make king over you one whom Yahweh your God will choose: one from among yourselves you shall make king over you, and not put a foreigner over you, one who is not your own kin (17:14).

However, this regulation is viewed from the perspective of a Mosaic fiction, or at least of the fictive setting of the book after Horeb but before entry into Canaan. It needs to be matched with a retrospective:

> Yahweh will bring you [sing.], and your king, whom you will set over you, to a nation that neither you nor your ancestors have known; and there you will worship other gods, wood and stone (28:36).

This can hardly be other than a reference to Babylon (the king of Israel was not taken into exile). Weinfeld (1972: 123) derives this element from Assyrian treaty curses, specifically citing those of Esarhaddon; but whether or not the *form* is so derived, the content almost certainly postdates 596, as indicated by the formula "other gods, wood and stone" (outside Deuteronomy the phrase is found in Isa. 37:19, Ezek. 20:32 and Dan. 5:23—thus everywhere else it reflects an explicitly "postexilic" context). We can, of course, discount this reference as a later addition, since it is not part of the central legal section that most scholars recognize as the original core. But it is significant that in 17:14 a foreign king is specifically forbidden. It is hard to imagine at what point in the monarchic period of Judah such a clause would have made any sense: it belongs most plausibly to Israel after 722 or Judah after 596 when the ruler of the lands was an imperial monarch.

The "law of the king" continues with the following (17:16–20):

> He shall not multiply horses to himself, nor cause the people to return to Egypt, in order to multiply horses: for Yahweh has said unto you, "You shall from now on return no more that way." Nor shall he take many wives, or else his heart will turn away: nor shall he accumulate silver and gold. And when he sits on the throne of his kingdom, he shall write for himself a copy of this law in the presence of the levitical priests. It shall remain with him, and he shall read it all the days of his life: that he may learn to fear Yahweh his god, observing all the words of this law and these statutes. Thus he will not exalt himself above his fellows, nor turn not aside from the commandment, either to right or left, so that he may prolong his days in his kingdom, he, and his descendants, in the midst of Israel.

The clause removes the twin basis of monarchic authority: justice and warfare. Instead, the conduct of war is subject to written rules, and the administration of justice to a written code written by someone other than the king. It is hardly conceivable that in monarchic Judah such a situation was imagined, let alone that it would have been implemented by any monarch. At what point in Judean history did any group acquire sufficient power and authority to effectively replace the monarchy? It has been suggested that Josiah, as a young king, was forced, or encouraged, into such a renunciation of power by other more powerful groups. But non-priestly groups (elders, landowners, local chiefs) depend upon monarchic authority for their own status. The implication is less plausibly of a weak, or young king but an *absent* king, an absent *monarchy*. Endorsement from a monarch is helpful, but the monarch need not be reigning: a righteous and dead one will do even better. And in the absence of a monarch, the Deuteronomic "reform" can be permanent and not subject to challenge by the king's successor. For the remainder of the account in 2 Kings does not suggest that any of Josiah's measures prevailed after his death. How, in such circumstances, would the programme of Deuteronomy have been sustained or revived? It is more economical, and more realistic, to suppose that it was in fact created after the end of the monarchy.

Law

While Deuteronomy contains individual stipulations characteristic of ancient Near Eastern law collections, it is not a royal code or edict. Because of its style of rhetorical address, it was identified by von Rad (1953) as originating in levitical sermons. Yet Deuteronomy appears to refer to *itself* as a law book, which even the king must obey. This reference reminds us of 1 Sam. 10:25: 'Samuel told the people the rights and duties of the kingship; and he wrote them in a book and laid it up before Yhwh.' Which historical context best fits such a notion, in which "the people" are entrusted with obeying a divinely-originated law? Taking the form of a speech to all members of the society, and representing itself as a book to be consulted and publicly read out, it implies a public ceremony in which members of the society are addressed and urged to behave in certain ways. What kind of context fits these requirements in a monarchic state? 2 Chronicles 20 describes a religious assembly addressed by the king and accompanied by a levitical "prophecy." Such a setting has no plausible historical setting under the Judean monarchy, but might reflect assemblies in the "Second Temple." The authors of Deuteronomy may well have had a similar setting in mind, and in its present form Deuteronomy has been provided with an actual audience.

Israelites/Canaanites

The definition of the society addressed in Deuteronomy is highly significant for determining its date. The name given to this society is "Israel." The Deuteronomic literature, and all modern scholarship, understands this as meaning a nation composed of twelve tribes, in existence before entry into the land, brought from Egypt and addressed in single assembly by Moses. But what this "Israel" is, is not actually specified in the material we are considering.

In the monarchic period, there existed two kingdoms, one called Judah and the other known (among other things) as "Israel." The possibility of a "united monarchy," currently in dispute, is not a relevant context to a document produced, by general consent, centuries later. When did such a society as Deuteronomy's "Israel" ever exist, or, more precisely, when might it have been *conceived* as an ideal? Josiah's kingdom was called Judah and the kingdom actually known as "Israel" had not existed for a century. The view that Deuteronomy is actually of "northern" origin and was brought to Judah after 722 would account for the use of the name, but not why this name would be adopted in Judah and retained as the title of the addressees. Why should Josiah's Judah be referred to as "Israel"?

Deuteronomy's "Israel" is also defined in terms of a differentiation from others. The legal section of Deuteronomy does not refer to "Canaan" or "Canaanites" (the terms occurs only once in the whole book, at 32:49, outside the supposedly original core). Two usages are employed. In some texts (14:2; 15:6; 17:4; 18:9, 14 and 26:19) the phrase "the nations" refers to all other nations, undifferentiated: "Israel" is to be quite distinct from these, creating the dichotomy Israel/nations that echoes throughout the Bible and in the later term "Gentiles." Within these, however, is a specific group: nations that will be "dispossessed" and shunned (7:1; 12:29–30; 14:2 etc.). For they occupy the land that "Israel" has been promised and also practise religious customs that are abhorrent to Yhwh, which "Israel" is not to imitate.

These nations and their culture are for destruction; intermarriage with them is also strictly forbidden. What kind of society gives rise to a notion of two nations (or ethnic identities) comprising distinct cultures but occupying the same space—one element indigenous and the other immigrant? These requirements fit the Mosaic fiction, but hardly the Judean monarchy. Who *are* the "Canaanites" in Josiah's kingdom? For the purposes of a religious reform under a monarch, such rhetoric is neither necessary nor helpful; there can be no point in a king endorsing a destruction or alienation of a *population* who comprise his subjects. Creating an alien "enemy within" is self-destructive and, indeed, unnecessary to religious reform. For a realistic context for such rhetoric, we need two categories of population, one "Israel," one "other," one indigenous, the other immigrant, where, moreover, the immigrant population seeks to separate from and ultimate displace the indigenous one.

This context is described in the following speech:

> "So their descendants went in and possessed the land, and you subdued before them the inhabitants of the land, the Canaanites, and gave them into their hands, with their kings, and the people of the land, that they might do with them as they wished" (Neh. 9:24).

> "All who have separated themselves from the people of the land…enter into a curse and an oath, to walk in God's law, which was given by Moses the servant of God… We will not give our daughters to the people of the land, nor take their daughters for our sons (Neh. 10:28–30).

In the book of Nehemiah, whatever its date or historicity, there is an identification of the "Canaanites" with a group living in Judah alongside the immigrants from Babylonia who are making a covenant and seeking exclusive claims to be "Israel." Whether or not the context described in Ezra–Nehemiah, of a single body of returnees is historically accurate, the ideology can be plausibly attributed to a group of Judeans whose membership and culture differed substantially from that of others in Judah and who were engaged in a struggle over legitimacy, over religious "orthodoxy" and thus over who really was "Israel."

The Origin of Deuteronomy

Deuteronomy is, on the arguments above, an improbable programme for religious and social reform produced for, or sponsored by, a king. Its representation of royal functions, its concept of law, its definition of "Israel" all point away from monarchic Judah. A deported population offers some plausible features, especially the self-government of a society under the direction of priests. But this community must have had a strong belief in its repatriation, and the destruction of Canaanites would be a programme for the future (the "Canaanites" can hardly be native Babylonians), and the use of the term "Israel" would signify an alliance of these Judeans with Israelites previously deported by the Assyrians. Deuteronomy might be a blueprint for a future society in Palestine with a constitutional monarch. But that is quite an improbable hypothesis. More plausible is a setting in which such conditions were not imagined but actually present; a society newly transplanted (or created), and an indigenous population with different religious practices. We must not draw too direct a comparison between the story of Nehemiah, which suggests a strong antipathy between Jerusalem and Samaria, whereas the books of Moses (including Deuteronomy) are also Samaritan scripture, and the sharing of this literature implies a commonality of the two communities at some point prior to their schism. The Elephantine letter (Cowley, 1923: *AP* 30/31) to Bagoas, governor of Yehud, refers to communication with Delayah and Shelemayah, sons of the governor of Samaria, while *AP* 32 mentions a joint declaration from the two governors, suggesting a degree of cooperation between the two provincial leaders over a matter of Jewish jurisdiction.

If Deuteronomy reflects a historical conflict—even an ideological one—between population elements, then it represents a particular viewpoint: the immigrant. The reinstatement of Jerusalem may have secured a political and religious victory equivalent to the story of Joshua, solving the "Canaanite" problem. Indeed, 2 Kings 22–23 implies that

Bethel was a rival to Jerusalem. But Bethel had been a major sanctuary in sixth century Judah (see Blenkinsopp, 2003). The narrative of Josiah's destruction of Bethel (and the prophecy of 2 Kings 13) fits very well what we can infer to have happened in the fifth or fourth century—the replacement of Bethel by Jerusalem and the destruction of the former.

Yet it is not certain that Deuteronomy specifies one single sanctuary. It plausibly eliminates all but Jerusalem in Judah, but not necessarily Samaria or Shechem, or else we should perhaps date it to the very late Persian period. Otherwise, the fifth century is perhaps the most likely context for the production of Deuteronomy. The Kings narrative is evidence of the document acquiring a wider authority, and with added features: in favour of Jerusalem as the exclusive sanctuary, against priests and sanctuaries from elsewhere, and as a Mosaic, not an anonymous, book.

Further clarification of Deuteronomy's origins and purpose depends on understanding its relationship to other canonized writings—the Pentateuch (and the *Book of the Covenant*), the Latter Prophets and the books of the Deuteronomistic History. In Pentateuchal criticism, the chronological sequence J-E-D-P, inherited from the Graf-Wellhausen hypothesis, has been under attack from several directions (for a convenient review, see Nicholson, 1998). Perhaps D's pivotal anchor in the seventh century needs to be shifted, too. But my purpose in this paper has not been to replace one implausible theory about Deuteronomy's origin with another more plausible one, but to argue that the continuity between monarchic and post-monarchic Judean religion that the theory of a Josianic reform endorses may be illusory. The story of the finding of the law book is not, in my view, an anticipation, in the monarchic age, of a postmonarchic society, but an attempt to *create* continuity, to give monarchic legitimation to a post-monarchic phenomenon, to assert "new" Israel as a reformed successor to "old" Israel. Historically, Deuteronomy represents something quite new: a new theory of religion and of society. It is one of the foundation documents of "early Judaism."

Chapter 6

The God of Cyrus and the God of Israel

"Second Isaiah" or "Deutero-Isaiah" (Isaiah 40–55) has, like Deuteronomy, secured a virtual scholarly unanimity over its time and place of composition. This chapter is a contribution to recent efforts at dislodging this poetry, also, from its assigned place, and so to revise some notions about the history of the cult of Yhwh and the origins of "early Judaism."

I begin with the explicit historical references in Isaiah 40–55, namely the mention of Cyrus in 44:28 and 45:1–7. The relationship between these passages and the famous inscription of the Persian king now housed in the British Museum (for the text see, e.g., Oppenheim in Pritchard, 1969: 315–16; Fish in Winton Thomas, 1958: 92) has been invoked and examined many times. According to the *Cyrus Inscription* the "lord of the gods" (Marduk), also "protector of his people," searched for a "righteous ruler to take his hand" and pronounced the name of Cyrus as future ruler of the world. Marduk "beheld Cyrus's good deeds and upright heart," as a result of which Babylon was overcome without any battle, and subsequently "all the kings of the world brought tributes" to Cyrus, while the new ruler of the world rebuilt cities and sanctuaries. Similarly, in Isaiah 45 Yhwh "grasps Cyrus's hand," to empower him to "subdue nations" and "open gates"; as a result, the wealth of Egypt and the Sabaeans will come to Cyrus.

These parallels, first noted almost a century ago (see Kittel, 1898) continue to be noted, but almost inevitably with the demurrer that the writer of the Hebrew poems cannot have been dependent on the inscription; they must have been written *before* Cyrus's capture of Babylon. This assertion carries the implication that the poetry is a genuine prediction, though only by a short period. At all events, the similarities between the texts tend for the most part to be regarded as each dependent on either a "Babylonian court style" (Gressmann, 1929: 59–60) or, with greater form-critical precision, the genre of "royal oracle" (Westermann, 1969: 154). Morton Smith (1963) proposed a more precise definition of the relationship, arguing that the parallels between the biblical texts and the inscription all involve only the first part of the inscription, which speaks of the king in the third person, and which, on Smith's view, represents propaganda from the Babylonian priesthood, originating from before Cyrus's arrival in Babylon, and paralleled only in Isaiah 40–48, whereas to the second part of the inscription there are "almost no parallels in II Isaiah" (415).

Smith's verdict is that "the parallels demonstrate literary dependence" (417). However, since the statements of Second Isaiah about the capture of Babylon are inaccurate, they must, he concludes, have been written before the peaceful capture of that city. The lack of parallels with the second part of the inscription, which tells of the favourable treatment of Babylon by its new ruler, are claimed to support this contention. Thus, the sentiments of the author of the Hebrew text are the result of successful Persian propaganda. The poet must, then, have been persuaded by agents of the Persian king, before Cyrus's arrival in Babylon.

Smith deduces further that contacts of the same kind might have led to the transmission of further Persian ideas, such as the creation of the world, a doctrine which (he claims) cannot be found in any Hebrew text whose origins we can securely date earlier than the sixth century. The extent to which Isaiah proclaims this doctrine, which he claims to have existed "of old" (40:21, 28 etc.) testifies to its very novelty (an observation typical of Smith's scholarship). And finally, he offers us a parallel between some texts from Isaiah 40, 44 and 45 and *Yasna* 44, one of Zoroaster's *Gathas*. The parallel texts deal with the supreme deity as the source of justice, creation of the heavenly and earthly beings, of light and darkness, of wisdom. These parallels, which involve the same material as the parallels to the *Cyrus Inscription* (chapters 40–48) suggest to Smith "relationship to the same tradition." Why such parallels might have been taken up by Second Isaiah is left by Smith deliberately unanswered.

I take note of Smith's suggestion because it raises the issue of whether the poetry of Isaiah 40–55 is influenced by the Zoroastrian ideology of the Achaemenid empire, which will be considered later. It seems to have been endorsed in large measure by Mary Boyce, who speaks of the "exalted trust in Cyrus which the unknown Persian propagandist had instilled in the prophet" (1982: 2, 45), and actually completes the circle from Smith's case by concluding that since the Zoroastrian influence came from Achaemenid agents, Cyrus must have been a Zoroastrian.

There are two objections to Smith's thesis, one minor and one major. The minor objection is that the parallels with Second Isaiah in the Cyrus inscription are not in fact restricted to the first part. Its final section includes the following passage:

> All the kings of the entire world from the Upper to the Lower Sea, those who are seated in throne rooms, (or) live in other (places), and all the kings of the Western lands living in tents, brought their heavy tributes and kissed my feet in Babylon.

This may be compared with Isa. 45:14

> "The wealth of Egypt and the merchandise of Ethiopia, and the Sabaeans, men of stature, shall come over to you and be yours, they shall follow you; they shall come over in chains and bow down to you. They will make supplication to you..."

There are differences between the two passages, but the parallel should not necessarily be excluded, even though the same sentiments are also present in the first part of the inscription.

The more important difficulty is that Smith's view requires Second Isaiah to have been in Babylon. But this agrees with the scholarly consensus. However, this consensus, having come about in a curious and rather uncritical way, has recently been challenged. An impressive review of the history of this consensus, and of the argumentation on which it is based, has been offered by Seitz (1992), who has added his weight to recent doubts that the author of Isaiah 40–55 is to be located in Babylon (205–207). These doubts are increasing as scholarly interest in the redactional history of the contents of the book of Isaiah as a whole has recently intensified.

Seitz reminds us (1992: 1–35) that for Duhm (1892), as well as for a number of other scholars earlier this century—Ewald (1867), Marti (1900), Hölscher (1914: 322), Torrey (1928) and Mowinckel (1931), there was no question of a Babylonian provenance for these poems. Duhm in fact stated forcefully that the author of Isaiah 40–55 was definitely *not* to be located there (1892: xviii). More recently Kapelrud (1960), Smart (1965), Barstad (1982), and Clements (1985) have also proposed objections against a Babylonian setting. Not all of the earlier scholars (including Duhm himself) opted for a setting in Palestine, though the more recent critics have been more in agreement with him. In Barstad's view, this shift in opinion has occurred because recent scholarship has questioned more persistently the biblical claim that Judah was virtually denuded of population, religion and culture after 586 CE (an analysis of the biblical ideology of the "empty land" can be found in Carroll, 1991). Barstad points out not only the existence of the book of Lamentations—which the scholarly consensus sets in Jerusalem—but its similarity in many respects to some of the ideas of Second Isaiah. (It may also be worth remembering that Martin Noth placed the composition of his "Deuteronomistic History" in Palestine during the sixth century, a view subsequently abandoned by most of his successors but worth reinstating; see Davies, 2007a: 108–15).

The exilic setting of these chapters is also being to some extent undermined (though less obviously) by the current trend towards denying the original independence of 40–55 from 1–39—the foundation of Duhm's own argument for a "Second Isaiah." Several scholars now suggest that Second Isaiah should be understood as either a commentary on a collection which corresponds to the present "First Isaiah" (see above), or even as the redactor of the entire book (e.g. Williamson, 2005). The view is partly supported by those who find "postexilic" material throughout First Isaiah (such as Vermeylen, [1977–78], Kaiser [1981] and Gosse [1992], who relates the redaction of the entire book of Isaiah to priestly circles, linking the process to elements in both the Psalms and Proverbs). The recent study by Jean Marcel Vincent (1977) assigning the whole of 40–55, with the rest of Isaiah, to the postexilic Jerusalem priesthood, has been virtually ignored, though Ronald Clements accepts some of Vincent's arguments, and, pursuing his own thesis that Isaiah 40–55 is developed consciously out of 1–39, observes that while a Babylonian setting remains likely for "at least some of the material," a Palestinian origin is "an increasingly probable deduction to make from so much of the recent research into the origin of these enigmatic chapters" (Clements, 1985: 110). The issue of single authorship versus redaction is not one which can be discussed here, important though it is. I note only that the separation of the "Servant Songs" from the remainder has long had substantial support. Otherwise, Kratz (1991) divides *Grundtext* from *Erweiterung* in 45:1–7, then, on the basis of that analysis, in the other Cyrus material (41:1–5, 21–29). The results are then further applied to an investigation of the growth of 40–55, seen as originally a collection of *ribs*, salvation-oracles and oracles against the nations, through which a greater role for Cyrus as world-conquering divine agent develops. Kratz finds the "Servant Songs" and the anti-idol polemic emerge as the product of secondary layers. Laato (1992) represents those who regard Isa. 40–55 as a literary unit: traditional themes and language of royal ideology, from both Judah and Assyria, inform the "Servant Songs" and are applied to Cyrus. Isaiah 40–55 is, in his view, an attempt to adapt an exilic messianic programme to the early post-exilic period, when there was no royal figure. Once the unity of Isaiah 40–55 is broken, of course, arguments for the historical setting have to be made for each unit, and we have to think of a sequence of poets of different times and possibly places. The collection and redaction itself would surely have to be placed in the post-exilic period, effectively destroying the image of an exilic "Second Isaiah." It certainly alters significantly the understanding of why and how—and for whom—the poems were written individually and collected as a series.

Having shown how the notion of an exilic poet asserted itself despite Duhm's opinion to the contrary, Seitz also provides a convenient summary of the arguments against a Babylonian exilic setting (1892: 205–207). The most compelling are as follows:

1. the opening call of 40:1–2 (and other places) addresses itself to Jerusalem and not to exiles.
2. The exiles to be gathered in are from all the parts of the world, not just from Babylon (43:5–6).
3. Cyrus is depicted as coming "from a far country" (46:11), which seems inappropriate for a Babylonian perspective.
4. The complaint about refusal to offer sacrifice (43:22–24) is invalid except in Jerusalem or some other sanctuary city.
5. The expression in 43:14 "I will send to Babylon" is inappropriate if the setting is itself Babylon.
6. Israel as "a people robbed and plundered ... trapped in holes and hidden in prisons" is not an apt description of life in exile.

Seitz adds that Zion itself is presented as in exile (49:21) without the sense of physical deportation. This is consistent with the well-known *topos* of exile as designating the state of Judah throughout the Persian and Greco-Roman periods (documented by Knibb, 1977). In short, the fate of Jerusalem and the promised return of its children is a theme that better suits a setting *in that city* rather than in exiled communities, while the notion of exile in these chapters is ideological rather than concrete and indeed a well-attested motif throughout the entire Second Temple era.

There are, by contrast, two possible indications of a Babylonian context for the poems. One is the reference to Babylonian gods, including specific mention of Bel and Nebo (the name "Marduk" is nowhere mentioned, let alone denounced in the Bible). The other piece of evidence is the inaccuracy of the prediction of Cyrus's bloody capture of Babylon. That suggests, the argument runs, that the poem was written when Cyrus's seizure of the city was imminent but before the *peaceful* surrender of the city to his forces—and this strongly implies Babylon as the place of composition.

These arguments are not particularly strong. On the first, Barstad notes (1982: 82–83), however, that since Judah had been under the Babylonian yoke for several decades before the exile, and was administered by the Babylonians as a province until the advent of Cyrus, references to alien gods might naturally name Babylonian deities (he cites in support Jer. 50:22; 51:44). As for the manner of Cyrus' capture of Babylon, one could, of course, fall back on the argument that while chapters 40–55 are *as a whole* later and non-Babylonian, there are one or two earlier poems that were not amended. But such argumentation is not necessary. The inaccurate prediction of Cyrus' destructive entry into Babylon establishes a date prior to 538 only if Second Isaiah lived in Babylon at about the time of Cyrus. But if the poet lived elsewhere or later, the error is explicable in other ways. The inaccurate "prediction" may be an inaccurate record or memory, or indeed a rhetorical point, since Babylon's destruction is meant as a retribution for Jerusalem's.

Indeed, this factor may be inconclusive either way on the questions of date and setting, since we do not know whether the city *was* taken peacefully: we have only an account emanating from Cyrus himself, who wished to appear as a welcome saviour (on this question see Kuhrt, 1990). There is yet another possibility. A half-century after Cyrus, Xerxes I is reported in Greek accounts as having razed the fortifications laid by Nebuchadnezzar, destroyed the *Esagila* and melted down the statue of Marduk. If these reports are correct (and they also may not be reliable: see Kuhrt and Sherwin-White, 1987), after 482 onwards, Babylon could be deemed to have been destroyed much as Jerusalem was in 586. There are no compelling, not even solid, arguments for an "exilic" setting for Second Isaiah, in whole or part.

And so we have to ask again: at what time and place does this collection of poems make the best sense? The starting point, as I stated earlier, must be the ideology of the collection taken as a whole. Accordingly, the best opening step is to look at the scope of the poetry, the wood rather than the trees. From such a perspective some interesting features appear—or fail to appear. For there is no address to returning exiles and little concern for them. Cyrus's role as liberator in Second Isaiah concerns only marginally (at best) his encouragement of deportees to leave for their original homelands (if indeed they really did receive such encouragement; see Kuhrt, 1983). In fact, such an act remains entirely to be inferred. He is proclaimed (see below) rather as world-conqueror and restorer of the fortunes of Judah and Jerusalem. The poetry expresses the aspirations, not of migrants about to return from deportation but of the inhabitants of an underpopulated, devastated city and its hinterland, awaiting a glorious future, and probably with some realistic hope from Persian initiatives. This observation supports Barstad's argument (Barstad, 1989) that there is no "second exodus" motif in Second Isaiah, but that the poet of Isaiah 40–55 wrote in the sixth century in Judah and offered wider promises to Judah of deliverance from the Babylonian yoke under which Judah lay during most of the sixth century. Barstad does in fact allow that one text (48:20–22), might link an exit from Babylon with the Exodus, though it is spoken from the perspective of Judah. Yet he is right to point out (as do several other commentators) that the call to "flee" here does not suggest a return home, but rather the avoidance of a catastrophe (Jer. 50:8; 51:6, 45 similarly calls on Judeans in Babylonia to escape the city's imminent fate).

I have reservations about Barstad's sixth-century date, however. First, we cannot be sure that in the sixth century, rather than the fifth, any realistic hopes of a political revival for Jerusalem could be entertained, or even that there was any significant migration from Babylonian to Judah, unless we rely on the chronological information in Haggai and Zechariah. But there are many problems with the scenario that these books offer: they imply that Jerusalem is already the capital and that the city has a high priest but not a temple. These books (and until recently most of their modern interpreters) have largely ignored the probable realities of the situation in Judah at the time; recent work (see Lipschits and Blenkinsopp, 2003; Lipschits, 2005; Lipschits and Oeming, 2006 and Edelman, 2005). A sixth century "Return" is almost certainly the product of later invention, simplifying a more complicated and lengthier process of political and religious transformation and obliterating the memory of Neo-Babylonian Judah in favour of an exclusive attention to the Judean "exiles," descended from people taken largely from Jerusalem and its immediate environment.

The lack of prominence given to a return of "exiles" in Second Isaiah is worth stressing, since this concern is so often taken for granted. But Barstad's arguments to the contrary are substantial. As he observes, the opening proclaims the coming of *Yhwh* ("the way of Yahweh, 40:3; cf. "behold your god," v. 9), not of immigrants; this divine presence is then contrasted with human feebleness ("all flesh is like grass," v. 6). The following image of the shepherd feeding and carrying the flock in v. 11 does not refer to a trek from Babylon to Jerusalem: there is no identifying of the flock with *exiles*: the nearest antecedent to the object pronoun here is the "cities of Judah" (v. 9). Nor is there a "new exodus" presented in 41:17–20, which refers to the blossoming of the desert, a time of prosperity (cf. Amos 9:11–15, etc.). In all other references to "leading," Barstad finds only the use of the kind of metaphorical language common throughout the Bible. The restoration promised by the voice does not have a return from Babylon especially in mind; where the gathering of exiles is mentioned, a general return from all areas is envisaged (a point also noted, as mentioned earlier, by Seitz [1992]). Thus, in 52:2–6 Zion itself is spoken of as "captive"; this is followed by a reference to enslavement in Egypt, then Assyrian oppression (of the kingdom of Israel, presumably). The Babylonian deportation is not mentioned, but presumably implied.

Shortly afterwards (52:11–12) comes "Depart, depart, go out thence, touch no unclean thing; go out from the midst of her, purify yourselves, you who bear the *kelim* of Yhwh. For you shall not go out in haste, and you shall not go in flight [*contra* 48.20!], for Yhwh will go before you, and the God of Israel will be your rearguard." The noun *hippazon* occurs elsewhere only in reference to the Exodus (Exod. 12:11; Deut. 16:3), but what are the *kelê yhwh*? Barstad suggests "weapons" and a holy war. Temple vessels are an alternative. Neither fits the Exodus story exactly, and if Exodus is being referred to, it is by contrast, since (at least according to the narrative in Exodus) it was accomplished in haste and as a flight. But is this call addressed to Judeans in Babylon? Although that is a plausible interpretation, there is in fact nothing in the context to require this at all and the words should not be required to bear too much weight.

Indeed, since the poetry in Isaiah 40–55 seems to comprise a sequence of independent pieces rather than a longer coherent composition, it is difficult to determine the precise meaning or reference of some of them. If, however, there is an overall perspective, this can only be determined by features that collectively characterize their theme and outlook. These are the creation of a world empire by Cyrus (including the punishment and degradation of Babylon), the gathering of the scattered nation of Israel from all corners of the world to Jerusalem and the rebuilding of the nation, with Jerusalem as the centre of worldwide worship of Yhwh.

Additional themes are criticism of the use of idols as vain and Yhwh as the supreme and creating deity.

These elements coalesce into a vision of a new historical order, in which under the one supreme god (named always simply as Yhwh, with the rare addition of a title or epithet) harmony will be achieved and sustained under a single ruler and a sanctuary in Jerusalem where the creator god will be aniconically worshipped and his own chosen people restored to a place of security, wealth and prestige (a similar vision is found in Hag. 2:1–9). The "servant" poems are not easy to fit into this general vision: if they do, they are probably to a large extent about the role of Israel in helping to bringing about this world order. The people will not achieve it themselves: rather, Yhwh and the Persians (led by Yhwh's anointed) will, and the suffering of the Judeans, their passivity and obedience, will be rewarded by a transformation of them and their beloved city. But it is not clear that a single identity (or any identity) for the "servant" can be identified; the purposes of Yhwh may be furthered by various types of "service," from suffering to ruling the word: "Israel" and Cyrus are, on this interpretation, partners in Yhwh's service. At all events, the poems elaborate on the roles of both Cyrus and "Israel" in Yhwh's new order.

Cyrus as World Ruler

The idea that the political future of the Judeans would be under a Persian king is more significant for dating than is often recognized. There is no expectation of a future *native* dynasty hinted at here. With this view we may contrast texts that suggest some kind of national royal or non-royal dynasty or ruler (e.g. Ezek. 34:23–24; Jer. 23:5, 33:15–17; Amos 9:11; Zech. 12:7–8). The poems here *take for granted* that the role of "anointed" has passed not just to Cyrus but to the Persians, for the role of Jerusalem as a centre for the kings of the world to come implies a world empire, and this can only be a Persian one. The fate of Jerusalem does not await the destruction of the Persian empire, but will be achieved within it. Jerusalem will be a city of the Persian empire, a major religious and cultural centre. This vision is an unusually percipient prognostication, not shared by any other Judean writings from the period. For in a few centuries the city was to become a metropolis of the Eastern Mediterranean. But the vision of a glorious future for Jerusalem, and apparently without any miraculous divine intervention "in those days," probably comes from a time when such an empire was already well and securely established, and the expectation of a native dynasty abandoned—and thus not in the time of Cyrus but rather of his successors.

Other biblical texts agree in giving Cyrus the credit for seeing this vision too, by making a priority the rebuilding of the Jerusalem Temple (2 Chron. 36:22–23=Ezra 1:1–2):

> Now in the first year of Cyrus king of Persia, that the word of Yhwh by the mouth of Jeremiah might be accomplished, Yhwh stirred up the spirit of Cyrus king of Persia so that he made a proclamation throughout all his kingdom and also put it in writing: "Thus says Cyrus king of Persia, 'Yhwh, the god of heaven, has given me all the kingdoms of the earth, and he has charged me to build him a house at Jerusalem, which is in Judah. Whoever is among you of all his people, may Yhwh his god be with him. Let him go up.'"

Whether it was really Cyrus who authorized the building of the Temple is dubious: according to the book of Ezra it was not completed until much later, and we may doubt whether it was in fact commenced as early as the reign of Darius I. The decree in Ezra 1:2–4 is of dubious authenticity (for a recent summary see Grabbe, 1992: I.32–36; Briend, 1996). Bedford (2001) takes a similar view of the authenticity of the decree, but argues that the temple building was commenced under Darius and that it was a local, not a Persian initiative, and undertaken without local opposition. Edelman (2005) takes the opposite view: it was part of a Persian initiative to restore Jerusalem and took place in the second half of the fifth century, not earlier. My own conclusion is that in Haggai, Zechariah and Ezra 1–6 we have, incorrectly but very understandably, an attribution of the Temple restoration to the founder of the Persian empire. To allow that it took a century or so before Jerusalem was again the centre of Judah was embarrassing and incompatible with Zionist ideology. We may compare the role of David as first temple builder (according to the Chronicler) with Cyrus's role as second temple builder, underlining the view that Cyrus and his successors are the truly chosen heirs of the native Davidic dynasty (the "anointed" of Yhwh).

Whether from political expediency or genuine benevolence, the biblical literature displays an almost unanimously benevolent attitude towards Persian world rule. The book of Esther also endorses the idea of a world order governed by the "law of the Medes and Persians" that can protect Jews as well as threaten them (and it also allows, as a mark of qualified approval, a Judean queen). Daniel, although tempered by the experience of oppressive (non-Persian) rule, retains in its older narratives (chapters 1–6) the idea of Yhwh the lord of history assigning government of the entire world to non-Judean kings, who in turn "inherit" his "kingdom" (2:37; 4:34ff.; 5:30).

The idea of a universal world order decreed by Yhwh is even retrojected into the Neo-Babylonian period. Jeremiah 27–29 represents Nebuchadnezzar as allotted the world empire by Yhwh, and in the closing verses of 2 Kings Evil-Merodach (Amel-Marduk) frees Jehoiachin from confinement and sits him at the "king's table" (25:29–30). Most commentators have detected here a hint of hope for the future of a Davidic dynasty; but it is equally likely that the hint is of the incorporation of the Davidic monarchy into the new world-empire: Evil-Merodach is here the inheritor of the "Davidic covenant." Indeed, Jer. 25:9, 27:6 and 43:10 refer to Nebuchadnezzar as Yhwh's "servant" (the other two "servants" in Jeremiah being Jacob and David). But this perspective of a series of world rulers under the patronage of Yhwh probably has its root in the favourable attitude of Judeans, and especially Jerusalemites, to the Persians who restored their city. From this (and not from the experience of deportation) came a Yahwistic ideology of world-empire, in which the Judean national god ensures the well-being and triumph of his own nation by means of benevolent world empires which he controls. This ideology presupposes a certain political order, one that did not develop until the fifth century when Jerusalem regained its status.

The Gathering of the Scattered Nation of Israel to Jerusalem

The idea of a regathering of Israel and Judah from their deportations is attested in several prophetic texts: Isa. 11:12 ("He [Yhwh] will raise an ensign for the nations, and will assemble the outcasts of Israel, and gather the dispersed of Judah from the four corners of the earth") distinguishes the two nations; Jer. 23:3 ("Then I will gather the remnant of my flock out of all the countries where I have driven them, and I will bring them back to their fold, and they shall be fruitful and multiply" belongs to a passage that most probably refers only to the kingdom of Israel (vv. 1–8). But an inserted section (vv. 5–6) associates them, and presumably Judah also, with a restored Davidic monarchy; Jer. 31:7–9 (v. 8: "Behold, I will bring them from the north country, and gather them from the farthest parts of the earth, among them the blind and the lame," etc.) also probably refers to the erstwhile kingdom of Israel. Ezekiel 11:17, however, envisages Jerusalem as the focus of a restoration of twelve tribes, Judah and Israel: "therefore say, 'Thus says the god Yhwh: I will gather you from the peoples, and assemble you out of the countries where you have been scattered, and I will give you the land of Israel.'"); other such texts include Mic. 2:12, 4:6 and Zech. 10:8–12.

The idea of a scattered Israel—a combined nation of Israel and Judah—to be restored in the future can be found in texts from throughout the Persian period and into the Hellenistic (for example, Daniel 9, the *Damascus Document*, 11QMelchizedek, I Enoch, Jubilees). Second Isaiah thus reflects a very common theme in the biblical literature. The poems of Isaiah 40–55 address the city of Jerusalem (and the cities of Judah) in promising this mother a return and increase of its lost children (49:20–25; 54:1), namely a population which comes from afar (49:22: "nations," "peoples"), brought from many places (49:23: "kings," "queens"): a vision best (if rather loosely) described as "eschatological." Such a prospect may have been prompted by the *hope* of an act of repatriation by Cyrus. But it is just as likely, and perhaps more likely, to have been based on some concrete action. From a rapidly growing volume of research it is becoming clear that under the Persians a new social structure emerged in Judah, including an enforced (not a permissive) repopulation of areas previously uninhabited, the goal being economic regeneration—followed in the time of Xerxes by military strengthening. Judah became a province of some regional importance, and the inhabitants of Jerusalem may have felt encouraged to hope that Jerusalem would become the major city of the Persian empire in the satrapy. But the writer is already using "god of Israel/holy one of Israel" of Yhwh and addressing his Judean compatriots as "Israel" and "Jacob," without, it appears, extending his view beyond the boundaries of Judah itself or considering the return of deportees from Samaria. But he may nevertheless have, like the Chronicler, assumed that Jerusalem was the rightful capital of the entire community of Yhwh-worshippers. At all events, the vision of Jerusalem as a major religious centre, economically prosperous and populous is one which at least fits (we can say no more) the perceived policy of the Persian empire towards the province of Yehud; the actions being taken could be viewed as steps toward the fulfillment of those hopes which Isaiah 40–55 expresses.

It should be added that the idea of a "nation" that comprised both Judah and Israel (and took the name "Israel" is much more problematic than has been recognized. In my view (for the arguments see Davies, 2007a), such an idea can only have emerged in Judah during the Neo-Babylonian period, when the identities and religious traditions of both former kingdoms were merged under Benjaminite leadership. Thereafter, Judah saw itself as part of this larger "Israel," as descendants of Jacob, but either the sole survivors (the perspective of Ezra-Nehemiah and in 2 Kings 17) of this nation, or as the senior partner (a view endorsed by the Chronicler but hinted at in the "united monarchy" of David and Solomon and those narratives in Genesis to Judges that give leadership of the "twelve tribes" to Judah). It is also highly developed in Ezekiel 40–48, which can hardly be assigned to a sixth-century Judean in Babylonia (whether any of the book belongs here is in any case questionable). These chapters and their vision belong in the Persian or possibly even the Ptolemaic period, when the political reunification of Judah and Samaria may have occurred.

Yahweh the Untouchable

Second Isaiah's antipathy to the worship of images is evident. The oft-expressed puzzle here (recognized too often to need citing) is that much of the invective is rather silly. Worshippers of deities that are represented in the form of idols do not make the mistake of thinking that these images *are* the gods: they do not worship the object but what it represents. But of course the attack—either implicitly or explicitly—is obviously against Judeans, but not because they are in danger of worshipping other deities—such worship is not criticized as such; monolatry is not the issue here, though it is elsewhere, and no doubt the poet hopes that eventually all the human race will worship the one true god. But in the anti-image passages the question is whether gods are to be represented in material form, and in making this point the poet is attacking, surely not other deities, but the iconic worship *of the god Yhwh*. This attack is supported by the claims that Yhwh is the creator (40:28) and cannot be created/made (as an image) and that he cannot be represented in any form (40:18) because he is to be invisible ("hidden": 45:15). The makers of idols who are castigated (44:9–21) are unlikely to have been non-Judeans fashioning statues of non-Judean gods, but Judean craftsmen making images of Yhwh.

The iconic worship of the old monarchic era Yhwh (and of his consort Asherah) was normal in Israelite and Judah, perhaps in the form of a bull—so, apparently at Bethel—and probably persisted into the early Persian period (see Schmidt, 1995). The much-discussed drachma coin from Judah/Yehud (Meshorer, 1967: 36–38 and plate I, coin no. 4; 1982: 21–28; cf. Grabbe, 1992: I.71–72) may display how the Persian authorities imagined Yhwh to look, namely as a warrior in a chariot. This is how Ezekiel 1 portrays him, too. But it also stresses the form of Yhwh as a human (or *like* a human: the force of the *kaph* is uncertain), just as texts from the Hellenistic period also represent him as such, together with the other minor deities who carry out his instructions (cf. Daniel 7 and 8–12 *passim*). It is possible that in the wake of the aniconic reform, or even as part of it, Yhwh was conceived as human in form, as Gen. 1.27 implies.

This new human-like but not-to-be-represented form is one of the features (along with the lack of consort) that distinguishes New Yhwh from Old Yhwh (another, mentioned earlier, is the merging of the Israelite "god of Jacob/Israel" with the Yhwh Sebaot of Jerusalem [see Jer. 7:3, 21; 9:15; 19:3 etc.]). Was he also becoming identified further with the high god of the Persian empire, Ahuramazda (who in Babylonia was identified with Marduk)? This is the impression given by the "edict of Cyrus" in 2 Chron. 36:22 and Ezra 1, where the name of Yhwh is put on Cyrus's lips. Such an identification would not only be logically necessary, but politically convenient. Among other things, it would of course authorize the rewriting of Mesopotamian myths which, in retrospect, would have been claimed as describing the acts of the creator Yhwh under other names. There is evidence that Ahuramazda was worshipped aniconically (as opposed to Anahita), but whether the attempt claimed by Xerxes to suppress *daiva*-worship (see Boyce, 1982: 173–77) is in any way connected with the reform of certain local cults is uncertain. But there is every reason to suppose, given the treatment of Persian kings in the biblical literature, that a tacit recognition of Marduk, Ahuramazda and Yhwh as the same high god was widespread in Judah, and that Second Isaiah gives us a glimpse into the process whereby the creation of the cult of the high god Yhwh was promoted in the temple city of Jerusalem so favoured, it seems, by the Persians. Yhwh became imperial: god of gods, king of kings, Most High, but his *real* capital city was Jerusalem.

We may finally return briefly to Morton Smith's wider interest in things Persian. Persian, specifically Zoroastrian influence on Judaism has been suggested many times (see Yamauchi, 1990 for a survey and unconvincing rebuttal). The idea was first mooted as early as the eighteenth century, and later, Bousset (1902) and Bertholet (1926) were its chief advocates. A number of scholars currently adhere to this view, but mainstream opinion does not seem to support the view, though the climate is changing. The claimed areas of influence are well-known: angelology, eschatology (including resurrection, judgment, heaven and hell), dualism, creation and, so Boyce (1982: 76–77) claims, purity. The obstacle to reaching a firm conclusion on this claim is the late date of most of the Persian sources. But it is equally difficult to date the biblical sources, and it does not seem from the material evidence or from a critical analysis of the biblical texts that such ideas were present in Israelite or Judahite religion during the monarchic period.

It is, in any case, unreasonable to assume that Persian religious ideas had no influence at all on the religion of a province whose temple was built, according to its own writers, by Persian decree, and whose religious leaders, again according to its own sources, came to Judah under Persian auspices. But in many respects Jewish doctrines also differ from Zoroastrian ones. The question is the extent to which the religion of Judah from the sixth or fifth centuries onwards was shaped by Zoroastrianism. And such an evaluation will obviously depend on one's estimate of the alternative influence—the religion of Judah itself in the pre-Persian era—which itself was shaped by imperial culture and religion.

Might we go as far as to claim that the cult of Yhwh in the Persian period was Zoroastrianism, localized and grafted onto an indigenous cult? Most scholars would probably regard this formulation as too extreme. But at all events, the influence of Persian religion was probably exerted continuously into the Greco-Roman period. The Parthians, after all, came to be the rulers of Babylon and close neighbours of Judah in the second century BCE onwards. They plundered Jerusalem in 40 BCE and were confronted by Herod the Great. How else do we explain the dualism of some of the Qumran writings, and the magi of Matthew's gospel? Whatever the role of Persian religion in the formation of early Judaism, Second Isaiah is the key witness.

Chapter 7

Jewish Apocalyptic

Questions of Definition

The study of Jewish apocalyptic has been greatly transformed in the last two decades. Despite efforts at clarification, it is perhaps even more difficult nowadays to use the term, even as an adjective, unselfconsciously. If not, it should be.

The view dominant until the mid-twentieth century regarded "Mosaic legalism" as the definitive form of Second Temple Judaism and consequently "apocalyptic" as a distinct phenomenon that arose during the Second Temple period in reaction to political, social and religious developments. It was, of course, appreciated as a literary and theological category, but one sufficiently curious to demand a historical explanation in the form of groups or even sects.

The apocalypse is certainly first and foremost a genre or group of genres. But the existence of a literary genre does not imply a correspondingly discrete social "genre." Prophetic texts were written by people who were not what we would classify as intermediaries. Even though they originate in certain discrete social contexts, genres are employed for certain functions, and it is the function of the apocalypse genre that I think has been insufficiently examined and which I intend to consider in what follows.

Is apocalypse a genre? From the late first century BCE most certainly, since we have works by that name and exhibiting common traits. The name was derived from an archetype that designated itself as "prophecy" but opened with the words "the revelation (*apokalypsis*) of Jesus Christ." After a series of letters, the book comprises a sequence of visions of heaven. Hence, just as "gospel" became a literary genre whose archetype is Mark (which opens "the beginning of the good news (*euaggelion*), so "apocalypse" acquired even in antiquity a secondary usage as the name of a writing containing the contents of a "revelation" (see Smith, 1983). In the last two centuries, however, and especially the last century, an abstract noun came into being: "apocalyptic." This designates something held to be the *content*, or the ideology of apocalypses—a set of ideas, a "theology," expressed either as individual dogmas or as a worldview. It is only one step from this reconstructed "apocalyptic" to a social-historical phenomenon including "apocalyptic" communities, groups defined and/or sustained by this "apocalyptic" ideology. Many scholars who have written recently on the problem recognize different levels of reference and the difficulties of interrelating all three. Some have wished to adhere as strictly as possible to a literary definition without wishing to extend the use of the term further (e.g. Rowland, 1982). Others regard as primary the genre "apocalypse" while maintaining that implied in its use is a certain "apocalyptic" worldview (Collins, 1979, 1984, 1986). Hanson (1975, 1976, 1985) has made the cleanest distinction, differentiating "apocalypse" (genre), "apocalyptic eschatology" (religious perspective) and "apocalypticism" (religio-social movement). But he still regards them all as somehow linked together conceptually under a wider rubric of "apocalyptic." If that link were not maintained, the notion of "apocalyptic" itself would be nonsensical. And I believe that it is nonsensical.

It is unwise to use the same word for phenomena belonging to three different categories. As if to illustrate this point, Collins has acknowledged that of the two "apocalyptic" communities he identifies in Greco-Roman Palestine—the Qumran community and the early Christians—the first produced no apocalypse and the latter just one: the archetypal book of Revelation (Collins, 1984: 140–41, 206). Most Jewish and Christian apocalypses were therefore written by "apocalyptic" individuals or by "non-apocalyptic" communities. In other words, anyone might write an apocalypse, just as anyone might write a biography, compose an oracle write a letter or make a speech. It is part of a repertoire of literary forms. Why should we take that classification further, when we do not for any other genre? It is not because the examples of the genre have much in common. That is entailed in a genre and does not indicate any other kind of identity among those who use it.

We might, on the other hand, use sociological categories and speak of "millenarian communities." But Collins (1984: 205–206) quite rightly comments that "there is only limited overlap between the Jewish apocalyptic literature and anthropological descriptions of millenarian movements." Indeed, he adds quite correctly that "the Jewish apocalypses were not produced by a single 'apocalyptic movement' but constituted

a genre that could be utilized by different groups in different situations."
But why "*single* apocalyptic movement"? Why should we imagine such
a things as an "apocalyptic movement" at all? For various reasons we
have inherited a notion that behind apocalypses lurks "apocalyptic." To
be fair, scholars in the past have also use the term "prophecy" to denote
a social function of mediation and a literary corpus (and have often
blended the two). But at least the prophetic texts feature characters
defined as "prophets," even if the prophecies in these books—and the
books themselves—are often the product of anonymous writers.

If the study of the genre of apocalypse begins, as it should, with the
book of Revelation, just as a study of "gospel" should commence with
Mark, it does not follow that either of these works invented a new
genre. The literary influences on Revelation are obvious: formally the
book of Daniel is the most prominent and as for the content of the
visions, motifs from other Jewish scriptures and the Enochic writings
can also be traced. Thus it is legitimate to consider Isaiah 26–27 and
Zechariah 9–14 or nearly all of the contents of 1 Enoch as being, or
containing "apocalypses." However, examples can also be found in Egypt
(the Demotic Chronicle) and Babylonia (there is a range of "Akkadian
apocalypses"), to say nothing of Greece and Rome. The fact is that the
genre was common in the Hellenistic period as is well illustrated by the
huge volume on *Apocalypticism in the Mediterranean World and the
Near East* (Hellholm, 1983). Just how far, then, do Jewish or Christian
apocalypses require their own distinct explanation? Naturally, the content
of their visions will reflect the beliefs of the authors and their readers,
but can one speak of "Egyptian apocalyptic" or "Greek apocalyptic" or
"Babylonian apocalyptic" rather than just "apocalypses." So why speak of
"Jewish apocalyptic"?

One reason is that Jewish and Christian apocalypses have been
approached as if the form entailed also a certain ideological value, as
if (to put the cart before the horse), apocalypses were the way in which
apocalyptic was expressed. In New Testament studies "apocalyptic"
was for a long time almost synonymous with "eschatological," and this
connection has found its way into modern culture: "Apocalypse" now
means a fiery end of the world. Yet, it is also clear (as Rowland, 1982 has
vigorously argued) that one cannot bind Jewish apocalypses to eschatology.
Graham Davies (1978) pointed to a concern with historiography, while
Stone (1976) points to an interest in the classification and interpretation
of natural phenomena, for example the movements of the heavenly
bodies, the origins of the winds—or even the succession of empires as in

Daniel. Even if Jewish apocalypses can be differentiated from non-Jewish ones (see Sanders, 1983; Nickelsburg, 1983), do they share anything that might point to the existence of something non-literary, something we could call "apocalyptic"?

What all apocalypses are essentially—and this definition is absolutely faithful to the prototypical Apocalypse—is "a literary communication of esoteric knowledge, purportedly mediated by a heavenly figure to (usually: not in the book of Revelation) a renowned figure of the past." This definition is close to Rowland, but slightly broader than Stone (1978) or Collins; it nevertheless permits us to divide the subject-matter of the knowledge into political, historical futuristic, astronomical, halakhic, *listenwissenschaftlich*. It is also broad enough to contain both Jewish and non-Jewish apocalypses. The content of an apocalypse, is therefore *esoteric* knowledge of a kind that could be acquired not by human observation or reason but by revelation. The supernatural origin of the revelation and the pseudonymous attribution of the literary report to a venerable figure of the past imply to the recipient that the knowledge is both irrefutable and powerful. Certain additional features can indicate the purpose and background of a particular apocalypse; for example, many Jewish apocalypses contain exhortation and consolation. The purpose of the revealed knowledge in these cases is to give assurance in the face of crisis or calamity (e.g. Daniel, 4 Ezra). If the content of the apocalypse is halakhic or quasi-historical (e.g. Jubilees, despite its historiographical guise), we may suppose that it represents a claim to the cosmic correctness of a certain way of behaving. None of these concerns could be said to *create* the genre, or to belong intrinsically with it, but they may explain why the genre is used in an individual case.

The conventions of the genre itself imply the belief in the existence and accessibility of heavenly secrets which enable one to understand, sometimes to predict, earthly phenomena. But that belief was so widespread in the ancient world that it cannot possibly be said to characterize apocalypses, nor to define a particular "apocalyptic" worldview. On the contrary, those who denied the existence of gods or of any reality beyond the present world (e.g. Epicureans) were a rather small minority.

The Invention of Jewish "Apocalyptic"

In view of the considerable number of reviews already in print (e.g. Nicholson, 1979; Hanson, 1976, 1985; Nickelsburg, 1983; Collins,

1984: 13–32; 1986; Sacchi, 1990: 13–30, 35–47; Kvanvig, 1988: 1–39; Tigchelaar, 1996: 1–15.) the following discussion can be fairly brief and will concentrate on the ways in which "apocalyptic" was redefined as a non-literary phenomenon.

A convenient starting point is Rowley (1944, 1963), for he represents a widespread set of assumptions, many of which were developed by Russell (1964). First, he was concerned only with *Jewish* apocalyptic; whether he recognized any external parallels is doubtful, since his account is given in terms of Jewish history, religion and literature alone. Second, he used "apocalyptic" somewhere between a literary and a religious phenomenon, but nowhere defined "apocalypse" formally: he was concerned mostly with the ideas expressed by the literature, although he remarks occasionally on literary features, such as pseudonymity (1963: 40ff.). It is therefore something like "prophecy," and indeed he believed that apocalyptic is a "child of prophecy"—both terms being used primarily to denote a set of ideas and an intermediary function. Third, Rowley understood "apocalyptic" to have arisen in the second century BCE, when it was "the re-adaptation of the ideas and aspirations of earlier days to a new situation" (15), that situation being the "crisis" under Antiochus IV. For the first and definitive apocalyptic writing was the book of Daniel.

At every level, the phenomenon "apocalyptic" was explained by Rowley in quite simple terms. The prophets addressed their contemporaries in times of historical crisis, or at least when a divine message was needed. The "apocalyptists" did the same, their crisis being one of persecution, and their emphasis being on prediction of an imminent salvation. The historical matrix of "apocalyptic" was therefore one of persecution and distress. What accounted for the use of the particular literary forms that Daniel exhibits (the court-tale and the symbolic vision) on this (or any) occasion was not addressed.

The revised edition of the book already acknowledges one major objection to its thesis: the dating of certain parts of Enoch, namely 6–36 and the "Apocalypse of Weeks" earlier than Daniel (Charles, 1913: 170–71). If correct, this view left much of Rowley's explanation (as he admitted, p. 31), "without basis." His refutation of that objection was robust, but it has now been almost universally accepted that parts of Enoch are older than the later chapters of Daniel. Rowley's view that all of Daniel was composed in the Maccabean period is also obsolete: chapters 1–6 are widely accepted as not only earlier, but reflecting a different social setting from the visions of 7–12. The chronological primacy of Daniel among the apocalypses and hence its claim to be the "typical" apocalypse has also waned. More problematic still, 1 Enoch and Daniel are rather different in character. Little of Enoch reflects either the influence of prophecy or a situation of persecution. The same objection arises regarding Jubilees. Hence the origin of "apocalyptic" cannot be explained from a single book. This is a problem for any unilinear account of "apocalyptic" whether as a literary, social or ideological phenomenon.

Rowley's account left two gaps: the historical, as opposed to doctrinal, connection between "prophecy" and "apocalyptic," and (as already noted) the identity of the producers of his first apocalypse, the book of Daniel. An attempt to fill these gaps was made by Plöger (1968), whose solution entails the same assumptions as Rowley's. Plöger's thesis, in more sophisticated and differing forms, may be discerned in the later proposals of Hengel and Hanson. Plöger attempted to account for the origins of the distinctive ideas of the book of Daniel. To the question "who wrote the book of Daniel?" he gave an answer already quite well established, but not loudly articulated: a group of Jews mentioned in 1 and 2 Maccabees by the name of *Hasidim or* "pious," loyal to the law and temporarily allies of the Maccabees (1 Macc. 2:42, 7:12f.). Two important features of these *Hasidim* were their organization into "conventicles" or small groups, and their embrace of eschatological hopes. The first feature is drawn from the mention of a "company" *(synagoge)* of *Hasidim* in 1 Macc. 2:42f., 7:13f. and the second from Daniel itself, assumed to be their product. The passive, loyal and eschatological attitude of Plöger's *Hasidim* is contrasted with the attitude of the Maccabees themselves, which was non-eschatological and more political.

Where, then, do the *Hasidim* and their beliefs derive from? Plöger accepted that eschatology suggested prophecy, but saw differences between prophetic and apocalyptic eschatology which he explained by developments in the religion and society of post-exilic Judaism. The nation had become a religious community rather than a political entity—that is, a theocracy, a constitution regarded by the religious establishment, represented in the Old Testament by the Priestly writers and the Chronicler, as an end in itself: the goal of life and history was the cult of divine worship of the one God in the one true Temple. In such an ethos of cult and law, there was no place for future hope. It was in conventicles—small, closed communities—which preserved, augmented and applied the older prophecies that eschatological traditions were sustained. On the one hand, stood the monolithic Temple establishment, on the other, the small "anti-establishment" groups.

This sharp duality of social and ideological character corresponds to what Plöger finds in the Maccabean period. To confirm his suggestion of a continuity throughout the post-exilic period, Plöger examines parts of the prophetic corpus which he regards as the products of such conventicles (Isaiah 24–27, Zechariah 12–14 and Joel). Thus was furnished not only a historical link between prophecy and apocalyptic literature but an explanation of that literature in terms of a social and religious movement (or movements).

The notion that apocalyptic writings were the product of conventicles was restated by Vielhauer (1965), but Plöger's ideas were taken up more fully by Hanson, though with a more refined definition of "apocalyptic," broken up into "apocalypse," "apocalypticism" and "apocalyptic eschatology." Hanson set out to explain the origin and development of the last of these only, and this from "prophetic eschatology," a derivation which, like Plöger he seems to have assumed from the outset. According to Hanson the evolution from the one to the other came about through the existence of a "deutero-prophetic" visionary tradition beginning early in the Second Temple period. Whereas prophetic eschatology had kept a balance between the heavenly and the earthly sphere, permitting human action some scope in the unfolding of history, the apocalyptic visionaries placed their trust in heavenly action, despairing of the redemption of human affairs by human activity. The eschaton could, in their view, only occur through a heavenly act. "Vision" and "reality," wedded in prophetic eschatology, were divorced in its apocalyptic successor.

Like Plöger, Hanson divided Second Temple Jewish society into two elements, and he focused on an analysis of deutero-prophetic writings, using a linguistic rather than a doctrinal analysis of the materials. He also recognized that the "apocalyptic eschatology" might have been carried by different groups at different times; finally, he laid stress on the use of ancient mythical themes which spoke of direct divine action in the world of human affairs, including the (much-loved at Harvard) motif of Israel's "divine warrior" and of the "heavenly court." Significantly, Hanson does not deal with Daniel—an aspect of his work for which he has been criticized, particularly by reviewers brought up on Rowley or Plöger. But what emerges as strongly from Hanson's as from Plöger's work is that apocalyptic ideas belong to the counter-establishment, to those deprived of their aspirations, those on the fringes of political and religious power. But it is hard, as we shall see, to find very many apocalypses which clearly point to such authors. Both the authorship and readership of such texts are more probably to be found about the privileged and even affluent (so Cook, 2003). The assumption that the political establishment, because it is in favour of the *status quo* is therefore anti-"apocalyptic" or anti-visionary is rather simplistic. Appeal to esoteric knowledge, heavenly revelation and the use of myth are all equally, if not more, characteristic of the methods by which ruling cliques justify their status and exercise ideological control. Both Daniel and the Qumran seem to have combined a reverence for the "established" priesthood and cult with a strong belief in an imminent eschaton, a reverence for prophecy and cultic legalism.

Hengel (1974) developed elements of Plöger's thesis in a different direction. Minimizing the link between prophecy and apocalyptic, he stressed a plurality of influences. Following Plöger in identifying the *Hasidim* with apocalyptic, he followed what was then a consensus in regarding this shadowy group as the ancestors of the Essene movement (identified with the "Qumran community"). Thus he could identify as the "bearers of apocalyptic" a specific community that could be identified and described. This permitted him a detailed description of the "First Climax of Jewish Apocalyptic" (1974: I.175). For Hengel, as for Rowley, the impact of the "Hellenistic reform" provided the impetus. The experience of persecution led to a new interpretation of history, a calculation of the time of the end, a concentration on the decision of the individual. Sociologically, the "apocalyptic" groups were characterized by strict adherence to the law (in the face of the laxity of the "Hellenizers") and a stress on penitence. Rejection of the entire post-exilic establishment took the form of denial that any restoration had taken place.

Hengel's contribution is perhaps of most value in his appreciation of the wider cultural connections of this earliest Jewish "apocalyptic climax": not only the influence of Israelite prophecy but also of Iranian and Babylonian mythology and Greek Orphic ideas. In particular, he recognized very clearly the stress on revealed wisdom and instruction in the earliest Jewish apocalyptic literature, and correctly observed that in this literature the "wise" acquired prophetic features and the prophets became inspired "sages." What he did not declare unequivocally (though he may have assented to the view) was that the mixture of prophecy and wisdom was characteristic of the Second Temple period generally, as illustrated by Barton (1986). As a literary phenomenon, biblical "prophecy," was, as Barton says, subject to interpretation as an ancient oracular source: it functioned in the way that omens did, as textual signs to the meaning of the present and future.

Hengel's rich description of the multifaceted character of Jewish apocalyptic writing in the Maccabean era was, curiously, yoked to a fairly narrow view of the social context in which it operated. There are new developments and alien influences in "Essene teaching" (1974: I.228), such as the intellectualization of piety, dualism (from Iran), the idea of the "plans of God" (i.e. determinism), angelology, interest in the stars and sun as indicators of a rational cosmic order, astrology, and manticism/magic. These characteristics are indeed prominent in apocalyptic literature, though Hengel illustrated them all from the Qumran literature. But can it be said that the Essenes (even if they constituted a wider movement than the Qumran scrolls imply) were the sole, or even the main, carriers of all these traditions? Might many of these features have been found more widely within the repertoire of early Judaisms? Should they be restricted to a particular sectarian stream?

Hengel's reconstruction has more specific weaknesses, too. The brief references to *Hasidim* do not demonstrate that they were a clearly-defined group, nor does it suggest any distinctive ideology, for according to the information in 1 Maccabees they participated in armed resistance (being remembered for their prowess), and were "devoted to the law." Like Judas Maccabee they also sought peace with Alcimus. The rest of Plöger's and Hengel's characterization is invention (Davies, 1977). Nothing about these reports points to a connection with the book of Daniel or with Essenes, or with the Qumran scrolls. On the other hand, the connections between Qumran and Enoch are broad and clear. Where has Enoch gone in this reconstruction of Jewish apocalyptic?

Apocalyptic and Manticism

The derivation of "apocalyptic" from "prophecy" which was almost universally accepted thirty years ago was challenged by von Rad (1965; but not for the first time: see Hölscher, 1919). Well-directed as this assault was, it was part of an "Old Testament Theology" and used "apocalyptic" as a theological category rather than a literary genre or a cultural feature. Von Rad's proposal to link "apocalyptic" with "wisdom" initially failed to convince, partly because his definition of "wisdom" created almost as many problems as did prophecy: the accepted setting of "wisdom" was the court-based worldly instruction of Proverbs, based on observation and deduction, and promoting social order. But von Rad had overlooked another sort of "wisdom" that is also represented in the Bible and makes better sense of Joseph and Daniel and of their Egyptian and Babylonian counterparts. This "wisdom," widely attested in the ancient Near East but especially Mesopotamian literature, was derived from a study of omens. To this art/science H.-P. Müller (1972) gave the name "mantic wisdom" and argued, in the end convincingly, that it provided the key element in the background of Daniel. The resurgence of interest in the books of Enoch—touched off by the discoveries of fragments at Qumran published by Milik (1976)—strongly supported Müller's contention: it is realized that much of the Enoch tradition, including the figure of Enoch himself, should be traced back to Babylonian manticism. Indeed, the placing of Enoch in the Genesis genealogy made him the counterpart of the ancestor of Babylonian mantic wisdom, Enmeduranki (see VanderKam, 1984). The worldview of the Babylonian mantics in fact provides a firmer basis for understanding apocalypses than the prophetic or wisdom literature in the Bible: although no formal account of the theory behind Mesopotamian manticism was ever left by its practitioners, we can enumerate the following elements (Wilson, 1980: 91; see also VanderKam, 1984).

First is the perception of all human experience as forming an "interlocking totality," which makes the associations of phenomena significant and potentially predictive. Nothing that happens, then, is arbitrary; the future is in principle discoverable through the application of the diviner's knowledge to the reading of signs. By cataloguing all instances of associations between, for example, the appearance of a comet or an abnormal birth with a subsequent plague, assassination or military defeat, the recurrence of the omen can be interpreted as predictive of the subsequent event.

How is this association understood? In what is perceived as an orderly universe, yet one created, controlled and inhabited by gods and other supernatural beings, irregularities are significant. This deduction is especially true of the nocturnal sky, where regular motions can be discerned, yet with occasional occurrences that disturb the regularity. Hence, the gods are implicated in human history and natural events are the outcome of divine decisions. Irregularities in the natural world, or in the celestial firmament, are the means by which irregularities in human history are forewarned—whether through specific individual manipulation or through some cosmic law that automatically linked the two does not matter. But in the arena of ethics (instructional wisdom) we find a similar nexus between human virtue and human fate: caution, thrift, honesty bring security, wealth, prestige, either through active reward or through the operation of a moral law. Indeed, we might well compare mantic and ethical wisdom with the traditional philosophical categories of metaphysics and ethics.

As Wilson observes, since in principle any natural occurrence could be an omen, the accumulation of such knowledge of "natural science" was seen to be necessary for understanding all reality, including the supernatural. Mantic lore is thus empirical, based on observation, as is instructional or "ethical" wisdom, the one concerned with the doings and decisions of the gods, the other with human behaviour.

Because of this empirical foundation, divination embraces both priestly practice and scribal "research." Behind divination lies a science (or a pseudo-science), which involves the accumulation of knowledge—written knowledge. If divination is the applied science, manticism is the pure science. The interpreters of omens are depicted in Jewish apocalyptic literature (and in the Joseph story) as "wise" not priests. The two groups were not mutually exclusive in any case, and their concerns overlapped considerably in Second Temple Judaism, where they are more easily recognized in the development of torah. There are overt priestly interests in both the Enoch literature and the Qumran scrolls. In the case of Daniel, we simply do not know: only that Daniel himself is not described as a priest. While mantic practice is a cultic activity, the recording of mantic lore and the pursuit of knowledge fundamental to it is scribal. It is from the study of mantic *lore*, not from its *practice*, that "apocalyptic" literature can be seen to develop.

We can see the connection in Daniel's feats of interpretation: dreams and wall-writing are signs with a meaning from the god(s) which the wise man can decipher. The biblical "prophecy" in chapter 9 is "interpreted" like an omen. It is an earthly phenomenon, a written text, but its meaning concerns the supernaturally determined course of history, the true significance being given not to the biblical prophet (who merely supplies the omen) but the mantic sage, whose inspired wisdom provides the decipherment. The Babylonian mantics were expected to have the cipher too, but from their own resources—from the training that Daniel himself underwent (chapter 1)—not by direct divine inspiration. Thus, the book puts the hero among a particular class of mantic—as he is in chapter 2, where he is sought for execution, along with the other mantics who had failed (having been given a task that could not possibly be accomplished merely with the aid of mantic lore).

But did the Babylonian mantics, or rather, their scribes, write apocalypses? One genre of texts has been labelled "Akkadian apocalypses" (Ringgren, 1983). These are not generically apocalypses, however, despite the name given to them, and some scholars prefer the term "Akkadian prophecies" (e.g. Grayson and Lambert, 1964). Some of these texts are *vaticinia ex eventu*, "predicting" the quality and length of the reigns of "future" kings. They offer a parallel to Daniel 11, which also provides a sequence of political events in the form of a prediction. Grayson and Lambert even include a text in which a king speaks in the first person, as in Daniel 4 (though they do not comment on the similarity). The parallels between these and the Enoch material are also thoroughly discussed by VanderKam (1984). In short, there is quite a broad range of literary and conceptual parallels between Babylonian mantic literature and the books of Daniel and Enoch. The parallels are not only more striking than any offered from biblical prophecy, but they also imply particular and identifiable social functionaries as the authors of the literature and transmitters of its contents.

The heroes of both Enoch and Daniel are mantic figures, but their knowledge comes from direct revelation and not from omen interpretation. This difference may be due in part to a lack of omen interpretation in Judah (which the scriptures imply). Possibly mention of such practices may simply have been suppressed, but if so, we still have to explain the disapproval of "divination." It is also possible, however, that manticism developed independently of divination, lost its cultic *Sitz im Leben* and occupied itself with explaining matters beyond direct human experience in the guise of esoteric knowledge directly acquired (and often fictitiously transmitted from heroes of the past. In any case, so-called "apocalyptic" literature still reflects a worldview determined by the premises and devices of manticism. J. Z. Smith (1975) has drawn attention to the Babylonian priest Berossus, who wrote his *Babyloniaka* during the Seleucid period. According to Smith (103), Berossus was a member of the Babylonian intellectual elite whose interests were "astronomy, astrology, mathematics, historiography and the recovery of archaic ritual lore. These Babylonian intellectuals...stood in continuity with ancient Babylonian scribalism, and unbroken tradition from the Sumerian period to the sages of the Babylonian Talmud." In this milieu Smith sees the link between scribalism and apocalyptic literature. Both, Smith argues (115), "depend on the relentless quest for paradigms, the problematics of applying these paradigms to new situations and the *Listenwissenschaft* which are the characteristic activities of the Near Eastern scribe." Smith notes, as have others, that Egyptian scribalism too produces apocalypses, such as the *Potter's Oracle* and the *Demotic Chronicle*.

The social background of "apocalyptic" writing thus furnished is more fully described and precisely documented by the activity of politically "established" and culturally cosmopolitan scribes than of visionary "counter-establishment" conventicles. The immediate reason for the production of any piece of apocalyptic literature may be persecution, polemics, or whatever; but the apocalyptic genre, the technique of disclosing heavenly secrets, is a long-established and well-embedded scribal convention.

The two matrices proposed for the origin and development of Jewish apocalyptic writing, "prophecy" and "wisdom," are false alternatives and misleading categories. And the label "apocalyptic" is unnecessary. If we recognize "mantic wisdom" and understand prophecy, whether social intermediation or literary corpus of "oracles of God," we can see that distinctions between them are overdrawn: the two categories are related (VanderKam, 1986; Barton, 1986). Barton demonstrates just how the distinction between the way prophets were understood corresponds very closely to what we would call mantic prediction—and in the course of this argument expresses his view that "apocalyptic" is a confusing and unnecessary concept.

Certainly, the symbolic vision represents a mantic device, whereby something observed is imbued with an esoteric meaning. This may involve a simple wordplay (e.g. Jer. 1:11–12; Amos 8:1–2) or a more developed perception, as in a dream (e.g. Zech. 1:7–17; Daniel 7) and can be stretched into a quite elaborate "historical" review from the mouth of an angelic intermediary (Daniel 10–12). Tempting as it is to convert this taxonomy into a diachronic development (Niditch, 1983), such an attempt should not be used to support the view that "apocalyptic" derives from "prophecy" as if the two terms stood in a clearly temporal relationship. If manticism is ancient and if the majority of biblical texts disapprove of divination, is it not equally plausible to argue (if one must have diachrony) that the "simpler" form of disclosure (biblical "prophecy") is a reaction against the more elaborate, that divine speech about earthly matters is theologically preferable to elaborate revelation of the transcendental world? In truth, neither kind of sequence is really plausible. More probably they represent different preferences. But an example of a reaction against the notion of celestial secrets knowable by humans is considered in the following chapter. The books of Job (as Cross [1969] suggested) and Qoheleth might also represent a rejection of the mantic belief that what is "above the sun" can be known by humans.

Apart from the appearance of mantic symbolism within the "prophetic" books, can we discern the culture of manticism elsewhere in early Judaism? We could consider ben Sira, whose connections with "apocalyptic" have recently been explored in more detail (Wright, 2005; on the "apocalyptic scribe" see also Orton, 1987). Ben Sira is universally accepted as typical of the Jerusalem scribal establishment: moderate, conventionally pious, well-off (for the social profile, see Hengel, 1974: I.131–53). But he accords to Enoch in the famous catalogue of eminent men more attention than the biblical allusions merit, being mentioned at the beginning and end (44:16; 49:14). The first of these mentions him as an example of repentance, suggesting an acquaintance with the kind of material found in 1 Enoch rather than in Genesis.

But ben Sira is not only acquainted with the Enoch of "apocalyptic." He also accepts a certain mantic element to his own profession. His description of the model scribe (39:1–11) includes not merely study of the law and the preservation of the discourse of ancient men, nor even appearing before rulers and travelling abroad, but also "seeking out the wisdom of the ancients" and the "hidden meanings of proverbs," the "obscurities of parables." Ben Sira concludes with the following sentiment:

> If the great Lord is willing
> he will be filled with the spirit of understanding;
> he will pour forth words of wisdom
> and give thanks to the Lord in prayer
> He will direct his counsel and knowledge aright,
> and meditate on his secrets.

The preoccupation with understanding hidden things, secrets, often preserved by the ancients, by means of a "spirit of understanding" does not confine ben Sira to teaching the law or tutoring in etiquette. The range of the ideal scribe's interests coincides reasonably well with those of the Seleucid scribal schools described by J. Z. Smith (1975). The centrality of Jewish law in Ben Sira nevertheless indicates that for the Jewish scribe the law revealed by God to Moses took the place of the catalogues of omens which formed the canon of the Babylonian scribe. The comparison is not fanciful: the notion of the scriptures containing hidden truths which inspired study could unlock is not found only in Daniel, Qumran and the New Testament but provides the basic rationale of rabbinic exegesis, although the rabbis, wary of charismatic or inspired exegesis formulated strict rules for interpretation.

What are missing from ben Sira, and thus divert attention away from his connection with "apocalyptic," are eschatology and a peripheral social location. Instead, he shows a great affection for temple and priesthood. But the authors of Daniel do not stand so far from ben Sira's location. Eschatology may seem to be a decisive difference in their outlook. But the eschatological vision of the book is developed in only a very rudimentary fashion. The emphasis is on divine judgment of the wicked, post-mortem vindication of the righteous and a future kingdom for the "holy ones." These themes are present, however, even in the cycle of court-tales which extols the virtues of the Jewish mantic and indeed present a Jewish version of a characteristic scribal genre (see Wills, 1990). These both celebrate the mantic abilities of the hero and chronicle his deliverance from persecution (with the punishment of the persecutors recorded in 5:30 and 6:24). The notion of a "plot" in history in the sequence of world-kingdoms (chapter 7), the hidden meaning of ancient books (chapter 9), the pseudo-predictions of political events (chapters 10–12), and ancient mythical motifs (chapters 2, 7) are all rooted in ancient Near Eastern scribal activity. (For possible direct dependence on the Babylonian *šumma izbu* series, see Porter, 1983.) All these features merely confirm what the book itself says about its authors: they are *maskilim*, scribal teachers who aspire to leadership. Nothing suggests they form a distinct social group, or that they are hostile to the "establishment"—the Temple or its cult, whose defilement so dominates the apocalyptic chapters. In a time of unprecedented and incomprehensible events, these scribes offered an explanation of the times using the techniques of their own scribal traditions plus traditional tales of a mantic hero which they themselves re-interpreted by means of the genre of the heavenly revelation, which blended well with the milieu created by the tales of chapters 1–6. If we need to explain the introduction of eschatology between ben Sira and Daniel (a gap of forty years), the events in Judah are sufficient. The Antichean crisis did provoke the creation of the book of Daniel, and of one or two of the Enochic apocalypses. But it not create "apocalyptic."

Indeed, since manticism is both ancient and widespread in the ancient Near East, we shall not find a "beginning" for it. But the earliest examples of Jewish writing in this genre are probably in 1 Enoch. Its most ancient section, the Astronomical Book (72–80) is an attempt to explain the workings of the cosmos through the medium of a narrative in which Enoch is guided through heaven by an angel. The purpose of this text is to demonstrate the order with which the universe has been created. Some of the demonstration is based on correct observation, some on an *a priori* scheme. One important purpose of the demonstration is the lack of symmetry between sun and moon, which is clearly a calendrical and hence a theological problem. The moon governs the months, the sun the days and seasons. The *Astronomical Book* shows that the moon is in error, moving contrary to the divine plan. The year which this text describes is not one of twelve lunar months (which would distort the seasons) but 364 days, a solar year (more or less). The *Sitz im Leben* for this erudite, speculative discourse is a scribal one in which the mantic culture is endemic. In a Jewish context (whether originally at home there or at some point imported from Babylonia), the heavens were of primary importance for the cultic calendar. Enoch's astronomy is therefore closely linked to the cult and suggests not merely a priestly context but a perplexity at a *lack* of order in the heavens and possibly a dispute over calendrical observance. Such a dispute can in any case be detected in some Enoch writings, in Jubilees and the Qumran texts.

Interest in the heavenly phenomena in this text is not therefore without serious implication. The lack of complete order in creation is disturbing. If humans must in the meantime ignore the moon, the creator deity must, in time, restore his original system. The present anomaly will obtain only "until the new creation" (72.1). This hint at the eschaton is considerably developed at the close, where further disruption in the heavens is predicted, with effects like the shortening of the day and increased wickedness in the earth. We noted earlier the mantic correlation between human and divine worlds, so that disorders in one create or precede disorder in the other. Biblical texts, priestly, wisdom and cultic, all suggest in their respective ways that early Judaism held disorder to be a symptom of cosmic or human evil.

The Apocalypse of Weeks (93.1-10 + 91.11-17), originally an independent composition, also involves calendrical calculation, but now applied to the past, which is organized, typically, into ten "weeks"— discrete units displaying an individual and collective structure. The author appears to be situated in the seventh week, in a time of maximum wickedness but at the dawn of progressive improvement leading to a reconstruction of creation. Daniel's periodization of history (chapter 9) is slightly different—seventy weeks of years—but this is inspired by the mantic interpretation of a scriptural text, which obliges it to commence with the Babylonian captivity and not Creation. The Melchizedek fragments from Qumran have a similar system which gives ten jubilees and thus the same total as Daniel's 490 years. Put simply (perhaps *too* simply, but it makes the point), the obsession with cyclical (days, months, years, Sabbaths, festivals) time evident in the observation of the heavenly bodies is extended to linear time—not controlled by movements above but, in the same way, by some divinely-engineered mechanism. But in both cases the system is faulty and therefore one must look forward to its eventual repair. Sun and moon will eventually harmonize again, and the course of history will culminate in permanent bliss. Daniel too is about disorder in history and in heaven, but it is differently described: kings on earth and angels above are in constant combat, under a divine plan that will be fulfilled in the destruction of evil. Calendrical issues are also present: the last wicked king alters the sacred calendar (7:25), and the days are marked by the mornings and evenings of the *tamid* (12:11): cultic time.

In both Daniel and Enoch disorder is the result of the presence of evil. Perhaps the issue became critical in the first half of the second century BCE, when internal and external conflict increased following the Seleucid conquest of Palestine. At any rate, Daniel has two explanations: the sin of rebellious monarchs (chapters 2–5) and the sins of Israel (chapter 9). For 1 Enoch the problem is ultimately not human sin, which is only a symptom: the origin is celestial. In the *Astronomical Book* (1 Enoch 72–82), this is matter of observation; but in the *Book of Watchers* (1–36) we find an explanation in the myth of a primordial rebellion in heaven that spilled over onto the earth.

It is undeniable that the calendrical issue resulted in sectarian division; the Qumran texts show this clearly enough. But the connection between "apocalyptic" ideas and sectarianism is not intrinsic, and neither Daniel nor Jubilees (nor some of the Enochic writings) imply a sectarian matrix. Yet the issues are undoubtedly conducive to a sectarian worldview. In the "Apocalypse of Weeks" (93:1–10; 91:11–17, included in reverse order) the preservation of a righteous group, the true "Israel" (a definition which might characterize a sect) is "foreseen," and thus presumably already in existence. In Daniel the *maskilim* form a distinct group, but as spiritual leaders of the nation, not as a sect. In 11QMelch the dualistic language (Melchizedek has a *goral*, a "lot," "party") may suggest a sectarian mentality—perhaps the fragments represent a Qumranic revision of an earlier composition. From the early second century BCE we have indications that some apocalyptic literature reflects sectarian tendencies: that is all. It seems that the authors of apocalypses (there are none at Qumran) did not belong to sectarian groups, and regarded themselves as responsible to the nation as a whole (this is apparently also the view of Collins, 1977: 191–224). But in the second century BCE apocalypses nonetheless reflect social and religious divisions, no doubt because these divisions became threatening to national unity. Reid (1983, 1989) has sought to identify the "Apocalypse of Weeks" and the "Animal Apocalypse" (85–90) with "a community of a rising élite which often offers material gain as a reward for membership" and which he defines as a "utopian community" (1983: 156). The analysis of Reid is suggestive but perhaps suffers from importing too much sociological theory into too little text. The social background of the "Epistle of Enoch" has been investigated more cautiously by Nickelsburg (1982, 1983), whose conclusion is that the Epistle highlights a tension between two groups (indicated by the language of "sinners" and "righteous"), the former appear as powerful and oppressive, and are accused of religious apostasy. Nickelsburg regards Enoch 92–105, the "Animal Apocalypse" and the *Damascus Document* as products of a "common religious movement, probably proliferated in its sociology" (1983: 645), suggesting that the Epistle might be called "pre-Essene" (1982: 347).

This last suggestion reminds us of the conclusions of Hengel, for whom, as we saw, the Essenes were the "bearers of apocalyptic." As noted earlier, like Nickelsburg, Hengel identifies the Qumran community as "the Essenes" and also perceives a "pre-Essene" "movement" in the *Hasidim.* But since this origin is suspect (see above), it may be worth mentioning the theory of Murphy-O'Connor (1974) that the Essenes originated with immigrants from Babylon in the third or second century BCE. More recently, Boccaccini (2005) has also argued that the Essenes are representatives of "Enochic Judaism" which, like Paolo Sacchi (1990), he identifies with what others call the Jewish "apocalyptic movement." The connections between various aspects of Jewish "apocalyptic" and Babylonia are certainly suggestive. The Babylonian origin of the Astronomical Book of Enoch has been proposed by VanderKam (1984), while significant agreements between accounts of the past in the "Epistle of Enoch" (91–108), *Jubilees* and the *Damascus Document* have also been noted, all of which commence with the exile to Babylonia (Davies, 1987: 107–34).

The question of Babylonian influence on early Judaism is too vast a topic to entertain here, and would have to include the Pentateuchal myths and laws. Unfortunately, we know too little about cultural communication between Babylonian and Judah from the sixth century onwards, but the Israelite/Judean/Jewish communities of the "eastern Diaspora" there presumably kept in regular touch with developments in Judah: there may have been continued migration in both directions. Babylonian forms of manticism can easily have been absorbed into Judaism, along with other cultural influence at any time from the sixth century onwards. We cannot confine such influence to a particular time-frame; in any case we know that cuneiform texts continued to be copied well into the Hellenistic era and also translated into Aramaic and Greek.

Although Jewish apocalypses predate the second century and arise from a mainstream cultural current, the effects of the "Hellenistic crisis" and its aftermath provided an opportunity for the use of the genre. The collective memories and customs of the Jewish people were under threat, but, in the view of the scribes (or some scribes) so was the order of creation which the Jewish God sustained. Accepting their role as the divinely-appointed teachers of the people, some scribes used revealed heavenly mysteries as a technique for articulating an explanation of the chaos of their own times and their society, predicting an imminent and radical change. Short-term predictions had long been the staple of mantic prediction or pseudo-prediction, but in the second-century apocalypses we find an intensifying of the view that climactic changes were happening and would result in divine intervention. By means of the authority of ancient mantic figures the compilers of the Daniel and Enoch texts "revealed" that the Jewish creator god was in control of both history and nature, that evil had an explanation and that it faced an imminent end. There is some variety among these explanations. There is no single "apocalyptic group" and no "apocalyptic movement." The literary genres which described divine revelation to an ancient seer (already in use) were adapted for a situation in which such explanations were especially demanded.

Thus far we have discussed only the origins and background of apocalypses in the third and second centuries BCE. It is interesting that few Jewish apocalypses appear again until after 70 CE (the *Parables of Enoch* is the major exception from this era), when we have 4 Ezra, 2 Baruch and the book of Revelation. The first two are apparently from within "mainstream" Judaism (so Collins, 1984: 169 n. 45), that is, they are not sectarian, and all respond to a recent crisis. But while there is little consolation in the two Jewish texts, the book of Revelation anticipates a glorious vindication. Gager (1975: 49–57) has no hesitation in treating this as a "millenarian" text, but this cannot be translated into "sectarian" or its author fitted into an "apocalyptic" community. We might consider Christianity in the first century still as a millenarian sect, but this is a dubious label for the growing religion(s) as a whole, especially those forms that stressed individual survival of death rather than political or social upheaval.

Non-Palestinian Jewish apocalypses should not be forgotten either. The (Jewish) Sibylline Oracles are derivative of the Roman Sibylline books, but draw also on local non-Jewish influences. According to Collins (1984: 94) "there was a tradition of prophecy in Egypt which looked for the restoration of native Egyptian rule and the demise of the Greeks." He refers to the *Demotic Chronicle* and the *Potter's Oracle*. These motivations do not seem dominant in the Jewish apocalypses, though Daniel's prediction of a "fourth kingdom" might, at least in chapter 2, be taken to reflect a national political hope. But a general survey of "apocalypses" shows them to be mantic genres used for a variety of purposes, sometimes political (anti-Hellenistic, nationalistic), but also for other purposes—inner-scribal *Listenwissenschaft*, polemics (*Jubilees*, *Epistle of Enoch*), theodicy (Daniel), consolation (4 Ezra), exhortation (Revelation). "Apocalyptic" is not a movement, nor a distinct set of ideas, for the belief on which divination was predicated—that the future could be foretold from signs—was everywhere.

Why should Jewish writings that contain disclosures of esoteric secrets acquire a distinct label, "apocalyptic" (which then becomes transferred to similar non-Jewish writings but without the theological and social baggage attached?) Perhaps this is because the Jewish scriptures display an aversion to divination itself: instead, transcendental disclosures come only as and when divinely prompted, and in either speech or vision, or a combination. Set within a scriptural context, apocalypses seem strange and even innovative, even though we can see examples within the prophetic books of scripture. Rather than continue to treat "apocalyptic" as a cultural curiosity, we might rather accept it as normal and ask instead why early Judaism, in its writings at least, took aversion to the disclosure of such secrets except on the divine initiative, preferring "prophecy" as the standard agency of intermediation. On the other hand, actual divination, the acquisition and interpretation of omens themselves, was unnecessary and even unhelpful. Just as (and not in Judaism only) written oracles, enshrined in texts, could replace live "prophecy" (intermediation), so esoteric knowledge could be acquired without omen, but rather by direct disclosure, mediated textually. "Apocalyptic" needs no explanation: much more curious is that the term, and the concept, were ever developed as a tool of scholarship. It tells us nothing useful about early Judaism that we cannot learn (and better understand) by doing without it.

Chapter 8

ENOCH AND GENESIS

I suggested in the previous chapter that 1 Enoch and Genesis 1–11 might be connected—might have common origins. Here I shall defend that claim. I begin with Gen. 6:1–4, a passage full of difficulties—Blenkinsopp (1992: 75) refers to "the garbled state of the text." Did the *Nephilim* perish in the flood? The story narrates that only Noah's family survived (7:1); but do the words "and also afterwards" suggest otherwise? Perhaps the author recalls that *Nephilim did* survive the flood; for these giants are encountered by the spies in Num. 13:33 (did one of the *nephilot* marry into Noah's family?) Another puzzle: the episode does not fit into any interpretative scheme for either Genesis 1–11 as it now stands, or for the "Yahwistic" narrative within it. Most interpreters find in these chapters (or at least in J's contributions) a pattern of human misdeeds or rebellions followed by divine retribution. But the language of 6:1–4 does not support that scheme. The gigantic offspring are called *gibborim* and *'anshey shem*, terms used approvingly elsewhere. And the retribution? No causal connection between the events and the flood is declared in the text: rather, the divine answer for the mixing of human and divine natures is a shortening of human lifespan. But again we are unclear: since the reason is that the divine spirit (*ruaḥ*) "shall not dwell (strive?) in humanity" (6:3). The "spirit" is presumably bestowed by the angelic beings. The additional comment "because they are flesh" seems to suggest that the limit is imposed on the lifespan of the giants only. But in any event, the Flood itself surely resolves all the problems posed by the episode. Interim measures are redundant. However, the Flood is *not* the divine response to this episode. The careless reader may think so, but attention to the wording rules that out.

The Flood follows immediately, but the reason given for it in 6:5 is human wickedness. This wickedness is presented as a fact, for which the stories of the garden, of Cain and of Lamech's song have possibly prepared us. These in fact comprise all of the previous J narrative and so the divine conclusion makes sense. After all, if we read only the J narrative there is no Seth: all humans are descended from Cain, whose lineage as far as Noah can be traced in 5:29, a J snippet in the middle of a section otherwise belonging to P (Davies, 2006). No allusion is made to any human wickedness entailed in the cohabitation with angels.

Genesis 6:1–4 is curious, tantalizing in its brevity and in its lack of connection with the immediate context. The use of the divine name suggests to us that the story belongs to J. Martin Noth proposed (1972: 28 n. 83) that these verses could well be an addition to the narrative later than either J or P. Yet he was unable to conjecture why such a story might have been added to complicate an otherwise coherent sequence of events. It is a reasonable deduction, therefore, that this story was *not* composed by J, nor added in by a later hand, but was already well anchored in the sequence of events when the J narrative was composed. What obstructs this deduction, however, is the view that J is the earliest of the documentary sources and that unless relying upon an even earlier written source, the sequence can only have existed in an oral form—or in Noth's hypothetical *Grundschrift* that underlay J, E and P—though hardly any source-critic now accepts that hypothesis.

Angelic Descent(s) in 1 Enoch

The problems of Gen. 6:1–4 all have a single and coherent solution, but the search takes us outside the Pentateuch. We have a fuller version of this story in 1 Enoch 6–11, where it seems probable that two versions of the story have been interwoven (Hanson, 1997; Nickelsburg, 2001: 171–72). Each version has a different name for the chief of the rebellious angels. Hanson's suggestion that a single account featuring Shemihazah has been converted into a double account by the addition of material about 'Asa'el; Nickelsburg mostly agrees, suggesting that the 'Asa'el material comes from a separate myth about a single fallen angel who brought with him hidden knowledge. But this obliges him to explain the accusation against 'Asa'el in 1 En. 13:1–3 of bringing sin as an "interpolation" (172). But, noting that Shemihazah is more common in the *Book of Giants*, while 'Azazel predominates in 4Q180 and in the "Animal Apocalypse" and "Parables," he also concludes that the name 'Azazel gradually supplanted Shemihazah. 'Azazel seems, at any rate, to have been an alternative for 'Asa'el. The form 'Azazel is used in the Qumran Aramaic fragment 4QEnGiants[a] (=4Q203) Stuckenbruck comments (1997: 77–87, esp. 82 n. 59): "The identification of 'As/zeal' or a comparable form…as the biblical Azazel does not constitute a problem as may initially seem." Stuckenbruck also discusses here the alternation of Shemiḥazah and 'Azazel/'Asael as leaders of the group (see also Milik, 1976: 131). It is enough, however, for our purposes to observe that a story about descending heavenly beings was known in more than one form and that the evidence of a conflation in the text of 1 Enoch and in the Qumran manuscripts points to a pre-history as well as some development within the preserved literary record.

In both versions of the story represented in 1 Enoch the descent of the heavenly beings is presented as the origin of evil on earth; in one, the Flood is sent to wipe out the evil, while the leader 'Asael/'Azazel) is bound and set under a rock in the desert; in the other, Shemiḥazah must first witness their offspring destroy each other, "for length of days they have not," then to be bound for seventy generations "underneath the rocks of the ground." The basis of both stories is that the corruption of the earth is brought about by heavenly interference. This doctrine fundamentally contradicts the Yahwistic narratives of Genesis 2–4, in which sin originates with human disobedience to the divine command. This contradiction is one obvious reason why the same author cannot make any connection between the angelic descent and humans—or punishment. Hence the *Nephilim* are not portrayed as evil and the incident is unconnected with the Flood. But such an explanation does not, of course, explain why the story is included in the first place.

Enoch in Genesis

The appearance of the story of angelic descent in the Enochic *Book of the Watchers*, to which there are allusions in other Enochic writings draws our attention back to the figure of Enoch in the early chapters of Genesis, where he receives brief but enigmatic treatment. In the geneaology of the Yahwist (4:17–18) nothing makes him stand out at all from other characters; he is the son of Cain, who built a city for him and named it after him. In P, however, Enoch is placed between Yared (in J Irad is his son) and Methuselah and it is said (Gen. 5:22–23) that he "walked with God after he begot Methuselah for three hundred years, and had sons and daughters: and Enoch lived for 365 years."

There are several strange things in the P record: most obviously, that Enoch apparently did not die; next, that he lived the number of years as days in a solar year; finally (and a little more conjecturally) that the name Jared means "descent" and so might be an allusion to the angelic behaviour. These hints give the impression that more is known by the author about Enoch than is recorded. What is hinted at we find spelled out in 1 Enoch, however, which has him teaching a solar calendar and records his translation to heaven. However, given that Genesis 5 is a brief genealogy, it is possible that P has omitted any fuller account of Enoch's "walking with God" and "being taken" by him. But this at any rate implies that such stories about Enoch were known. Otherwise, none of these curious hints makes sense. But if that is true, as it must be, then J's treatment of Enoch is rather surprising. An antediluvian patriarch who did not die is surely worth mentioning. But, as with 6:1–4, such an event would contradict the punishment of mortality brought upon humanity in chapter 3. Again, there is a good reason for suppressing this feature of Enoch's story.

Genesis and 1 Enoch

What is the relationship between the material about Enoch in the Genesis material and in the 1 Enoch stories? Astonishingly, it has long been an assumption that the accounts in 1 Enoch are elaborations of the Genesis text (see, e.g., Nickelsburg, 1997; Collins, 1984: 38f.; Delcor, 1976). But this solution does not work, though only a few scholars have rejected it. Milik (1976) proposed that the Enoch story was earlier than Genesis; Black (1985: 124–25) favours this opinion but remains open to the alternative that both Genesis and Enoch go back to an earlier source. Black's conclusion is by far the most probable. The reason why the majority of scholars have opted for the least likely view is probably that none of those interested in Enoch were also interested in the problems of the Pentateuch and assumed that Genesis was finalized as it now stands well before any Enochic composition was created. But the questions raised purely by the Genesis text itself, which have been discussed earlier, cannot be set aside: they are part of the wider problem.

The relationship of the two sets of textual data, biblical and Enochic, is not fundamentally difficult to deduce. There is no reasonable explanation for the creation of the story of Gen. 6:1–4 by the Yahwist, since it clearly makes no sense in its context and threatens to obscure his account of the origin and nature of sin. Hence it is a story already known. If such a story was known to the Yahwist, it was also known to the writers of 1 Enoch. The same is true of other features of Enoch's story, which P at least was aware of. The writers of 1 Enoch would not need to expand the enigmatic references in Genesis when they could utilize the fuller story to which references allude.

Another important piece of biblical evidence also shows that the Enoch story of the Watchers is not an elaboration of Gen. 6:1–4. The ceremony of the scapegoat in Leviticus 16 concludes with the sending out of a goat bearing the sins of Israel, a goat "to" or "for Azazel" who is sent away "in the wilderness to Azazel" (v. 10). Neither the meaning of the name nor the significance of the ritual are explained, but the purpose of the ceremony is the removal of the sins of the people. Again, the account in 1 Enoch of the imprisonment of Azazel and his group provides the explanation (although in 1 Enoch the name of the leader is Shemihazah, Azazel is given in 4Q180). The angels await punishment for the sins they have caused humans to perpetrate, and the sins of Israel are thus being returned to their source, upon whom their punishment will ultimately fall. Again, it is implausible that the authors of 1 Enoch are providing a rationale for a scriptural ritual: in any case the ritual seems to have continued, with embellishments and variations to the end of the Second Temple period (see *M. Yoma* 4–6). Those who participated in the ritual or witnessed it must have had knowledge of what was being done and of who Azazel was. The conclusion is almost unavoidable that the story of an angelic descent and the scapegoat ritual are not independent but related and that the authors of the Enochic version were not creatively connecting two enigmatic scriptural texts into a single coherent myth but repeating the story that underlay both of them and that was known not only to the writers of Genesis and Leviticus but to almost every Jew, especially living in the vicinity of Jerusalem.

The conclusion should be drawn that a story common to both the book of Genesis (J and P) and to the writers of 1 Enoch (and their sources, too) is given fairly fully in 1 Enoch but not in Genesis, where we find only allusions to Enoch's unusual life and character (and only in P), and a curious, truncated story about angels descending to earth (only in J). The problem is, as I remarked earlier, less about 1 Enoch than about Genesis. Given that the story of the angelic descent—and with it other stories about Enoch—is older than both texts, its reproduction in 1 Enoch needs less explanation than its treatment in Genesis.

Enoch in Genesis (Again)

Why would Genesis suppress stories connected with Enoch? Sacchi (1990: 32–71), followed by Boccaccini (1998, 2002) has argued that the kernel of the Enoch story is a view of the origin and nature of sin, and that a competing view understood sin as arising from human disobedience (I suggested earlier that this view itself may have a connection with astronomical observations of the solar and lunar cycles). In illustrating this phenomenon, Boccaccini proposes that a compromise of "Enochic" and its alternative (which he calls "Zadokite") views appear in works such as ben Sira, Daniel and the Qumran scrolls. Ben Sira is an extremely important testimony because his book seems to reflect a wider range of options (despite Boccaccini's arguments, 2002: 134–50). For instance, he celebrates an Adam that corresponds to the figure of Genesis 1 (made in the divine image) rather than the fallen creature of Genesis 2–3—in other words, P's Adam. He does state that woman is the origin of sin and that because of her we all die, however. Whether this recalls the disobedience of Eve, or reiterates the generally wary attitude of biblical Wisdom literature to women is unclear. As noted earlier, he also grants Enoch (44:16; 49:14) a more prominent status than does Genesis. However, unlike Boccaccini's "Enochic Judaism," ben Sira does not believe in an afterlife or an eschatological judgment. If his views are representative of his class, the scribal worldview at the beginning of the second century BCE espoused a fluid notion about the nature and origin of sin. At all events, he does not endorse the myth of Genesis 2–3 as we now have it. Indeed, the story of Eden is generally less prominent in Jewish and Christian writings of the Greco-Roman period than the myth of an angelic fall. Argall (1995) gives a nuanced analysis of shared features of ben Sira and 1 Enoch and for an appraisal of ben Sira's connection between women and sin, and other theories of the origin of evil in early Judaism, see Davies (2002).

The evidence that Boccaccini presents for a negotiation between "Zadokite" and "Enochic" Judaisms, if perhaps channelled rather too narrowly, is quite persuasive and provides a realistic context for a solution to the problems we are facing in Genesis 1–11. For in advocating a myth that human sin originates in primordial disobedience, J's narrative opposes the myth of a heavenly origin. As we have seen, such a doctrine has no place for an angelic descent, nor for a figure such as Enoch (or the stories connected with him). Nor does it have a place for an angelic leader of evil spiritual forces—a figure of some complexity in both Judaism and Christianity. The agency of human temptation in the garden is a creature that Yhwh made, not a fallen angel in disguise, despite the efforts of later Christian mythology. Hence the angels who descend in 6:1–4 are benign, have no leader, and do not bring on a destructive Flood. This is not the story as the Yahwist is likely to have known it.

But J's treatment of the Enochic myth goes a good deal further. There are elements in his narrative that suggest a deliberate reworking of the story of the heavenly descent, transposed into the alternative story. In the *Book of the Watchers* the angels bring knowledge of arts and sciences to humans; the birth of the giants leads to bloodshed, and the earth cries out and its voice is heard in heaven. The chief perpetrator of all this does not die but is imprisoned in the wilderness. All these features, absent from Gen. 6:1–4, reappear in connection with the figure of Cain.

In Genesis 4 it is the descendants of Cain (who, let us remember, J presents as the ancestor of *all* humans) who invent the arts and sciences; it is after Abel's murder that the earth cries out because of the blood and is heard in heaven, and it is Cain who is banished to the wilderness. His words "my sin is too great for me to bear" (4:13) may allude to the fate of the "Azazel" goat itself, condemned *not to die* but to wander in the desert under the weight of Israel's iniquities. It is an impossible coincidence that all these features of Enoch recur in the case of Cain. The only solution is that Azazel has been transformed into a human, a prototype of all human wickedness appropriate for J's overall conception. This strategy, as suggested above, can be fitted into a context of conflict between different "Judaisms" characterized by different views of evil and sin. It fits into that negotiation that Boccaccini has discussed at such length within Second Temple Jewish literature.

The issue here is not one of chronological priority as between 1 Enoch and Genesis or specifically the *Book of Watchers* and the Yahwistic narrative in Genesis 1–11. Assigning specific dates to these texts and to stories is extremely difficult: both are usually products of ongoing rewriting and retelling. What can sometimes be reconstructed, however, is a relative chronology: certain stories (or versions of stories) imply the existence of others. As far as the relationship between Genesis and 1 Enoch is concerned, we know that the earliest extant manuscript of 1 Enoch is older than the earliest copy of Genesis; but that proves little. In any case, 1 Enoch itself often shows an awareness of other scriptural texts. But we can conclude that the myth in the *Book of the Watchers* is not elaborated from Genesis but represents a combination of versions of a story of heavenly descent that is older, and older than the Yahwist, who has retained elements of it but in radically revised forms. (Bedenbender [2003] has recently described this process in terms of "mythological competition" and "counter-reactions.") We are presented with perhaps the clearest case that biblical narratives participate in the process by which early Judaism was formed and do not necessarily provide a starting point for those processes.

The Yahwist versus P and Enoch

Our enquiry has one further step, however. The attitude towards Enoch in J and in P is quite different. The Yahwist's view of the origin and nature of sin is clear enough: what is the Priestly writer's stance on the question? In fact, P gives us no account at all. In 1973, Cross had correctly observed that "There is no account of primordial human rebellion in the Priestly strata of Genesis 1–11. Save for the rubric in Genesis 2:4a, P is absent in chapters 2 and 3... That a Priestly narrative once existed without an account of man's rebellion and sin is very hard to believe" (Cross, 1973: 306). It is indeed hard to believe; but it is also possible to infer P's view from textual clues. Having insisted (Genesis 1) that when God created the world it was good, P states, at the onset of his own Flood narrative (6:11) that "the earth also was corrupt before God, and the earth was filled with violence." It is an abrupt and enigmatic assertion. Westermann (1992: 53) seems to suggest that P is not interested in the reason for the Flood, only the decision to bring it. But that is not the case: P *does* give a reason—the *earth* was corrupt, and not just the human race living upon it. There are several clues to P's understanding of this state of affairs, however. The most indirect of these are that P is aware of at least something of the Enoch story, as 5:21–23 shows; furthermore, P is ideologically and probably literarily connected with the authorship of Leviticus, in which the scapegoat ceremony appears, and in which the eating of blood is forbidden (Leviticus 17). More directly, P's contribution to the Flood narrative contains a calendrical reckoning similar to that used in the Enochic literature, namely months of thirty days each (see most recently Najm and Guillaume, 2004). Finally, and perhaps conclusively, the Noachic covenant (9:1–7) focuses on the *shedding of blood*, a transgression for which there is no other antecedent than the widespread bloodletting that according to the Enochic story was the result of the giant offspring. The phrase "the *earth* was corrupt" rather than "*humans* were corrupt" fits exactly such an act: in 1 Enoch the earth cries out because of the blood shed on it. For P the Flood is an appropriate remedy for the earth as well as its inhabitants: the earth is washed clean, the inhabitants killed. The language is, as most scholars recognize, indicative of renewed creation, but on this occasion the earth is not chaotic or formless but polluted. These arguments all point towards the Priestly writers having viewed the Flood, and the origin of evil on the earth, exactly as did 1 Enoch: as the punishment for the sins of the angels who descended to earth and of their offspring.

However, we have no such narrative in P, but only in J, and the scholarly consensus is that P is later than J. Hence, either P had no such account, or the Priestly writer (or an editor) found no reason to duplicate an existing J narrative of the event. Elsewhere, P narratives stand alongside J narratives as doublets (creation: chapter 1/chapters 2–4; spread of humanity: chapter 10/chapter 11:1–9: genealogies: 4:17–24/chapter 10) or, as in the case of the Flood, combined (chapters 6–9). There is no other case of any episode in J that does not have a counterpart in P—so much so that it is possible to recover two complete versions of the entire story from creation to Abraham. Hence the conclusion (see above) that P simply did not contain any story explaining the origin of sin or the precise reason for the Flood. This view can be held if J and P existed as originally separate sources that were later combined by a third party. It is not conceivable that if P himself were responsible for the final form of the narrative he would have left 6:1–4 in contradiction of his own understanding. But it is almost as inconceivable that P would have omitted to give his own account in the first place. For, as we observed earlier, Gen. 6:1–4 is not an invention of the Yahwist, but a retelling of a story that was already well-known—and for that reason could not be omitted but only transformed. If, as I have argued, the story as related in Enoch corresponds closely to what P implies, P's silence is inexplicable.

Either we have come to a frustrating end, or we need to re-examine the relationship of J and P in Genesis 1–11. In his own analysis of these two sources, Blenkinsopp has provided a solution to the problem, but accidentally. For while he accepts that "The P version of human origins has no explicit account of what happened to bring about the deluge" (Blenkinsopp, 1992: 79) he finds the reason embedded in the genealogies with their decreasing lifespans. But on this view, P still offers no account of the origin of wickedness in a world created "good" (chapter 1), but merely observes the symptoms.

However, on entirely different grounds, Blenkinsopp has argued that within Genesis 1–11, what is called J is in fact a supplement to what is called P (he does not commit himself on whether these two sources, and especially J, belong with the J and P of the remainder of the Pentateuch). To my knowledge, his suggestion has not gained widespread acceptance, though I have not seen his arguments refuted, either. But he has actually missed the most important argument in favour of his conclusion. For only this view of the relationship of J and P is able to explain the problems we have met. It permits us to conclude that J's narrative in Gen. 6:1–4 is a revision of a story of a heavenly descent similar to that found in Enoch, *that was included in P*. This conclusion explains better than any other why there is no longer a P account of the origin of sin and why the Yahwist was obliged to rewrite it (and not just in 6:1–4 but in creating the Cain story) rather than merely delete it. I would go as far as to suggest that the purpose of the J material in Genesis 1–11 is *precisely* to provide a different account of human origins that contradicted the view upheld in 1 Enoch and in P, which celebrated a world created perfect, a glorious Adam bearing the divine image, and a corruption caused by angelic beings—and perhaps (as 1 Enoch at least proposes), still affected by this spiritual source of evil on the earth, until the final day of judgment. For J, however, humanity was corrupted by its own disobedience, without any angelic intervention: mortals are made of clay and crumble into clay and their lives are a misery.

Conclusions and Implications

I have concluded that the narratives interwoven in Genesis 1–11 engage in different ways with an earlier story of primeval origins that is also preserved in the Enochic literature. The P account will have followed the lines of the story we find in 1 Enoch's *Book of the Watchers*. The Yahwist replaced the earlier myth, together with its glorious Adam and its transported beings. The view that 1 Enoch is a later development of this writer's account in 6:1–4 is the very opposite of the truth. What we find in Genesis 1–11 is evidence of a conflict of mythologies and in particular, evidence of a deliberately anti-Enochic writer. While that conclusion provides us with no certain historical context, it is very likely, given the evidence of ben Sira and of P the Priestly writer, that this controversy belongs in the Hellenistic period, perhaps even as late as the second century BCE. It is not improbable that the controversy forms part of the background to the production of the Qumran scrolls themselves, which include many examples of the rewriting of Genesis (and no awareness of J's own version of the origin of sin or the cause of the Flood). Indeed, this new myth failed to make any immediate impact on early Jewish or Christian mythology. On the contrary, the Yahwist's attempt to obliterate the wicked angel by insisting that temptation to sin came originally from an earthly, created being—a snake—spectacularly failed: in Christian mythology he was quickly transformed into Satan himself.

Chapter 9

Eating and Drinking in the Qumran Texts

This essay and the one following are both concerned with eating and drinking, offer highly contrasting studies of "early Judaism." This study of the Qumran yahad *is facilitated by detailed literary description and the "Judaism" in question is expressed in a discrete sectarian body. "Diaspora Judaism" on the other hand, is much less accessible, but, on the sources we do have, much more diverse. Between them, the essays illustrate extreme definitions of "early Judaism" and of the ways in which we can, and cannot, come to understand its various manifestations.*

Thesis: The Body and Society

On the subject of boundaries, in her seminal *Purity and Danger* (Douglas, 1995: 115–29) Mary Douglas argued (116) that:

> The body is a model which can stand for any bounded system... We cannot possibly interpret rituals...unless we are prepared to see in the body a symbol of society, and to see the powers and dangers credited to social structure reproduced in small on the human body.

She cited a number of examples of "excremental magic," and then asked (122), "Why should bodily margins be thought to be specially invested with power and danger?" Her answer is that in any bounded society "margins are dangerous" (122). She continues:

> We should expect the orifices of the body to symbolise its specially vulnerable points. Matter issuing from them is marginal stuff of the most obvious kind.

Douglas's treatment concentrates on what *issues* from the bodily margins, which is more obviously seen as polluting, even in modern society. She includes within her range of examples the treatment of bodily emissions in the Hebrew Bible, especially from Leviticus. In Leviticus 15 (and partly Leviticus 12) a range of human bodily emissions are deemed to convey impurity, including, as well as irregular and diseased discharges, any male seminal discharge and a female menstrual discharge. Indeed, sexual intercourse renders the participants unclean for the remainder of the day.

Leviticus 15 does not regard either urinating or defecating as examples of unclean emissions. Deuteronomy 23:12–14 *does* regard defecation as in some way unclean (Deuteronomy does not share Leviticus's system of classification), but not as causing uncleanness, as does an emission of semen. Thus, while semen and blood (including menstrual blood and skin sores, but not blood caused by wounding) bring impurity, perhaps because of their connection with the life-principle, the expulsion of digested food and drink does not; nor do tears or sweat. Why sexual functions are in Leviticus in principle unclean, yet defecation not, inevitably attracts the curiosity of the interest of anthropologists as well as the expert on Jewish law.

In applying corporeal functions to social ones, Douglas points out that control over entry and exit from the "body" tends to be of particular importance in a *minority* society, in which one might expect to find taboos regulating what may be eaten or drunk, symbolizing an assertion of control over its own boundaries (Douglas, 1995: 125):

> [W]hen rituals express anxiety about the body's orifices the sociological counterpart of this anxiety is a cultural unity of a minority group.

and again she immediately recalls the ancient Israelites:

> The Israelites were always in their history a hard-pressed minority. In their beliefs all the bodily issues were polluting: Blood, pus, excrement, semen, etc. The threatened boundaries of their body politic would be well mirrored in their care for the integrity, unity and purity of the physical body.

Now, the Hebrew Bible does not regard all bodily issues as impure, nor were Israelites always in a minority within a larger society, although the ideology is often exploited in respect of the "peoples" round about, or the Canaanites in the land. Israel is often depicted as a vulnerable and even besieged society, as when constituted in the wilderness as a military camp (Numbers) or defined as a tightly-regulated legally-constituted society with strict rules of membership into the "congregation" (Deuteronomy), or represented as a sphere of especial "holiness" amid a world of uncleanness. Just how and why this image was fostered and sustained is a large question, but it can be taken for granted that Jews were often encouraged to believe that they belonged to a society whose existence depended, or was felt to depend, on a certain level of perceived and maintained distinction between itself and all other societies—which were for the most part undifferentiated, simply "the nations."

But why the emphasis on bodily emissions? There is no reason why body-as-society should be construed largely in terms of points of *exit* rather than *entry*. Douglas's discussion of society as a human body briefly addresses consumption, but her argument concentrates on what *leaves* the body. Yet in any society (or body) entry is as important as exit, death as much as life, marriage in as much as marriage out. The way is open for an investigation of how entry *into* the society/body is transacted within a formally constituted society and a definitely minority one.

What follows is thus generated by Douglas's suggestion, but is not a mechanical application of it, for several reasons: first, as stated, Douglas does not focus on eating and drinking as much as on bodily emission; second, hers is an anthropological approach, and indeed a structural-anthropological approach, and does not take account of religious or theological dimensions; and thirdly, she was not dealing with a unique historical phenomenon, a Jewish sectarian movement reflected, though as yet still not very clearly, in an archive of ancient texts.

In considering the applicability of Douglas's thesis to the Qumran texts, it would be useful to point out that the distinction between "clean" and "unclean," "holy" and "unholy," "Israelites" and "Gentiles" (*goyim, 'ammim*) characterizes a symbolic order that overlaps, but does not merge with, the symbolism of the body-as-society and a corresponding concern with orifices (nor am I concerned with Douglas's interesting mapping of society onto the sacrificial body). I am therefore not engaging with all the aspects of Douglas's theory about purity in the Jewish scriptures; these have been extensively utilized by Wenham (1979) and critiqued, among others, by Milgrom (1991: 766–68; 1000–1004). To some extent the worldview that such a taxonomy articulates does entail the creation and maintenance of boundaries—"dividing" between light and dark (at Sabbath), good and evil, holy days and profane days, and so on. The boundaries between a society and its *Umwelt* can be symbolized equally by geographical (the "camp," the "land of Israel") or legal ("children of the covenant") or genetic ("descendants of Abraham") codes, some of which can also accommodate a patrolling of the points of transition, of entry and exit. In this function such symbolizations of social integrity overlap with the symbolization of society-as-body. But there seems to me a good reason not to confuse the different symbolic systems that generate such phenomena as blood avoidance, *kashrut* and the topic of this paper, ingestion.

So what follows is a study of bodily and social orifices, and of the control that may be exercised within a society over ingress into the body, individual or corporate. This essay is dealing not with "Jewish society" (which does not mean anything, but see the next chapter) but with a Jewish sect. According to Bryan Wilson (1970: 22), sects are

> self-conscious attempts by men to construct their own societies, not merely as political entities with constitutions, but as groups with a firm set of values and *mores*, of which they are conscious. Such groups have a carefully ordered structure of social relationships and clearly established patterns of behaviour and control.

Among the distinguishing marks that Wilson attributes to the sect are the following (26–35): voluntary nature of membership; administering of a test of merit; strong sense of self-identity; complete and conscious allegiance; self-perception as an elite; exclusivity. Exhibiting all or nearly all of the characteristics mentioned by Wilson, a number of the Qumran scrolls (which he does not include in his treatment) fit the typology very well. Furthermore, a group that consciously constructs itself as "Israel" asserts itself to be the true and proper bearer of that identity. Thus, it is surrounded by that which it most resembles and that which at the same time most threatens it. To preserve its identity, a sect must enforce the boundaries between this immediate and threatening surrounding by both psychological and physical means.

Hence, the sects described in the scrolls are depicted as Israels, and live in closed communities with carefully controlled access. It is not so much the *character* of their beliefs that makes them a "sect" (though this makes an important contribution) so much as the social structure on which the texts also insist: these sects require to be clearly separated from the society that surrounds them, yet of which they constitute the true representatives.

As I have argued several times previously (1994, 1995), and it seems to be fairly widely accepted, there are two major sects described in the Qumran scrolls. One was scattered into several settlements ("camps" and "cities") and is described in the "Damascus" manuscripts (D); the other (the *yahad*) is more likely to have occupied a single settlement and is reflected especially in the *Serek ha-Yahad*, or "Community Rule." There are good reasons for thinking that the latter is a splinter of the first. The ability to differentiate between the two societies promises a marvellous opportunity for examining the issue of boundaries and thus

of ingress: for we can employ a scheme of three concentric "Israels."
On the literary level, the outermost might be defined by the scriptural
Israel, but since this is represented by each of the others as the model for
itself, that system does not work. The outer Israel is thus the society of
Judah, which from the viewpoint of the sects within it is the excluded;
the rejected, invalid "Israel" that lies outside. The second circle is the
Israel of the "Damascus" covenant, and the third is the Israel within that
sect, a splinter group. Each circle represents itself as the true version,
embodiment or remnant of the circle immediately outside it. In what
follows we shall begin from the inside.

Inscribing Society on the Body 1: The Yahad

What functions of a sectarian society might be inscribed on the individual
member? Douglas (1995: 123–24) lists four kinds of social pollution (to
which I have added in parentheses the Qumran manifestations):

1. danger pressing on social boundaries (=apostasy)
2. danger from transgressing the internal lines of the system (=penal
    codes)
3. the margin of the lines (=hierarchical divisions)
4. internal contradiction (=e.g. dualism, authority)

The first of these is illustrated in corporate (rather than corporal)
terms by the danger of apostasy, a problem addressed explicitly on both
CD and 1QS; the second by the disciplinary codes operating within both
sects, especially the penal code; the third is (if I have understood Douglas
correctly here) illustrated by the hierarchical system evident especially
in the *yahad*; and the fourth I would see exemplified in the tension
between a dualistic and predestinarian doctrine that divides humans
into damned and saved (presumably corresponding to the population
inside and outside the sect) and the contradictory recognition that there
is evil even inside the sect (and thus possible good outside it?). Thus,
in a society of "perfect holiness" tight discipline is necessary, for Belial
does not respect boundaries. A further potential contradiction is that
between scriptural and charismatic or sectarian authority. Both require
absolute allegiance and thus threaten each other. Accordingly, the two
sources have to be made to accord with each other.

But we wish to explore how these dangers will also be reflected in the
body. This is rather more evident in the *yahad*, where, as a group of quasi-
priests, the members minister in the appropriate state of holiness to a

sanctuary that is not there, and thus become the building stones of that sanctuary themselves (1QS 8:7–10). The holiness of the entire community thus depends crucially upon the holiness of every individual, for every individual is a building stone, an altar—and a gateway. What enters every individual enters the community, enters the holy sanctuary.

Commensality within the *yahad* is not a gesture of fellowship, nor a quasi-sacrificial act, nor a social convenience, nor an occasion to do communal business. It may or may not incidentally be any or all of these. But from the perspective of a Douglasian analysis, the physical control over what members eat and drink, and how they eat and drink, is to be seen primarily as maintaining of the integrity of the sectarian body through the individual bodies that make it up.

Eating and drinking are also incorporated into the physical boundary maintenance of the *yahad*. 1QS 6:8–7:26 contains a set of disciplinary rules with the heading "This is the Rule (*serekh*) for the assembly of the Many (*rabbim*)." Under this heading come regulations that affect admission. During the first of his two years of "probation," a new member of the *yahad* is forbidden to touch the "purity of the Many" (*tohorat ha-rabbim*) and during his second year, while allowed this, he is still forbidden the "drink of the Many" *mashqeh ha-rabbim*. After two years, if judged fit, he is admitted "among his brothers in the order of his rank, for instruction (*torah*), judgment and *tohorah*; his property is also merged with that of the community. Likewise, anyone who lies in respect of property is excluded from the *tohorah* for a year (and foregoes a quarter rations); the same punishment awaits anyone who has insulted a priest, or another member. One who has "walked in the stubbornness of his heart" is deemed to have left the community and is excluded, like the new entrant, from the *tohorah* in the first year and the *mashqeh* in the second year of his penance. Finally, and importantly, any member who has shared food or property with a member who has defected shall be expelled. This last offence merits the most serious punishment because it threatens the integrity of the communal holiness. If one member becomes unclean through sharing food with a non-member, he can transmit that to those who share the table in the community.

There are further occurrences of the phrase *tohorat ha-rabbim* in 1QS 8:16–7:24–25, which apply to any who "turn aside from anything that is commanded," or who have inadvertently broken any part of the law of Moses. And in 1QS 5:13 occurs a passage which, although preceded by a blank, and is rather clumsily phrased, must refer to a member of the sect who is regarded as apostate (1QS 5:13–18):

They shall not enter the water in order to share in the purity (*tohorah*) of the men of holiness, for they have not been cleansed unless they turn away from their wickedness, for he is unclean, among all who transgress his word. No-one shall associate with him in his work or in his possessions, so as not to involve himself with guilty sin. Instead, he must remain far from him in every matter, since it is written as follows: "You shall remain far from everything false." None of the men of the *yahad* shall obey them in any law or rule. No-one shall eat or drink anything that is his, or take anything from him, unless paid for, for it is written: "shun the man in whose nostrils is breath, for how much is he worth?"

From these passages, we have a reasonably clear portrait of the kinds of persons who may be excluded from the *tohorat ha-rabbim* (and by implication, *a fortiori* the *mashqeh* as well [Avemarie, 1997: 217]): what they have in common is a breach of the holiness of the *yahad*. Partly due to parallels in rabbinic literature and partly to the accompanying phrase "drink of the Many," the usual interpretation of the phrase *tohorat ha-rabbim* is that it refers to the food of the community members which was eaten in conditions of ritual purity. But why is the meal so important? Because on this occasion the holiness of the community is corporate and not individual; in the ritual of sharing food holiness is also shared—and any impurity transmitted, not just from one individual to another but to the entire body. Because of the sharing of food (and drink is even more susceptible to transmitting uncleanness), the impurity of one becomes the impurity of all. The food is therefore part of the corporate holiness of the community. *You are what you eat.*

Inscribing Society on the Body 2: The Damascus Sect

Among the fragments of the "Damascus Document" from Cave 4 (but not in CD) appears a version of the code in 1QS, which is now commonly termed the "Penal Code" (for a comparison of the two versions, see Baumgarten [1992, 1996]). There is a high degree of verbal correspondence between the two, but Baumgarten's attention has focused on the differences in the nature of the penalties. Hempel (1997) has refined the comparison and concludes, rightly in my view, that there must have been a penal code within the Damascus community that was modified within the *yahad*. But she also points out further important differences. One is the existence of legislation involving women in the D material; another is the absence of the word *rabbim* ("Many") from D, which uses *'edah* for the community. But the most intriguing difference between the two codes concerns eating and drinking. While both prescribe a reduction of rations as one form of penalty, and both use the term "penalizing" (√*ns*), S has exclusion "from the *tohorah* and *mashqeh* of the *rabbim*," while the D penal code uses the term "keeping apart" (√*bdl*). However, since S sometimes imposes a reduction of rations and sometimes exclusion from the *tohorah* and *mashqeh* of the *rabbim*, and sometimes both (see, e.g., 1QS 6:25) it is clear that the two measures are not to be confused. One case simply uses privation as a punishment (and Baumgarten supposes that on a basic diet, a reduction of any food at all would be a severe penalty) but the other case, exclusion from the *tohorah* and *mashqeh* is of a different order. It symbolizes something that we do not find in the Damascus community. The two communities appear to have a different conception of the function and significance of commensality.

Let us consider this possibility, beginning with the Damascus sect. Its language is frequently that of "separation." Thus, in CD 6:15–7:10, where a basic set of principles governing communal behaviour is listed, the opening word is *hibbadel* ("keep apart") from the "children of perdition" (*bene shahat*); later (6:17), to "make a distinction"(*hibdil*) between clean and unclean; later still (7:30), to "keep apart (*hibbadel*) from every form of uncleanness."

The mechanism of "keeping apart" members who have infracted the rules of the D community is thus entirely in keeping with the perception of the community as "separated." But there is no hint of exclusion *specifically from a common food consumption*. Why not? The answer may have to do with the social structure of this sect. For at least part of the sect was constituted in households. This in itself is interesting, because a household creates its own set of symbolic boundaries. Wives, children and slaves are a good example (Davies, 1994, 1995). CD states— immediately after the passage just mentioned (7:7)—that "if they (i.e. male members of the D sect) live in camps and take wives and beget children, these (obviously the family members) shall walk according to the law." The boundary between the world inside the sect and that outside is thus drawn *around*, and not *within*, the families that belong to it. But slaves constitute another possible fault-line (as the Christian apostle Paul found also in writing to Philemon). Thus their status has to be carefully defined: "Nor may he sell his male or female slave to them, since they have come with him into (or: "since they belong, like him, in"), the covenant of Abraham" CD 12:10–11. I have argued (1994) that slaves were *not* members of the Damascus sect (not members of the "new covenant in the land of Damascus" that constituted the sect), but were nevertheless expected to be Jewish. A non-Jewish slave would be entirely improper within this sect (he or she would probably have to be freed); but a member of the sect could hardly be a slave within it. The dilemma of the slave well illustrates to what extent it was still a household structure than the Damascus sect preserved—among its married members at least. We do not know how the non-married communities understood themselves, but since there is no evidence of a different understanding of eating and drinking, in this respect they may have regarded themselves as a "family."

Most characteristic of all household activities (and especially Jewish households in which a concept of pure and impure food was meaningful) are food preparation and consumption. Rules about these matters are lacking in D, and so we should probably conclude that consumption of food and drink did not symbolize, let alone represent, the corporate integrity of the sect, and so did not require sectarian regulation. The *yahad* is probably to be understood as single community, as is still generally agreed, though the matter has nevertheless recently received renewed discussion (Regev, 2003; Collins, 2005; Metso, 2005). For some, the name *yahad* means a "union" of several groups: for others, it means "unity" and describes a corporate identity. But for the D community, its constituent "camps" and "towns" did not lend itself to a strong sense of corporate holiness expressed in the physical act of commensality, while the relatively greater degree of interaction with outsiders (contact with non-Jews is mentioned in the D "Laws") suggest a less intense ideology of "holiness." The concentration of "holiness" in the communal meal of the *yahad* makes sense even if there were more than one such group (which I doubt); the important difference being that each *yahad* would symbolize itself as a discrete "body" with both physical and social boundaries: such could not be the case for the "Damascus" groups.

Hempel (1996) has suggested that the original form of 1QSa, the *Rule of the Congregation*, was originally a description of meals in the Damascus community, including women and children. If she is correct, it seems to me more likely that these meals were not every day but on special occasions and, of course, took place in each of the various locations. Whether or not she is correct, it is probable that such ceremonies did occur (possibly at Passover). In this case, it is quite likely (following the description in 1QS 6:2–6) that the *yahad* meal, was taken over and adapted from its parent group, the Damascus sect. The description of this meal in 1QSa is, however, clearly influenced by the description of the biblical "congregation," including the classes of excluded persons such as physically disabled, and nowhere are such exclusions mentioned in connection with membership. Possibly this element of the description has been introduced as part of the presentation of the meal as an "eschatological banquet." In any case, we do not find the language of holiness, let alone the term *tohorah* in the description. Then I therefore doubt that we can assign to the Damascus sect a highly symbolic corporate function of regular eating and drinking. This is not to say that commensality was not practised, especially among celibate members, nor to deny that such a practice may have been carried over into the *yahad*, rather than invented by it. But if so, such commensality was symbolized only by the *yahad*.

The "Purity of the Rabbim"

With a different social structure, then, and a different self-awareness, the *yahad* sought to provide in its commensality a symbolization of society as body. This symbolization implies the levitical purity of food and drink (Licht, 1965: 294–303; see the review of Licht's position in Avemarie, 1997: 218–20). Licht's opinion has been confirmed in the eyes of those for whom Qumran halakhah is a precursor and possible ancestor of rabbinic halakhah (so Schiffman, 1991) and is supported explicitly or implicitly by a rapidly-growing corpus of essays on Qumran halakhah prompted by the publication of the Temple Scroll, the *Halakhic Letter* (4QMMT) and the Cave 4 D fragments. In this case, certainly, the similar (not identical) rabbinic terminology of *tohorot and mashqin* seems compelling (see Neusner, 1999; though he is less enthusiastic about continuities between Qumran and rabbinics).

These other halakhic texts, both Qumranic and rabbinic, permit us to confirm that the "purity of the *Rabbim*" refers to their solid food, and it is distinguished from their drink. The "Halakhic Letter" (4QMMT), like the rabbinic halakhah (but more stringently), regards liquids as more susceptible to contamination than solids. Hence, food and drink cannot be treated equally. Yet the issue of concern here is not the degree to which food and drink can convey uncleanness, but the fact that they are regarded, under levitical rules, as so doing. But why the levitical rules?

There were, as we know, Jewish groups in the late Second Temple period who gathered to eat meals in levitical purity (*haburot*). But the *yahad* was, it seems, more than a haburah. As a sect of a sect, and as (so I have assumed) a small, single, and ideologically highly-charged entity, the *yahad*, unlike its "Damascus" parent, seems to have entirely withdrawn from all contact with the Jerusalem Temple. This enabled it to transfer to itself (in rather the same way that the liturgy of the "Songs of the Sabbath Sacrifice" may have transferred Temple liturgy) the centre of holiness, with each member following the priestly rules as a consequence of this holy status (a status that allowed them, according to 1QS 8:3 to "atone for sin"). Priests on temple service, of course, ate portions of meat that had been sacrificed. But I have suggested a further dimension to this, a further level of symbolization. The orifices of each member were gateways into and out of the holy precincts of the *yahad*. Hence, to eat with an outsider or a lapsed member was a highly serious offence, because it was to eat or drink an uncleanness, *which then passed into the human sanctuary* and defiled it.

Jesus is credited with saying that "it is not what goes into someone that defiles, but what exits" (Mt. 15:8; Mk 7:15). For the *yahad*, while the exit was also important, what went in was even more so, since it involved the holiness not merely of the person, but of the whole sectarian body: whatever any of its members ate, they all ate. And so, any infringement, or possible infringement, of that holiness, whether through unclean food or an unclean mouth, needed to be watched for.

It is unfortunate that the Qumran manuscripts tell us little about the actual conduct of a meal, nor about how the community corporately rid itself of such uncleanness (though it presumably involved rituals of purification). The danger was, of course, that such infringements might not be detected: hence the stringency by which infringements were to be punished. 1QS 6:2–6 prescribes that the members shall eat together, as they also bless and deliberate together. This makes it clear that all these activities were seen as corporate. As for the conduct of the meal, we are told only that the priest shall first bless the first fruits of the bread or the wine. But the conduct of the meal itself is unimportant. Each member at table was conscious of being a part of a whole, but an important part. His body was part of a larger body. Communal meals were, of course, used widely as a ritual of solidarity: societies, clubs and organizations regard their occasional "dinner" as an expression of their shared identity. The Sabbath meal and the Passover Seder, though without the ideology of priestly holiness, also express Jewish solidarity. But outside these rituals, our modern consumer society, for whom ingestion is becoming more and more signifying of pleasure, desire, status, even ethics (vegetarianism, holistic food, ethically sourced food, unhealthy food, GM products) stands in other respects at a great distance and exploit a vastly different set of symbols.

Chapter 10

Eating and Drinking in the Roman Empire

The study of "early Judaism" should not be confined either to Judah or to literary texts, though the bulk of our evidence falls into either one or both categories. Most Jews in the Greco-Roman world neither lived in Judah nor are found through texts. In "Diaspora Judaism" we are not, for example, dealing with a single society. Are there any common features to speak about? What, if anything, is distinctive about "Jewish" eating and drinking throughout the Roman Empire? Can we do more than describe that variety? And even so, from what perspective? How Jews interpreted what they did? How their neighbours understood them? How should we balance literary sources that purvey the author's understanding of food and drink with archaeological and epigraphic clues which at least reflect, however poorly, what was actually done? How should the rich resources of cultural anthropology be used? If nothing else (and the following essay is a very superficial review of the question) it is important to be reminded that any description of "early Judaism" or even "early Judaisms" remains at some distance from the complexities of daily Jewish life, especially outside Judah, where the ultimate decisions about Jewish identity and the character of Judaism were finally made, at a time before rabbinic definitions made any social or political headway outside Judah (and perhaps even inside it), and when the loss of Temple and then land removed the notion of centre even further into the symbolic realm. In that sense, this final chapter is deliberately an antidote to all previous discussion of "early Judaism."

Theory versus Data

I have decided to adopt a functionalist approach to the ritual of eating and drinking, partly because without some kind of approach the topic cannot be handled with any order, and partly because I have previously (see previous essay) used such an approach in analysing eating and drinking in the Qumran texts relating to the *yahad*. The theory is that social rituals express a system, and that such a system can be expounded in terms of a worldview. In the case of the sect, I suggested that the individual body functioned as a microcosm of the whole (a suggestion I adopted from Mary Douglas who kindly commented on an early draft of that essay). But Judaism as a whole is a different matter: and without a corresponding "society" can any common "worldview" or "symbolic system" be predicated? Within the Roman Empire, were any groups sufficiently autonomous or independent of external influence to develop a distinctive social system or worldview? What we know of Diaspora Jewish communities suggests that they assimilated a good deal, though in varying degrees (see, e.g., Barclay, 1996; Gafni, 1997; Gruen, 1998, 2002; Schwartz, 2001). We cannot speak of a single religious system for "Diaspora Judaism" in any holistic sense (*pace* Goodenough, 1953–1988) and surely not of eating and drinking. As for the literature, what the rabbis, or Philo, or Josephus might say, or even what the scriptures might imply, is not direct evidence of Jewish social behaviour in general or in any particular. The social world of each Jewish community or household in the Roman Empire was composed of various elements, only some of them Jewish. That is to say, even where Jewish ethnicity is predominant, there are always other constitutive elements of identity that have to be considered relating to local politics, trade or profession, social networks.

Barclay's superb study of the Mediterranean Diaspora (1996) has demonstrated that in his own words, there is no "scripted response" (82) in the Egyptian Diaspora to Egyptian history, nor any "package deals" (83) that Diaspora Jews bought. He has suggested three categories: assimilation, acculturation and accommodation, within which specific indices can be used, such as attendance at the Greek theatre (one indication of assimilation), scholarly expertise (acculturation) and antagonsim to Greco-Roman culture (accommodation). But within all three is a range of creating together a wide spectrum of responses.

But this does not mean that worldviews and social systems were not operative. Each Jewish community, and each individual Jew, represents a space in which various symbolic systems or worlds intersected. We cannot describe exactly how each space was filled, but we can perhaps indicate some of the available ingredients, using a "multi-functional" approach. The value of such an exercise is not in discovering how any particular community or individual behaved, but in exploring how decisions about behaviour might have been influenced and determined—a way of reminding ourselves that defining "Judaism," especially outside Judah itself, was ultimately a private and local matter, and we can only try to identify what kinds of criteria may have been in force and how they may have applied.

We can, in other words, attempt to catalogue the Jewish and non-Jewish components from which Jewish social identity, and specifically the culture of food and drink, *might* be manufactured: the myths, the discourses, the idioms, the memories, the language, the rituals, the literature. What we cannot do is predicate how that mix might work in individual cases. At different places *and on different occasions*, the mix would be different. Ethnicity is always a matter of negotiation, because it depends on the assertion of identity and difference, and these are not fixed, but relative to others. On the other hand, ethnicity is stubborn and resilient. To a great extent it was no doubt held together by beliefs, and practices, including rituals. But it was also maintained by a network of cultural codes that did not construct a fixed system but afforded materials for different constructions. To take the most elementary example: we can assume with some confidence—indeed, we can take it as almost axiomatic—that the patterns of behaviour between Jews were different from those between Jews and non-Jews.

The long debate between "humanistic" and "social-scientific" historical paradigms and methods is well known. While a humanistic approach that respects the individuality, even the uniqueness, of each event and circumstance *describes* well but *explains* poorly, a social-scientific approach *explains* well but *describes* poorly. While ideally the two should be harnessed together, the nature of the evidence sometimes requires one rather than the other.

Practice

It is probably safe to say, with most cultural anthropologists, that in eating and drinking, groups and societies tend to express most strongly their solidarity, identity and relationships, internal and external. Meals symbolize relations within and between groups. (The modern ethnicity of food—Italian, French, Greek, Vietnamese—represents in part a commodification of the role of diet and cuisine in identity-formation.) Alongside such generalization, however, something needs to be said about the *realia*. Quite apart from geographical distribution, even in a single city, such as Rome there is no evidence that the eleven synagogues so far discovered (see Smallwood, 1999: 173) formed a single Jewish "community." Sometimes a Jewish community was officially recognized as an "association," but often not. Some synagogues offered places for communal dining (the Theodotus synagogue in Jerusalem, or in Stobi, Macedonia, for example), but probably not most. The main locus of eating and drinking among Jews (as with everyone else) was the household. An important social context is also the "neighbourhood," perhaps even the "quarter," a part of the city in which Jews might cluster and which would certainly play a significant role in the maintenance of a social world; and the city itself furnished a wider context.

From an etic point of view, it would be interesting to ask how far the sharing of table in an exclusive manner was dictated by dietary customs or by religious taboos (i.e. on meat that may have been subject to a non-Jewish religious ritual), rather than by a concern to preserve social and cultural identity. How far, in the Roman Empire, *was* diet shaped by ethnicity? Is it true in the case of the Jewish Greco-Roman Diaspora that food in general marked differences in social affiliation? For the most part, a Jewish diet was much like anyone else's (see the useful review in McGowan, 1999: 33–88). Diet depends on availability, and is hugely subject to local variation. The Jews of Egypt thus ate an "Egyptian" diet, the Jews of the Peloponnese a "Peloponnesian" diet, and so on. Poorer people rarely ate meat or fish, the staple being cereals, supplemented by fruit, vegetables, olive oil, salt, cheese depending on availability. Cooking at home was not the norm, and bread was probably usually bought rather than baked at home. Wine was sometimes drunk; water more commonly. Meat was occasionally available, especially on public festivals and from sacrifices or acquired by an association for a communal celebration. Most commonly eaten by Romans was pork— but most of the population of the Roman Empire were not Romans. A non-meat, non-wine diet was thus not remarkable, and the Jewish diet therefore not distinctive and, moreover, not demanding of exclusive dining. If there were Jewish butchers or even Jewish wine-merchants in the vicinity, abstention from these commodities would not be necessary, either. In short, *kashrut*—to the extent that it was acknowledged as part of Jewish life—need not have been a predominant issue at all for the poor.

The rich, of course, could afford regular meat and fish, and in addition to the usual meals, would banquet, often with a following *symposium*. Both these events, and especially the latter, would have included religious actions: prayers, hymns, libations. Excess was not uncommon;

conversation *de rigueur*. Such occasions obviously have to be separated from everyday consumption, and they afford a very rich resource for analysis of culture. It is also probable that the Jewish Passover meal was influenced, perhaps even inspired, by the banquet. Apart from this ritual meal, Jewish communities understanding themselves (and being understood) as "associations" would behave accordingly and arrange banquets for their members.

Thus, it is likely that a Jew might not normally be distinguishable in diet or in eating habits from anyone else; and even where formal Jewish meals were taken, these followed to some extent the pattern of the society in which they took place. This is all rather obvious and does not take us very far, except to underline that Jewish eating and drinking was not at all immune to the cultural environment or even clearly exceptional within it.

What, if any, were the *distinctive significations* of *everyday* eating and drinking among Jews in the Roman Empire? Introducing the word "distinctive" means eliminating all those significations they might have shared with others. "Everyday" means I ignore the *Seder, qiddush* or, say, the fish meal at the beginning of Shabbat. Finally, "significations" in the plural means I recognize that a range of meanings, beyond practice, is always potentially or actually present, and that only a few such meanings may have been shared by all or most Jews or Jewish groups (for a detailed account of such significations, see McGowan, 1999, and Feeley-Harnik, 1994, both of whom explore these as a background to the Christian eucharist).

Did Jews eat with non-Jews? One might ask this of any ethnic minority, and come up with the same answer: "it depends." If food is an index of ethnicity, then sharing is always a delicate and special matter. But in some groups—perhaps the majority—hospitality is a virtue. And as long as the host was Jewish, what reason would there be for excluding non-Jews from a Jewish table? It is the sensibility of the non-Jewish guest, not the Jewish host that matters here. I have personally never been offered meat when dining in a vegetarian household (and resisted my temptation to bring my own). But like most carnivores I expect vegetarian guests to bear the sight of others eating meat at my table. Reasons for sharing or not sharing the table with non-Jews would more usually, I suspect, be social and political than religious. Many Jews might nevertheless wish not to eat meat (possibly drink wine) as guests, and *their* reasons might well be religous. Injunctions against idolatry and eating blood are well-documented and the Jewish practice well-attested.

Let us consider a different case. An ancient Jewish merchant might well have to accommodate himself to various practices and Jewish cultures as he travelled across the Empire, but his receptivity to a range of Jewish cultural constructions would enable him to remain a Jew within whatever local Jewish community he was welcomed, and thus he would not be obliged to reflect upon any of the values that made him a "Jew." He would, however, if he were in a place without a Jewish community (which we may nevertheless consider to be rather unusual). During his travels, this merchant's Jewish ethnicity would in effect be newly renegotiated, without being either questioned or challenged. He would recognize and be recognized by others who were also Jewish (for a forceful exposition of this viewpoint, see Alter, 1979).

The Example of Daniel

We should not assume that Jewish eating was consciously dictated by doctrinal or any other explicit ideology. But what if a Jew were asked about reasons for avoiding non-Jewish dining, if that was in fact practised? We can suggest, with support from literary sources, the kinds of reasons or rationalizations that might be offered. In fact, we can do that by considering a single biblical passage dealing with an archetypal Jewish "Diaspora Jew": Dan. 1:8–12:

> Daniel made up his mind that he would not defile himself with the king's ration of food or wine and he requested from the head of the household that he should not defile himself.

Here is a story of Judean aristocrats who are brought to the royal court in Babylon. They refuse to eat the king's food but insist instead on a very simple diet, with the consequence that they appear healthier than those enjoying the regular royal rations. What does the food and drink symbolize here? The fact that this is not explained in the story has led commentators, ancient and modern, to propose different solutions (none of which excludes the others):

1. *Sovereignty*: God as the true provider of food to his people
2. *Purity*: the separation of Jew from non-Jew as "holy to God"
3. *Asceticism*: moral and physical superiority; discipline
4. *Exile*: the status of food outside the "homeland"
5. *Sacrifice*: food consumption and the Temple

1. *Sovereignty*

Sovereignty is, of course, one of the pervading themes of the book of Daniel, and as with a good deal of Jewish literature, from the Bible to the classical period, a non-Jewish king is the foil. The issue of Jewish loyalty to both their god and their emperor was represented, and formally resolved, by the sacrifice *on behalf of* the Roman emperor at the Jerusalem Temple. But understandably it remained a tension. Under this topic we can also recognize an aspect of the theme of *idolatry* and of *sacrifice*: in Daniel 2, as in imperial Rome there is the question of a cult of the king/emperor.

Distribution of food was among the imperial measures necessary from time to time and it seems to me probable that, as with the emperor's head on the coin (Mt. 22:15–22), the emperor could claim, implicitly or explicitly, to be the feeder of his people. (I will discuss below how, as the Empire itself took over from the city as the political cosmos, the personal figure of the Emperor came to be ever more closely associated with meat and its provision.) One way of reading Daniel 1, then, is as a conflict of sovereignty between king and God as provider of food (and possibly as a contrast to the last Judean king and fellow-exile, Jehoiachin, who, according to 2 Kgs 25:30, took the Babylonian king's food.

The theme of "God as feeder" is discussed by Feeley-Harnik, who cites (1994: 71–76) numerous passages from the Jewish scriptures to support her suggestion, including Ps. 104: 24, 27–30, the Eden story and the giving of manna in the Sinai desert. One can argue, further, that the dietary laws themselves imply the notion of God as provider of food, just as circumcision signifies divine ownership of the human body. We do not know for certain how far the custom of reciting a blessing over food was usual in Jewish households: the rabbinic form of the blessing over food is given in *M. Berakot* 6–7. For Qumran, see 1QSa 2:19, and perhaps 4Q343, if it is, as has been claimed, a "grace after meals," while the Paternoster is of course a further example of the practice. If this was a common practice, the theme of God as provider of food is possibly the most fundamental, as well as distinctive aspect of everyday Jewish consumption.

The familiar parable of the king who invites to a banquet (rabbinic literature and New Testament *passim*) also suggests that the relationship between Israel and its god was easily symbolized in terms of hospitality, presence at a banquet, with God as the host. The eschatological overtones of this, in terms of a "messianic banquet," though more fully attested in

Christian than in Jewish texts, are also no doubt rooted in late Second Temple Judaism, and not confined to the Passover Seder.

As a final note on this theme: the episode of Daniel 1 is of course narrated as a miracle (*pace* Josephus, see below), and as such serves, as in the other Daniel stories, to underline the superiority of divine feeding to human feeding.

2. *Purity*

This verb *g'l* in Dan. 1:8 usually connotes ritual defilement in the Bible. Some commentators have thus suggested regarding Daniel's act as obedience to Jewish dietary laws. In his discussion of the verse, Collins (1993: 142–43) concludes that the defilement in question is undoubtedly ritual. As he concedes, there is no ban on wine in the Torah, but only of Gentile wine in the Mishnah (*Abodah Zara* 2:3; 4:8–12; 5:1–12). But the diet is "in the spirit of the biblical laws" (142). He also points to the Old Greek of Est. 14:17, where Esther claims she has never eaten from the king's table "nor drunk the wine of the libations." The wording suggests that the impurity of the food and drink here lies in its dedication to other gods. He also cites Tobit (1:10–11) and Judith (12:1–4), which imply that all non-Jewish food may be suspected of being unclean. Alongside these are Jub. 22:16 which forbids eating with non-Jews because of pollution and 1 Macc. 1:61–62 which refers to "unclean food" of non-Jews.

These passages could in fact suggest either that all non-Jewish food was *suspect* (though the specific reasons are not given). Possibly its not having been tithed provided a pretext, in which case the reason falls under the previous category of giving due recognition to the deity (see also under "exile" below). But unlike that category, it is extremely unlikely that most Jews in the Roman Diaspora could possibly apply this reason, on practical grounds. The priests sent to Rome under Nero (Josephus, *Vita* 14) were said to have taken with them a store of figs and nuts. But these are priests, and from Jerusalem, and this behaviour tells us nothing about lay Jews in the Diaspora.

This does not rule out the possibility of the notion that Jewish food could be pure and non-Jewish food not. Gastronomic chauvinism can always likely to be co-opted as a mark of ethnic affiliation anyway. But we are hardly speaking here about the *kind* of food (apart from meat and wine) but about its *provenance*. Few Jews in the Diaspora could survive on food guaranteed to have been produced by Jews and in accordance with tithing laws.

3. Asceticism/Vegetarianism

Asceticism and vegetarianism can be linked here for brevity but also on the grounds that eating meat was often associated with wealth and indulgence. Among interpreters of the Daniel episode Josephus readily illustrates this interpretation. Daniel and his companions had resolved to adhere to a strict diet, to abstain from food from the royal table, and refrain from meat…they had pulse (seeds) and dates for their food, *and anything else, apart from meat, that they wanted.* Arioch, the king's officer, noticed their improved appearance, and gave the other youths the same diet, with the result that

> "their souls were in some measure purer, less burdened, and fitter for learning, and their bodies in better shape for hard work, for they were not oppressed and heavy with a variety of meats, nor were the others effeminate, for the same reason (Ant. 10.10:2).

We can also add Philo to Josephus' testimony. In his *Special Laws* (4:96–97), for example, he condemns gluttony and notes that Moses legislated against excess in food and drink, which are a "hindrance to piety."

How distinctively Jewish is this code? The virtue of abstinence from meat is a Greek as well as a Jewish theme. In the Jewish scriptures it is hinted in Gen. 1:29 and perhaps also 2:6 that the first humans were vegetarian; and this becomes clear in Gen. 9:3–4. Several Greek philosophers also advocated abstinence from meat, of whom the best-known is Pythagoras, and, as in Genesis, a primordial state of vegetarianism was sometimes imagined (see McGowan, 1999: 70ff.). For possibly different reasons, such as its association with wealth, the Cynics also tended to avoid eating meat.

It is therefore possible that Josephus is imputing good Greek philosophical notions to his Jewish heroes. What may be an important link between the Jewish and Greek traditions, however, is an aversion to sacrificial cultic practice (see below). Among Greeks, however, this extended often to an aversion against religion itself. A Jew might find it convenient to cite a Greek principle rather than risk the charge of xenophobia or lack of hospitality. But not where this pretext attracted the charge of atheism (and Josephus does not seem to have worried about this). But while the Daniel story can be claimed as demonstration of the virtues of abstinence from meat and wine, it is equally likely to imply that this was the first of several instances of divine intervention and so not a direct consequence of their ingestion but of their piety. And in any case, a vegetarian lifestyle was, as noted earlier, the norm for most

Jews: only the wealthy or privileged, such as the Flavian client Josephus, would be able to enjoy a regular carnivorous lifestyle.

4. *Exile*

The story of Daniel 1 opens with the account of the deportation, and immediate confrontation with a court that is not the royal court of Jerusalem, wisdom that is not that of Judah and food that is not Jewish. Daniel's diet might thus be seen as one of the issues in which accommodation between "familiar" and "strange," home/non-home is necessary. In exile he eats a different diet from most of his fellow-exiles, either because he is not yet ready to accept this fundamental fact of exile ("you are what you eat," i.e. you will become foreign) or perhaps as some kind of response to exile as divine punishment, in a form of self-discipline or even self-mortification (though his state of health shows that this interpretation is unlikely!)

The one thing that all Diaspora Jews shared was a recognition that they were not in the ethnic "homeland." This state of affairs applied to many *ethne*, and of course few Diaspora Jews had been born in Judah. But the role of the Temple (and the existence of a Jewish king) provided a stronger link to the "homeland" than most other Diasporas, and the land of Israel/land beyond Israel. The biblical and Mishnaic regime of purity applies, of course, to the land of Israel alone and, as Neusner has extensively argued, the problematic of sustaining Jewish purity outside the land is the key to the Mishnah itself, at a time when the centre, the land of Israel, had effectively disappeared from the real, contemporary geography of Judaism.

The notion that food of Assyria is "unclean" occurs already in Hos. 9:3–4, which suggests that the Israelite food will be unclean because it cannot be offered to Yhwh (either as sacrifice or as tithe: it would be very helpful if we could date this verse!). It is nevertheless likely that the perception of "unclean food" as characteristic of the diasporic environment was quite widely and deeply recognized and that, following the ideology of Numbers and Leviticus, "outside the camp" uncleanness was the rule, and the condition of exile was defined precisely by that: living among the unclean.

How far did Diaspora Jews actually live and act as if "outside the camp": did they feel an estranged part of "Israel"? Among recent treatments of this question, van Unnik (1993) argues that since the Greek word *diaspora* is largely used in the negative sense of "scattering, dispersion," in the LXX and in other texts of the Greco-Roman period, it meant to

Jews more than exile: it was the decomposition of Israel. For Kraabel (1987), however, the negative biblical image of exile is transformed in the Diaspora into a positive one, expressed in the reconstitution of the local Jewish community into a Hellenistic "association." Gafni (1997) and Scott (1997) have also considered this question, and concluded that a great many Diaspora Jews did indeed feel a strong sense of estrangement, though not without means of redemption, such as being a "light to the Gentiles." Studies of such "exiled" communities suggest, however, a deep ambivalence in attitudes to the "homeland" and its claims and the phenomenon of "Jewish local patriotism" is a reminder of the danger of imposing an ideology of "exile" too readily on the Jews of the Roman Empire. Rather, such a perspective as something to be negotiated and not simply accepted. A similar tension can be observed, and analyzed, within Jews living outside Israel.

But in what ways might an ideology of Diaspora affect food and drink? Whether as a divine punishment or as a "light to Gentiles," Diaspora might provoke either rejection of or openness to commensality with non-Jews.

5. Sacrifice

A final interpretation of Daniel 1, rather more distant from the surface of the scriptural text than the others, might link it with the theme of the defiled Temple that grows to dominate the closing chapters of the book, and see in it a response to the cessation of the divine diet of meat in the Jerusalem Temple, added to by the removal of temple vessels to Babylon (and, in chapter 5, their provocative use by Belshazzar).

The association of table and altar in Mary Douglas's famous essay "Deciphering a Meal" (Douglas, 1971) is not easy to apply to Diaspora communities and individuals. In the Greco-Roman world meat was above all connected with sacrifice. Such meat was also sometimes taken home from the altar and eaten there, or sold. Wine was not in the same way a part of a sacrificial cult, but since consumption of wine was usually attended by libation or some other religious practice, its connection with sacrifice was still close. (However, since these religious acts took place during consumption, Jews would find the association easier to counter.)

Just as the daily sacrifice of the Jerusalem Temple was represented as sustaining the world (in Daniel the cessation of the *tamid* must lead to the end of the present world order), so also in the Roman Empire, the maintenance of sacrifice preserved harmony between gods, human, animals and nature. The culture of sacrifice was not a small part of social life in the Diaspora that a Jew might simply avoid, even if sacrificial food itself could be evaded. Moreover, as numerous Jewish and Christian stories recognized, sacrifice was also a political act. In the Roman Empire, the altar extended into the kitchen, as it did to the entire household (where, of course, altars might also be found).

Not so in the scriptural theology of Judaism, where one temple alone hosted sacrifices to the Jewish god, and thus afforded employment to priests, and where domestic cuisine was non-sacrificial. The cultural geography of Diaspora Jews and most other populations of the Empire was in this respect different. Through sacrifice the Empire, and increasingly the Emperor, was present everywhere, in the consumption of meat. But among Diaspora Jews sacrifice was remote: Jerusalem remained physically the place where Israel and its god met in sacrifice, and nowhere else.

Such abstinence from a sacrificial culture, where maintained, may have emphasized the Passover meal as a single exception, the one time of the year in which a Jewish banquet could celebrate the meat of a sacrifice. We do not know whether Diaspora Jews refrained from eating lamb on that occasion, even though the lamb was not sacrificed in Jerusalem (and note also the importance of wine in the meal). They had scriptural warrant in Exodus, if not in Deuteronomy. *Baba Bathra* 60b states that many Jews abstained from meat and wine after the destruction of the Temple, since these were no longer being brought to the altar. Whether or not such a habit was really adopted just after 70 CE, the destruction of the Temple might just possibly have been invoked as a rationale for avoiding meat and wine, especially if that custom were already being observed. The Talmudic passage, however, refers to the Jews in question as *perushim*, and thus not applicable to most Jews. Given the Pharisaic interest in extending levitical laws of purity to the dining table, a strong ideological connection between abstinence from meat and the Temple cult is not unlikely among these Jews. How far Pharisaic practices were in evidence outside Judah is another matter. (Against the claim of Mt. 12:15 about Pharisaic conversion, see Goodman, 1992)

It is unlikely that the destruction of the Temple in Jerusalem had any major effect on the daily practice of Jewish eating and drinking, unless it actually weakened (rather than strengthened) certain inhibitions about eating meat.

Conclusions

I have suggested ways of looking at the range of options that might have been available to Diaspora Jews in negotiating the question of eating and drinking. My suggestion is that, insofar as any rationale was felt to be needed, the use of these "codes" (for they do represent elements of a worldview) would have varied from place to place, and even from time to time. Individually or together they offered the opportunity to signify and sustain Jewish identity flexibly, and make it possible for a Jew to eat and drink, as a Jew, in a number of different local regimes and various social situations. In the end, of course, we are dealing with something ultimately inaccessible: the insides of people's heads, where all semiotic systems come to life and where the root of Jewish identity lodges.

Finally, it should be stressed that my determination to include individual Jews as well as members of a "community" is deliberate and perhaps I have not stressed it enough. It is not that I am reading back modern notions of "individuality" into a society in which it was less developed, but that the boundaries between "Jew," "non-Jew" and "Jew-ish," or "semi-Jew" were not hard and fast. Many non-Jews adopted lifestyles that were "Jewish," and many "Jews" adopted lifestyles that were not noticeably so. The penumbra of many Jewish communities, and of "Jewish society" as a whole, was considerable. It seems inescapable that the individual's own claims to Jewish identity were regulated and annotated by the attitudes of others (Jewish and non-Jewish) and that table fellowship was an important mark of the extent to which an individual was "in" or out." Literary sources have a tendency to clarify the boundaries between "Jew" and "non-Jew" in ways that help self-identity; but in everyday life such distinctions are usually much more blurred. Commensality can certainly be seen as an important and practical way in which the boundaries of Judaism, of "Israel" were drawn, but these boundaries were not the biblical ones that were not to be moved. Perhaps they were indeed one means of attracting non-Jews into Judaism (and might conversely have drawn Jews further out).

In the end, a strong case can be made for saying that "Judaism" has to be what Jews say it is, and while Jews have never agreed on any definition, outsiders have often found it important to make the determination, whether Roman tax officials, Christian authorities or more recent anti-Jewish regimes. But whether Jewish or not, all of us in the end have to be human and humanity does not have such boundaries.

BIBLIOGRAPHY

Aaron, David H., 2006. *The Emergence of the Decalogue*. London: T&T Clark.

Alexander, P. S., 2002. "The Enochic Literature and the Bible: Intertextuality and its Implications." In Edward D. Herbert and Emanuel Tov (eds.), *The Bible as a Book: The Hebrew Bible and the Judaean Desert Discoveries*: 57–69. London: The British Library and Oak Knoll Press in association with The Scriptorium: Center for Christian Antiquities.

Alt, A., 1953. "Die Heimat des Deuteronomiums." Kleine Schriften II; Munich: C. H. Beck: 250–75.

Alter, Robert, 1979. "A New Theory of *kashrut*." *Commentary* 68: 58–65.

Argall, R. A., 1995. *1 Enoch and Sirach: A Comparative Literary and Conceptual Analysis of the Themes of Revelation, Creation and Judgment*. Atlanta: SBL.

Avemarie, Friedrich, 1997. " 'Tohorat Ha-Rabbim' and 'Mashqeh Ha-Rabbim': Jacob Licht Reconsidered." In Bernstein, *et al.*, 1997: 215–29.

Barclay, John M. G., 1996. *Jews in the Mediterranean Diaspora from Alexander to Trajan (323 BCE–117 CE)*. Edinburgh: T&T Clark.

Barstad, Hans, 1982. "Lebte Deuterojesaia in Judäa?" *NTT* 83: 77–87.

— 1989. *A Way in the Wilderness: The "Second Exodus" in the Message of Second Isaiah*. Manchester: University of Manchester Press.

Barton, John, 1986. *Oracles of God: Perceptions of Ancient Prophecy in Israel after the Exile*. London: Darton, Longman & Todd.

Baumgarten, Joseph M., 1992. "The Cave 4 Versions of the Qumran Penal Code." *JJS* 43: 268–76.

— 1996. *Qumran Cave 4: The Damascus Document (4Q266–273)*. DJDXVIII; Oxford: Clarendon Press.

Bedenbender, A., 2003. "Traces of Enochic Judaism within the Hebrew Bible." In Boccaccini, 2003: 39–48.

Bedford, Peter, 2001. *Temple Restoration in Early Achaemenid Judah*. Leiden: Brill.

Bergren, Theodore A., 1997. "Nehemiah in 2 Maccabees 1:10–2:18." *JSJ* 28: 249–70.

Bernstein, M., F. García Martínez and J. Kampen (eds.), 1997. *Legal Texts and Legal Issues: Proceedings of the Second Meeting of the International Organization for Qumran Studies. Published in Honor of Joseph M. Baumgarten*. Leiden: Brill.

Bertholet, Alfred. 1926. *History of Hebrew Civilization*. London: Harrap.

Black, M. 1985. *The Book of Enoch or 1 Enoch. A New English Edition*. Leiden: Brill.

Blenkinsopp, J., 1987. "The Mission of Udjahorresnet and Those of Ezra and Nehemiah." *JBL* 106: 409–21.

— 1991. "Temple and Society in Achaemenid Judah." In Davies, 1991: 22–53.

— 1992. *The Pentateuch: An Introduction to the First Five Books of the Bible.* New York: Doubleday; London: SCM Press.

— 2003. "Bethel in the Neo-Babylonian Period." In Lipschits and Blenkinsopp, 2003: 93–107.

Boccaccini, G., 1991. *Middle Judaism: Jewish Thought 300 BCE to 200 CE.* Minneapolis: Augsburg Fortress.

— 1998. *Beyond the Essene Hypothesis: The Parting of the Ways between Qumran and Enochic Judaism.* Grand Rapids: Eerdmans.

Boccaccini, G. (ed.), 2002. *Roots of Rabbinic Judaism: An Intellectual History, from Ezekiel to Daniel.* Grand Rapids: Eerdmans.

— 2003. *The Origins of Enochic Judaism. Proceedings of the First Enoch Seminar. University of Michigan, Sesto Fiorentino, Italy June 19–23, 2001.* Freiburg: Herder.

— 2005. *Enoch and Qumran Origins: New Light on a Forgotten Connection.* Grand Rapids: Eerdmans.

— 2007. *Enoch and the Messiah Son of Man: Revisiting the Book of Parables.* Grand Rapids: Eerdmans.

Boccaccini, G., and John J. Collins (eds.), 2007. *The Early Enoch Literature.* Leiden: Brill.

Bohak, Gideon, 1996. *Joseph and Aseneth and the Jewish Temple in Heliopolis.* Atlanta: Scholars Press.

Bousset, Wilhelm, 1902. *Die Religion des Judentums im späthellenistischen Zeitalter.* Tübingen: Mohr.

Boyce, Mary, 1982. *A History of Zoroastrianism.* Handbuch der Orientalistik; 2 vols.; Leiden: Brill.

Briend, Jacques, 1996. "L'édit de Cyrus et sa valeur historique." *Transeuphratène* 11: 33–44.

Broshi, M. (ed.), 1992. *The Damascus Document Reconsidered.* Jerusalem: Israel Exploration Society, 1992.

Carmichael, Calum, 1992. *The Origins of Biblical Law. The Decalogues and the Book of the Covenant.* Ithaca: Cornell University Press.

Carroll, Robert P., 1991. "Textual Strategies and Ideology in the Second Temple Period." In Davies, 1991: 108–24.

Carter, Charles E., 1994. "The Province of Yehud in the Post-Exilic Period." In T. C. Eskenazi and K. H. Richards (eds.), *Second Temple Studies. 2. Temple and Community in the Persian Period.* Sheffield: Sheffield Academic Press.

— 1999. *The Emergence of Yehud in the Persian Period.* Sheffield: Sheffield Academic Press, 1999.

Charles, R. H., 1913. "Book of Enoch." In Charles (ed.), *Apocrypha and Pseudepigrapha of the Old Testament II*: 163–277. Oxford: Clarendon Press.

Clements, R. E., 1985. "Beyond Tradition-Hisory: Deutero-Isaianic Development of First Isaiah's Themes." *JSOT* 31: 95–113.

— 1989. *Deuteronomy.* Old Testament Guides; Sheffield: JSOT Press.

Clines, D. J. A., 1990. "The Perils of Autobiography." In Clines, *What Does Eve Do To Help? And Other Readerly Questions to the Old Testament*: 124–64. Sheffield: JSOT Press.

Cohen, Shaye J. D., 1987. *From the Maccabees to the Mishnah.* Philadelphia: Westminster Press.

— 2000. *The Beginnings of Jewishness: Boundaries, Varieties, Uncertainties.* Berkeley: University of California Press.

Collins, John J., 1977. *The Apocalyptic Vision of the Book of Daniel.* Missoula, MT: Scholars Press.

— 1984. *The Apocalyptic Imagination.* New York: Crossroad.

— 1986. "Apocalyptic Literature." In Kraft and Nickelsburg, 1986: 345–70.

Collins, John J. (ed.), 1979. *Apocalypse: The Morphology of a Genre.* Semeia 14; Missoula, MT: Scholars Press.

— 1993. *Daniel.* Hermeneia; Minneapolis: Fortress Press.

— 2005. "The *Yahad* and the Qumran Community." In Charlotte Hempel and Judith Lieu (eds.), *Biblical Traditions in Transmission: Essays in Honour of Michael A. Knibb*: 81–96. Leiden: Brill.

Cook, Stephen L., 2003. *The Apocalyptic Literature.* Nashville: Abingdon.

Cowley, A. E., 1923. *Aramaic Papyri of the Fifth Century B.C.* Oxford: Clarendon Press.

Cross, F. M., 1969. "New Directions in the Study of Apocalyptic." *JTC* 6: 157–65.

— 1973. *Canaanite Myth and Hebrew Epic: Essays in the History of the Religion of Israel.* Cambridge, MA: Harvard University Press.

Crüsemann, Frank, 1984. "The Unchangeable World: The 'Crisis' of Wisdom in Koheleth." In W. Schottroff and W. Stegemann (eds.), *God of the Lowly: Socio-historical Interpretations of the Bible*: 57–77. Maryknoll: Orbis.

Davies, Graham I., 1978. "Apocalyptic and Historiography." *JSOT* 5: 15–28.

Davies, Philip R., 1977. "Hasidim in the Maccabean Period." *JJS* 28: 127–40.

— 1982. *The Damascus Covenant.* Sheffield: JSOT Press.

— 1987. *Behind the Essenes.* Atlanta: Scholars Press.

— 1992. *In Search of Ancient Israel.* Sheffield: JSOT Press.

— 1996. *Sects and Scrolls: Essays on Qumran and Related Topics.* Atlanta: Scholars Press.

— 1994. "The 'Damascus' Sect: and Judaism." In John C. Reeves and John Kampen (eds.), *Pursuing the Text: Studies in Honor of Ben Zion Wacholder*: 70–84. Sheffield: JSOT Press.

— 1995. "Who Can Join the 'Damascus Covenant'?" *JJS* 46: 134–42.

— 1998. *Scribes and Schools: The Canonization of the Hebrew Scriptures.* Louisville: Westminster John Knox Press.

— 2000. "Food, Drink and Sects: The Question of Ingestion in the Qumran Texts." *Semeia* 84: 139–51.

— 2001. "Judaeans in Egypt: Hebrew and Greek Stories." In L. L. Grabbe (ed.), *Did Moses Speak Attic? Jewish Historiography and Scripture in the Hellenistic Period*: 108–28. Sheffield: Sheffield Academic Press.

— 2002. "The Origin of Evil in Early Judaism." *Australian Biblical Review* 50: 43–54.

— 2006. "And Enoch Was Not, for Genesis Took Him." In C. Hempel and J. M. Lieu (eds.), *Biblical Traditions in Transmission. Essays in Honour of Michael A. Knibb*: 97–107. Leiden: Brill, 2006.

— 2007a. *The Origins of Biblical Israel.* London: T&T Clark.

— 2007b. "'Old' and 'New' Israel in the Bible and the Qumran Scrolls: Identity and Difference." In F. García Martínez and M. Popović, *Defining Identities: We, You, and the Other in the Dead Sea Scrolls: Proceedings of the Fifth Meeting of the IOQS in Groningen*: 33–42. Leiden: Brill.

Davies Philip R. (ed.), 1991. *Second Temple Studies, 1: Persian Period*. Sheffield: JSOT Press.

— 2007–2007b. "'Old' and 'New' Israel in the Bible and the Qumran Scrolls: Identity and Difference." In F. García Martínez and M. Popović, *Defining Identities: We, You, and the Other in the Dead Sea Scrolls: Proceedings of the Fifth Meeting of the IOQS in Groningen*: 33–42. Leiden: Brill.

Delcor, M., 1976. "Le mythe de la chute des anges et de l'origine des géants comme explication du mal dans le monde dans apocalyptique juive: Histoire des traditions." *RHR* 190: 3–53.

Dever, W. G., 2001. *What Did the Biblical Writers Know and When Did They Know It?* Grand Rapids: Eerdmans.

Douglas, Mary, 1971. "Deciphering a Meal." In C. Geertz (ed.), *Myth, Symbol, and Culture*: 61–81. New York: Norton.

— 1966. *Purity and Danger: An Analysis of the Concepts of Pollution and Taboo*. London: Routledge.

Duhm, Bernhard, 1892. *Das Buch Jesaja*. Göttingen: Vandenhoeck & Ruprecht.

Edelman, Diana, 2005. *The Origins of the "Second Temple." Persian Imperial Policy and the Rebuilding of Jerusalem*. London: Equinox.

Eskenazi, T. C., 1988. *In an Age of Prose: A Literary Approach to Ezra-Nehemiah*. Atlanta: Scholars Press.

Evans, C. A., 1993. "Mishna and Messiah." In "Context: Some Comments on Jacob Neusner's Proposals." *JBL* 112: 267–89.

Ewald, Georg, 1867. *Die Propheten des alten Bundes I*. Göttingen: Vandenhoeck & Ruprecht.

Falk, Z. W., 1978. *Introduction to Jewish Law of the Second Commonwealth*. 2 vols.; Leiden: Brill.

Feeley-Harnik, Gillian, 1994. *The Lord's Table: The Meaning of Food in Early Judaism and Christianity*. 2nd edn; Washington and London: Smithsonian Institution Press.

Finkelstein, I., 1988. *The Archaeology of the Israelite Settlement*. Jerusalem: Israel Exploration Society.

Finkelstein, Israel, and Neil Asher Silberman, 2001. *The Bible Unearthed: Archaeology's New Vision of Ancient Israel and the Origin of its Sacred Texts*. New York: Free Press.

— 2006. *David and Solomon: In Search of the Bible's Sacred Kings and the Roots of the Western Tradition*. New York: Free Press.

Fishbane, M., 1985. *Biblical Interpretation in Ancient Israel*. Oxford: Oxford University Press.

Flesher, Paul V. M., 1988. *Oxen. Women, or Citizens? Slaves in the System of the Mishnah*. Atlanta: Scholars Press.

Fried, Lisbeth S., 2004. *The Priest and the Great King: Temple Palace Relations in the Persian Empire*. Winona Lake: Eisenbrauns.

Gabba, E., 1989. "The Growth of Anti-Judaism or the Greek Attitude towards Jews." In W. D. Davies and Louis Finkelstein (eds.), *The Cambridge History of Judaism* II: 614–56. Cambridge: Cambridge University Press.

Gafni, I. M., 1997. *Land, Center and Diaspora: Jewish Constructs in Late Antiquity*. Sheffield: Sheffield Academic Press.

Gager, John G., 1975. *Kingdom and Community: The Social World of Early Christianity.* Englewood Cliffs, NJ: Prentice-Hall.

Glasson, T. F., 1961. *Greek Influence on Jewish Eschatology.* London: SPCK.

Goodenough, Erwin R., 1953. *Jewish Symbols in the Greco-Roman Period.* 13 vols.; New York: Pantheon Books.

— 1988. *Jewish Symbols in the Greco-Roman Period.* Revised and abridged by Jacob Neusner; Princeton: Princeton University Press.

Goodman, Martin, 1987. *The Ruling Class of Judaea.* Cambridge: Cambridge University Press.

— 1992. "Jewish Proselytizing in the First Century." In Judith Lieu, John North and Tessa Rajak (eds.), *The Jews among Christians and Pagans*: 53–78. London: Routledge.

— 2007. *Rome and Jerusalem: The Clash of Ancient Civilizations.* London: Allen Lane.

Gosse, Bernard, 1992. "Isaïe 1 dans la rédaction du livre d'Isaïe." *ZAW* 104: 52–66.

Grabbe, Lester L., 1991. *The Jews from Cyrus to Hadrian.* 2 vols.; Minneapolis: Fortress Press.

— 1992. *Judaism from Cyrus to Hadrian.* 2 vols.; Minneapolis: Fortress Press.

— 1998. *Ezra-Nehemiah.* London: Routledge.

Grayson, A. K., and W. G. Lambert, 1964. "Akkadian Prophecies." *JCS* 18: 7–30.

Green, W. S. (ed.), 1987. *Judaisms and their Messiahs in the Beginning of Christianity.* New York: Cambridge University Press.

Gressmann, Hugo, 1929. *Der Messias.* Göttingen: Vandenhoeck & Ruprecht.

Gruen, Erich S., 1998. *Heritage and Hellenism: The Reinvention of Jewish Tradition.* Berkeley: University of California Press.

— 2002. *Diaspora: Jews amidst Greeks and Romans.* Cambridge, MA: Harvard University Press.

Hanson, Paul D., 1975. *The Dawn of Apocalyptic.* Philadelphia: Fortress Press.

— 1976. "Apocalypticism." In *Interpreter's Dictionary of the Bible, Supplementary Volume*: 30–31. Nashville: Abingdon.

— 1985. "Apocalyptic Literature." In D. A. Knight and G. M. Tucker (eds.), *The Hebrew Bible and its Modern Interpreters*: 465–88. Philadelphia: Fortress Press; Chico: Scholars Press.

— 1997. "Rebellion in Heaven, Azazel, and Euhemeristic Heroes in Enoch 6–11." *JBL* 96: 195–233.

Hanson, Paul D. (ed.), 1983. *Visionaries and their Apocalypses.* London: SPCK; Philadelphia: Fortress Press.

Harrison, C. Robert, Jr, 1997. "Qoheleth among the Sociologists." *BI* 5: 160–80.

Hayward, Robert, 1982. "The Jewish Temple at Leontopolis: A Reconsideration." *JJS* 33: 429–43.

Hellholm, D. (ed.), 1983. *Apocalypticism in the Mediterranean World and the Near East.* Tübingen: Mohr-Siebeck.

Hempel, Charlotte, 1996. "The Earthly Essene Nucleus of 1QSa." *DSD* 3: 253–69.

— 1997. "The Penal Code Reconsidered." In Bernstein, *et al.*, 1997: 337–48

— 2000. *The Damascus Texts.* Sheffield: Sheffield Academic Press.

Hengel, Martin, 1974. *Judaism and Hellenism.* 2 vols.; London: SCM Press.

Hjelm, I., 2000. *The Samaritans and early Judaism: A Literary Analysis.* Sheffield; Sheffield Academic Press.

— 2004. *Jerusalem's Rise to Sovereignty: Zion and Gerizim in Competition*. London: T&T Clark.

Hoffmann, H.-D., 1980. *Reform und Reformen. Untersuchungen zu einem Grundtheme der deuteronomistischen Geschichtsschreibung*. Zürich: Theologischer Verlag.

Hölscher, G., 1914. *Die Propheten*. Leipzig: J. C. Heinrichs.

— 1919. "Die Entstehung des Buches Daniel." *TSK* 92: 113–39.

— 1922. "Komposition und Ursprung des Deuteronomiums." *ZAW* 40: 161–255.

Horsley, R. A., 1987. *Jesus and the Spiral of Violence: Popular Jewish Resistance in Roman Palestine*. Minneapolis: Fortress Press.

Hultgren, Stephen, 2007. *From the Damascus Covenant to the Covenant of the Community*. Leiden: Brill.

Jackson, Bernard, 1988. "Biblical Laws of Slavery: A Comparative Approach." In L. Archer (ed.), *Slavery and Other Forms of Unfree Labour*: 86–101. London: Routledge.

— 1989. "Ideas of Law and Legal Administration: A Semiotic Approach." In R. E. Clements (ed.), *The World of Ancient Israel*: 185–202. Cambridge: Cambridge University Press.

Jolowitz, H. F., and B. Nicholas, 1972. *Historical Introduction to the Study of Roman Law*. Cambridge: Cambridge University Press.

Kaiser, Otto, 1981. *Das Buch des Propheten Jesaja: Kapitel 1–12*. 5th edn; Göttingen: Vandenhoeck & Ruprecht [ET London: SCM Press; Philadelphia: Westminster Press, 1983].

Kapelrud, Arvid, 1960. "Levde Deuterojesaja in Judea?" *NTT* 61: 23–27.

Käsemann, E., 1969. "The Beginnings of Christian Theology." (ET) *Journal for Theology and Church* 6: 17–46.

Kessler, R., 1992. *Staat und Gesellschaft im vorexilischen Juda. Vom 8. Jahrhundert bis zum Exil*. Leiden: Brill.

Kippenberg, H., 1978. *Religion und Klassenbildung im antiken Judäa*. Göttingen: Vandenhoeck & Ruprecht.

Kittel, R., 1898. "Cyrus und Deuterojesaja." *ZAW* 18: 149–64.

Knibb, Michael A., 1977. "The Exile in the Literature of the Intertestamental Period." *Heythrop Journal* 18: 253–72.

Koch, Klaus, 1972. *The Rediscovery of Apocalyptic*. London: SCM Press.

Kraabel, A. T., 1987. "Unity and Diversity among Disapora Synagogues." In L. Levine (ed.), *The Synagogue in Late Antiquity*: 49–60. Philadelphia: ASOR.

Kraemer, D., 1993. "On the Relationship of the Books of Ezra and Nehemiah." *JSOT* 59: 73–92.

Kraft, K. A., and G. W. E. Nickelsburg (eds.), 1986. *Early Judaism and its Modern Interpreters*. Philadelphia: Fortress Press; Atlanta: Scholars Press.

Kratz, Reinhard G., 1991. *Kyros im Deuterojesaja-Buch. Redaktionsgeschichtliche Untersuchungen zu Entstehung und Theologie von Jes 40–55*. Tübingen: Mohr.

Krauss, F. R., 1960. "Ein zentrales Problem des altmesopotamischen Rechts: Was ist der Codex Hammurabi." *Genava* 8: 283–96.

Kreissig, H., 1973. *Die sozialökonomische Situation im Juda zur Achämenidenzeit*. Berlin: Akademie Verlag.

Kuhrt, Amélie, 1983. "The Cyrus Cylinder and Achaemenid Imperial Policy." *JSOT* 25: 83–97.

— 1990. "Nabonidus and the Babylonian Priesthood." In Mary Beard and John North (eds.), *Pagan Priests, Religion and Power in the Ancient World*: 119–55. London: Duckworth.

Kuhrt, Amélie, and S. Sherwin-White, 1987. "Xerxes' Destruction of Babylonian Temples." In H. Sancisi-Weerdenburg and A. Kuhrt (eds.), *Achaemenid History II: The Greek Sources. Proceedings of the Groningen 1984 Achaemenid History Workshop*: 69–78. Leiden: Nederlands Instituut voor het Nabije Oosten.

Kvanvig, H., 1988. *Roots of Apocalyptic: The Mesopotamian Background of the Enoch Figure and of the Son of Man*. Neukirchen: Neukirchener Verlag.

Laato, Antti, 1992. *The Servant of YHWH and Cyrus: A Reinterpretation of the Exilic Messianic Programme in Isaiah 40–55*. Stockholm: Almqvist & Wiksell.

Lemche, N. P., 1992. "The Old Testament—a Hellenistic Book?" *Scandinavian Journal of the Old Testament* 55: 81–101.

Levenson, Jon D., 1987. "Why Jews Are Not Interested in Biblical Theology." In J. Neusner *et al.*, *Judaic Perspectives on Ancient Israel*: 281–307. Philadelphia: Fortress Press.

Licht, Jacob, 1965. *The Rule Scroll: A Scroll from the Wilderness of Judaea. 1QS, 1QSa, 1QSb. Text, Introduction and Commentary*. Jerusalem: Bialik.

Lipschits, Oded, 2005. *The Fall and Rise of Jerusalem*. Winona Lake: Eisenbrauns.

Lipschits, Oded, and Joseph Blenkinsopp (eds.), 2003. *Judah and the Judeans in the Neo-Babylonian Period*. Winona Lake: Eisenbrauns.

Lipschits, Oded, and Manfred Oeming (eds.), 2006. *Judah and the Judeans in the Persian Period*. Winona Lake: Eisenbrauns.

Lipschits, Oded, Gary N. Knoppers and Rainer Albertz (eds.), 2007. *Judah and the Judeans in the Fourth Century B.C.E.* Winona Lake: Eisenbrauns, 2007.

Lohfink, N., 1985a. "Zur neueren Diskussion über 2 Kön 22–23." In Lohfink, 1985b: 24–48.

Lohfink, N. (ed.), 1985b. *Das Deuteronomium*. Leuven: Peeters.

McBride, S. Dean, 1987. "Polity of the Covenant People." *Interpretation* 41: 229–44.

McCready, Wayne O., 1993. "Sectarian Separation and Exclusion—the Temple Scroll: A Case for Wholistic Religious Claims." In Bradley H. McLean (ed.), *Origins and Method: Towards a New Understanding of Judaism and Christianity. Essays in Honour of John C. Hurd*: 360–79. Sheffield: JSOT Press.

McGowan, Andrew, 1999. *Ascetic Eucharists: Food and Drink in Early Christian Ritual Meals*. Cambridge: Cambridge University Press.

McKay, Heather A., 1994. *Sabbath and Synagogue: The Question of Sabbath in Ancient Judaism*. Leiden: Brill.

Maccoby, H., 1973. *Revolution in Judea: Jesus and the Jewish Resistance*. London: Ocean Books (2nd edn; New York: 1980).

Marshall, J., 1993. *Israel and the Book of the Covenant: An Anthropological Approach to Biblical Law*. SBLDS, 140; Atlanta: Scholars Press.

Marti, K., 1900. *Das Buch Jesaja*. Tübingen: Mohr.

Mendels, Doron, 1992. *The Rise and Fall of Jewish Nationalism: Jewish and Christian Ethnicity in Ancient Palestine*. Grand Rapids: Eerdmans.

— 1983. "Hecataeus of Abdera and a Jewish 'patrios politeia.'" *ZAW* 95: 96–110.

— 2004. *Memory in Jewish, Pagan, and Christian Societies of the Graeco-Roman World*. London: T&T Clark.

Mendels, Doron (ed.), 2007. *On Memory: An Interdisciplinary Approach*. Oxford: Peter Lang.

Meshorer, Y., 1967. *Jewish Coins from the Second Temple Period*. Tel Aviv: Am Hassefer and Massada.

— 1982. *Ancient Jewish Coinage, I: Persian Period through Hasmonaeans*. New York: Amphora.

Metso, Sarianna, 2005. "Whom Does the Term Yahad Identify?" In Charlotte Hempel and Judith Lieu (eds.), *Biblical Traditions in Transmission. Essays in Honour of Michael A. Knibb*: 215–35. Leiden: Brill.

Middendorp, T., 1973. *Die Stellung Jesu ben Siras zwischen Judentum und Hellenismus*. Leiden: Brill.

Milgrom, J., 1991. *Leviticus 1–16*. Anchor Bible; New York: Doubleday.

Milik, Jozef T., 1976. *The Books of Enoch*. Oxford: Clarendon Press.

Mowinckel, Sigmund, 1931. "Die Komposition des Deuterojesanischen Buches." *ZAW* 8: 87–112, 242–60.

Müller, Hans-Peter, 1972. "Mantische Weisheit und Apokalyptik." In P. A. H. de Boer (ed.), *Congress Volume, Uppsala 1971*: 268–93. VTSup 22; Leiden: Brill.

Murphy-O'Connor, Jerome, 1974. "The Essenes and their History." *RB* 81: 215–44.

Na'aman, Nadav, 1992. *The Kingdom of Judah under Josiah*. Tel Aviv: Institute of Archaeology.

Najm, S., and Ph. Guillaume, 2004. "Jubilee Calendar Rescued from the Flood Narrative." *JHS* 5: 1 (http://www.arts.ualberta.ca/JHS/Articles/article_31.pdf).

Negev, A., and S. Gibson, 2003. *Archaeological Encyclopedia of the Holy Land*. London: Continuum.

Neusner, Jacob, 1973. "The Mishna in Philosophical Context and Out of Canonical Bounds." *JBL* 112: 291–304.

— 1994. *The Judaism the Rabbis Take for Granted*. Atlanta: Scholars Press.

— 1988. *Testament to Torah*. Englewood Cliffs: Prentice-Hall.

— 1999. "The Religious Meaning of Bodily Excretions in Rabbinic Judaism: The Halakhah on Leviticus Chapter Fifteen: Zabim and Niddah." In Jacob Neusner (ed.), *Approaches to Ancient Judaism*: 177–240. Atlanta: Scholars Press.

Newman, K. S., 1983. *Law and Economic Organization*. Cambridge: Cambridge University Press.

Nicholson, Ernest W., 1979. "Apocalyptic." In G. W. Anderson (ed.), *Tradition and Interpretation: Essays by Members of the Society for Old Testament Study*: 189–213. Oxford: Clarendon Press.

— 1986. *God and His People: Covenant and Theology in the Old Testament*. Oxford: Clarendon Press.

— 1998. *The Pentateuch in the Twentieth Century: The Legacy of Julius Wellhausen*. Oxford: Clarendon Press.

Nickelsburg, George W. E., 1982. "The Epistle of Enoch and the Qumran Literature." *JJS* 33: 333–48.

— 1983. "Social Aspects of Palestinian Jewish Apocalypticism." In Hellholm, 1983: 641–54.

— 1997. "Apocalyptic and Myth in 1 Enoch 6–11." *JBL* 96: 383–405.

— 2001. *1 Enoch 1: A Commentary on the Book of 1 Enoch: Chapters 1–36; 81–108*. Ed. Klaus Baltzer; Minneapolis: Fortress Press.

Niditch, Susan A., 1983. *The Symbolic Vision in Biblical Tradition*. Chico: Scholars Press.

Niehr, H., 1987. *Rechtsprechung in Israel: Untersuchungen zur Geschichte der Gerichtsorganisation im Alten Testament*. Stuttgart: Katholisches Bibelwerk.

Nodet, Etienne, 1997. *A Search for the Origins of Judaism*. Sheffield: Sheffield Academic Press.

Noth, Martin, 1972. *A History of Pentateuchal Traditions*. Englewood Cliffs, NJ: Prentice-Hall. (=*Überlieferungsgeschichte des Pentateuch*. Stuttgart: Kohlhammer, 1948.)

Orton, David E., 1987. *The Understanding Scribe*. Sheffield: JSOT Press.

Patrick, D., 1985. *Old Testament Law*. Louisville: John Knox Press; London: SCM Press.

Paul, M. J., 1985. "Hilkiah and the Law (2 Kings 22) in the 17th and 18th Centuries." In Lohfink, 1985b: 9–12.

Paul, Shalom, 1970. *Studies in the Book of the Covenant in the light of Cuneiform and Biblical Law*. Leiden: Brill.

Phillips, Anthony, 1983. "The Decalogue: Ancient Israel's Criminal Law." JJS 34: 1–20. Reprinted in A. Phillips, *Essays in Biblical Law*: 2–24. London: Sheffield Academic Press, 2002.

— 1985. *Ancient Israel's Criminal Law*. Oxford: Blackwell.

Plöger, Otto, 1968. *Theocracy and Eschatology*. Oxford: Blackwell.

Porter, Paul A., 1983. *Metaphors and Monsters*. Lund: CWK Gleerup.

Pritchard, J. B. (ed.), 1969. *Ancient Near Eastern Texts Relating to the Old Testament*. 3rd edn; Princeton: Princeton University Press.

Purvis, J. D., 1986. "The Samaritans and Judaism." In R. A. Kraft and G. W. E. Nickelsburg (eds.), *Early Judaism and its Modern Interpreters*: 81–98. Philadelphia/Atlanta: Fortress Press/Scholars Press.

Regev, Eyal, 2003. "The Yahad and the Damascus Covenant: Structure, Organization and Relationship." *RQ* 82: 233–62.

Reid, Steven Breck, 1983. "1 Enoch: The Rising Elite of the Apocalyptic Movement." *SBL Seminar Papers* 1983: 147–56.

— 1989. *Enoch and Daniel: A Form Critical and Sociological Study of Historical Apocalypses*. Berkeley: BIBAL Press.

Rhoads, David M., 1976. *Israel in Revolution: 6–74 C.E. A Political History based on the Writings of Josephus*. Philadelphia: Fortress Press.

Ringgren, Helmer, 1983. "Akkadian Apocalypses." In Hellholm, 1983: 379–86.

Römer, Thomas, 2007. "La construction d'une 'vie de Moïse' dans la Bible Hébraïque et chez quelques auteurs hellénistique." In G. J. Brooke and Thomas Römer (eds.), *Ancient and modern Scriptural Historiography (L'historiographie biblique, ancienne et moderne)*: 109–25. Leuven: Leuven University Press.

Rowland, Christopher, 1982. *The Open Heaven: A Study of Apocalyptic in Judaism and Christianity*. London, SPCK; New York: Crossroad.

Rowley, H. H., 1944. *The Relevance of Apocalyptic*. 2nd edn, 1963; London: Lutterworth.

Russell, D. S., 1964. *The Method and Message of Jewish Apocalyptic*. London: SCM Press.

Sacchi, Paolo, 1990. *Jewish Apocalyptic and its History*. Sheffield: Sheffield Academic Press.

Sanders, E. P., 1977. *Paul and Palestinian Judaism: A Comparison of Patterns of Religion*. London: SCM Press.

— 1983. "The Genre of Palestinian Jewish Apocalypses." In Hellholm, 1983: 447–60.

— 1992. *Judaism, Practice and Belief 63BCE–66CE*. London: SCM Press; Philadelphia: Trinity Press International.

Schaper, J., 1995. "The Jerusalem Temple as an Instrument of the Achaemenid Fiscal Administration." *VT* 45: 528–39.

Schiffman, L. H., 1991. *From Text to Tradition: A History of Second Temple and Rabbinic Judaism*. Hoboken, NY: Ktav.

Schmidt, Brian, 1995. "The Aniconic Tradition." In Diana Edelman (ed.), *The Triumph of Elohim*: 75–105. Kampen: Kok Pharos.

Schürer, Emil, 1973–87. *The History of the Jewish People in the Age of Jesus Christ*. 3 vols; revised and edited by G. Vermes, F. Millar and M. Goodman; Edinburgh: T.&T. Clark.

Schwartz, Daniel, 1992. *Studies in the Jewish Background of Christianity*. Tübingen: Mohr.

Schwartz, Seth, 2001. *Imperialism and Jewish Society 200 B.C.E. to 640 C.E.*. Princeton, NJ: Princeton University Press.

Scott, James M., 1997. "Exile and the Self-Understanding of Diaspora Jews in the Greco-Roman Period." In J. M. Scott (ed.), *Exile: Old Testament, Jewish, and Christian Conceptions*: 173–218. Leiden: Brill.

Seitz, Christopher R., 1992. *Zion's Final Destiny. The Development of the Book of Isaiah: A Reassessment of Isaiah 36–39*. Minneapolis: Fortress Press.

Smallwood, E. Mary, 1999. "The Diaspora in the Roman Period before CE 70." In William Horbury, W. D. Davies and John Sturdy (eds.), *The Cambridge History of Judaism III: The Early Roman Period*: 168–91. Cambridge: Cambridge University Press.

Smart, James D., 1965. *History and Theology in Second Isaiah: A Commentary on Isaiah 35, 40–6*. Philadelphia: Westminster.

Smith, Jonathan Z., 1975. "Wisdom and Apocalyptic." In B. A. Pearson (ed.), *Religious Syncretism in Antiquity*: 131–56. Missoula, MT: Scholars Press.

Smith, Morton, 1961. "The Dead Sea Sect in Relation to Ancient Judaism." *New Testament Studies* 7: 347–60.

— 1963. "II Isaiah and the Persians." *JAOS* 83: 415–21.

— 1971. *Palestinian Parties and Politics that Shaped the Old Testament*. New York: University of Columbia Press.

— 1983. "On the History of APOKALYPTO and APOKALYPSI." In Hellholm, 1983: 9–20.

Spieckermann, H., 1982. *Juda unter Assur in der Saronidenzeit*. Göttingen: Vandenhoeck & Ruprecht.

Sprinkle, J. M., 1994. *The "Book of the Covenant." A Literary Approach*. Sheffield: Sheffield Academic Press.

Stern, Menaham (ed.), 1976 *Greek and Latin Authors on Jews and Judaism*, I. Jerusalem: Israel Academy of Sciences and Humanities.

Stone, Michael, 1976. "Lists of Revealed Things in the Apocalyptic Literature." In F. M. Cross, W. E. Lemke and Patrick D. Miller (eds.), *Magnalia Dei: The Mighty Acts of God. Essays on the Bible and Archaelogy in Memory of G. Ernest Wright*: 414–52. Garden City, NY: Doubleday.

— 1978. "The Book of Enoch and Judaism in the Third Century BCE." *CBQ* 40: 479–92.

Stuckenbruck, L., 1997. *The Book of Giants from Qumran*. Tübingen: Mohr Siebeck.

Sweeney, M., 2000. *King Josiah of Judah: The Lost Messiah of Israel*. New York: Oxford University Press.

Thomas, D. Winton (ed.), 1958. *Documents from Old Testament Times*. London: Nelson.

Tigchelaar, E., 1996. *Prophets of Old and the Day of the End: Zechariah, the Book of Watchers and Apocalyptic*. Leiden: Brill.

Torrey, C. C., 1910. *Ezra Studies*. Chicago: University of Chicago Press.

— 1928. *The Second Isaiah: A New Interpretation*. New York: Charles Scribner's Sons.

Van Seters, J., 1983. *In Search of History: Historiography in the Ancient World and the Origins of Biblical History*. New Haven, CT, and London: Yale University Press.

— 2003. *A Law Book for the Diaspora: Revision in the Study of the Covenant Code*. Oxford and New York: Oxford University Press.

van Unnik, W. C., 1993. *Das Selbstverständnis der jüdischen Diaspora in der hellenistisch-römishen Zeit*. Leiden: Brill.

VanderKam, J. C., 1984. *Enoch and the Growth of an Apocalyptic Tradition*. Washington: CBA.

— 1986. "The Prophetic-Sapiential Origins of Apocalyptic Thought." In J. D. Martin and Philip R. Davies (eds.), *A Word in Season: Essays in Honour of William McKane*: 163–76. Sheffield: JSOT Press.

— 1992. "Ezra-Nehemiah or Ezra and Nehemiah?" In E. Ulrich *et al.* (eds.), *Priest, Prophets and Scribes: Essays on the Formation and Heritage of Second Temple Judaism in Honour of Joseph Blenkinsopp*: 55–75. Sheffield: JSOT Press.

Vermeylen, J., 1977–78. *Du prophète Isaïe à l'apocalyptique. Isaïe i–xxxv, miroir d'un demi-millénaire d'expérience religieuse en Israël*. 2 vols.; Paris: Gabalda.

Vielhauer, P., 1965. "Apocalypses and Related Subjects." In E. Hennecke and W. Schneemelcher (eds.), *New Testament Apocrypha*: II.581–607. London: SCM Press; Philadelphia: Westminster.

Vincent, J. M., 1977. *Studien zur literarischen Eigenart und zur geistigen Heimat von Jesaja, Kap. 40–55*. Frankfurt/Bern: Peter Lang.

von Rad, Gerhard, 1953. *Studies in Deuteronomy*. London: SCM Press.

— 1965. *Old Testament Theology*. Edinburgh: Oliver & Boyd.

Watson, Alan, 1974. *Law Making in the Later Roman Republic*. Oxford: Clarendon Press.

Watts, James S. (ed.), 2001. *Persia and Torah: The Theory of Imperial Authorization of the Pentateuch*. Atlanta: SBL.

Weinberg, Joel, 1992. *The Citizen-Temple Community*. Sheffield: Sheffield Academic Press.

Weinfeld, M., 1972. *Deuteronomy and the Deuteronomic School*. Oxford: Oxford University Press (repr. 1992; Winona Lake: Eisenbrauns).

— 1991. *Deuteronomy 1–11: A New Translation with Introduction and Commentary*. Anchor Bible, 5; New York: Doubleday.

Welch, A. C., 1923. *The Code of Deuteronomy: A New Theory of its Origins*. Edinburgh: T&T Clark.

Wenham, Gordon J., 1979. *The Book of Leviticus*. Grand Rapids: Eerdmans.

Westbrook, R., 1988. *Studies in Biblical and Cuneiform Law*. Paris: Gabalda.

— 1991. *Property and the Family in Biblical Law*. Sheffield: Sheffield Academic Press.

Westermann, Claus, 1969. *Isaiah 40–66: A Commentary*. London: SCM Press.

— 1992. *Genesis: An Introduction*. Minneapolis: Fortress Press.

Williams, Ronald, 1990. "The Sage in Egyptian Literature." In J. G. Gammie and L. Perdue (eds.), *The Sage in Israel and the Ancient Near East*: 19–30. Winona Lake: Eisenbrauns.

Williamson, H. G. M., 2005. *The Book Called Isaiah: Deutero-Isaiah's Role in Composition and Redaction*. Oxford: Oxford University Press.

Wills, Lawrence M., 1990. *The Jew in the Court of a Foreign King: Ancient Jewish Court Legends*. Minneapolis: Fortress Press.

Wilson, Bryan, 1970. *Religious Sects: A Sociological Study*. London: Weidenfeld & Nicolson.

Wilson, R. R., 1980. *Prophecy and Society in Ancient Israel*. Philadelphia: Fortress Press.

— 1993. "The Role of Law in Early Israelite Society." In B. Halpern and D. W. Hobson (eds.), *Law, Politics and Society in the Ancient Mediterranean World*: 90–99. Sheffield: Sheffield Academic Press.

Wright, Benjamin G., III, 2005. "Putting the Puzzle Together: Some Suggestions Concerning the Social Locations of the Wisdom of Ben Sira." In B. G. Wright and L. M. Wills (eds.), *Conflicted Boundaries in Wisdom and* Apocalypticism: 89–112. Atlanta: SBL.

Würthwein, E., 1976. "Die josianische Reform und das Deuteronomium." *ZTK* 73: 395–423.

Yamauchi, Edwin, 1990. *Persia and the Bible*. Grand Rapids: Baker Books.

Zevit, Ziony, 2001. *The Religions of Ancient Israel: A Synthesis of Parallactic Approaches*. London: Continuum.

Index of References

Index of Authors

Breinigsville, PA USA
04 April 2011
259041BV00003B/1/P